TRADE POLICIES TOWARDS DEVELOPING COUNTRIES

Trade Policies towards Developing Countries

Edited by

Ippei Yamazawa
Professor of Economics
Hitotsubashi University, Tokyo

and

Akira Hirata
Senior Research Officer
Institute of Developing Economies, Tokyo

St. Martin's Press

© Institute of Developing Economies, Tokyo 1993

First published in Great Britain 1993 by
THE MACMILLAN PRESS LTD
Houndmills, Basingstoke, Hampshire RG21 2XS
and London
Companies and representatives
throughout the world

This book is published in association with The Institute of
Developing Economies, Tokyo.

A catalogue record for this book is available from the British Library.

ISBN 0–333–55723–9

Printed in Great Britain by
Ipswich Book Co Ltd, Ipswich, Suffolk

First published in the United States of America 1993 by
Scholarly and Reference Division,
ST. MARTIN'S PRESS, INC.,
175 Fifth Avenue,
New York, N.Y. 10010

ISBN 0–312–08557–5

Library of Congress Cataloging-in-Publication Data
Trade policies towards developing countries / edited by Ippei Yamazawa
and Akira Hirata.
p.   cm.
Includes index.
ISBN 0–312–08557–5
1. Japan—Foreign economic relations—Developing countries.
2. Developing countries—Foreign economic relations—Japan.
3. European Economic Community countries—Foreign economic
relations—Developing countries.   4. Developing countries—Foreign
economic relations—Developing countries.   5. United States—Foreign
economic relations—Developing countries.   6. Developing countries-
-Foreign economic relations—United States.   I. Yamazawa, Ippei,
1937– . II. Hirata, Akira.
HF1602.15.D44T73   1993
337.5201724—dc20   92–18929
                                                        CIP

Contents

v

Notes on the Contributors

Jamuna P. Agarwal is a senior research fellow at the Kiel Institute of World Economics. He has written many books and articles in professional journals.

Ulrich Hiemenz is Professor at the Kiel Institute of World Economics and head of the development economics department. He is also chairman at the Scientific Advisory Council to the German Ministry of Economic Cooperation. Areas of specialisation include international trade and capital flows, structural adjustment and regional integration.

Akira Hirata is a senior research officer at the Institute of Developing Economies, Tokyo, and has been working on the trade aspect of development with a focus on East and Southeast Asian countries.

Hirokazu Kajiwara is Associate Professor of Economics at Chiba Keizai University. He was previously a research officer at the Japanese Embassy in Manila. He has been working on the quantitative aspect of economic development in many Asian developing countries, including Korea and India.

Hirohisa Kohama is Associate Professor at the University of Shizuoka. He previously worked at the International Development Center of Japan for thirteen years.

Rolf J. Langhammer is a senior research fellow at the Kiel Institute of World Economics. He has been a consultant to various government departments in the Federal Republic of Germany and to the Commission of the European Community in Brussels.

Toru Nakakita is Associate Professor of Economics, Toyo University, Tokyo. He has worked at the Ministry of Foreign Affairs and the Research Institute on the National Economy. Development and industrial structure are his main fields.

Takashi Nohara has been working for the Institute of Developing Economies for almost three decades, with a break to serve as an economic officer at the Asian Development Bank for four years. Quantitative trade analysis is his main field.

Satoru Okuda is a research officer at the Institute of Developing Economies. Besides trade, he has worked on Korean affairs.

Kinya Onoda is Associate Professor of Economics at Kyorin University, Tokyo. He started his academic career with work on intra-industry trade, but has expanded his research to trade policy for development.

Hiroshi Osada joined the newly established Graduate School of Development, Nagoya University, in 1991 after spending nineteen years at the Institute of Developing Economies, where he worked on the compilation of the international input–output tables for Asia and economic forecasting, as well as on trade and development.

Jörg-Volker Schrader is a senior researcher at the Kiel Institute of World Economics. He was previously a researcher at the International Institute of Applied Systems Analysis, Luxemburg, Austria and a research scholar at the University of California, Berkeley. His main research areas are international agricultural policy analysis and raw material markets.

Dean Spinanger, senior research associate and research group head at the Kiel Institute of World Economics, joined the Institute in 1972, and has extensively researched and published in development economics with particular emphasis on international trade as well as labour markets. He has worked as a consultant for the World Bank, USAID, ILO, UNCTAD and GTZ.

Volker Stüven is a research fellow at the Kiel Institute of World Economics.

Stuart K. Tucker was until December 1991 a fellow at the Overseas Development Council in Washington, DC, and is now a freelance writer, editor, and statistician. He is a public policy analyst and an economist working primarily on international trade policy and Latin American development issues.

Shujiro Urata is Associate Professor of Economics at Waseda University, Tokyo. He has worked at the Brookings Institution, Washington DC, and the World Bank. His main fields are international trade and industrial organisation.

Ippei Yamazawa is Professor of Economics at Hitotsubashi University, Kunitachi, Tokyo. His research focuses on trade and development in such countries as Japan and Asian developing countries. He has been active in promoting economic cooperation in Asia and the Pacific.

Kazuhiko Yokota is a research officer at the Institute of Developing Economies. Majoring in development economics, he spent one year at Thammasat University, Bangkok, before joining the Institute.

Introduction

The title of the present project reminds me of the well-known book by the late Professor H. G. Johnson with the similar title, *Economic Policies toward Less Developed Countries* (The Brookings Institution, Washington, DC, 1967). In the early 1960s, President Kennedy's proposal for the Declaration of the Decade for the United Nations Development was adopted, and the first United Nations Conference on Trade and Development (UNCTAD I) was held in Geneva in 1964. At the Conference, the establishment of the New International Economic Order promoting development in developing countries was advocated, and the need to attain it by export promotion from developing countries was emphasised.

Two major proposals were made there, both from developing countries. One was the Generalised System of Preference (GSP) for the promotion of manufactured exports, and the other was the International Commodity Agreement on major primary products. Thus export promotion was the key objective.

The book was written at such a time to help the United States government and citizens to evaluate the requests from developing countries. Professor Johnson criticised the tendency of the request to distort the free trading regime, but he also stressed the need to improve export opportunities for developing countries and warned against protectionism by developed countries.

The present project tries to review the same topic after twenty years. During the period, there have been various changes. Firstly, developing countries themselves have been diversified. Some have successfully launched industrialisation in both production and exports. They have already been treated differently from the rest of the developing countries – as newly industrialising countries (NICs), as their manufactured exports penetrate developed countries and threaten domestic producers there. Some other developing countries with less than certain levels of industrialisation and income (the least developed countries, LDCs) have received specially generous treatment.

Secondly, parallel to trade liberalisation protective measures have strengthened. In developed countries tariffs have been substantially reduced through the GATT negotiations of the Kennedy Round (1962–67) and the Tokyo Round (1973–79), while such restrictive measures as voluntary export restraints (VERs) and anti-dumping actions have been more frequently used. These measures do not necessarily violate the GATT rules. The former is called a 'grey area measure': it is not consistent with the rules but has never been the subject of appeals to the GATT panel. The latter is consistent with the rules but has been administered in a restrictive manner. Both are often exercised against the NICs.

Thirdly, major developed countries differ in their economic situation and in their trade policy management. This project covers three major developed countries, Japan, the United States, and the European Community. The EC is a group of twelve countries but is treated as a single entity as the EC Commission exercises a common external trade policy on behalf of all member countries. Each of the three has its own peculiar economic problem.

Japan, with its persistent trade surplus, has switched from export-oriented to domestic demand-led growth, promoted economic restructuring, and increased imports through improved market access.

The United States, in contrast, suffers from a huge trade deficit twice as big as Japan's surplus. She has become very sensitive to further increases in imports and has been trying hard to promote exports through bilateral negotiations. Some advocate a strategic trade policy which assists the strengthening industry competitiveness and export promotion from the United States.

The EC faces yet another type of issue. It has admitted the application for entry from such European NICs as Greece, Spain and Portugal, and aimed at the single European market towards 1992. Intra-regional adjustments have been a preoccupation and recent events in Eastern Europe have further complicated matters. It is not certain in what direction they would adjust common external trade policies.

Fourthly, in addition to commodity trade, we are facing very active services trade and various types of foreign direct investments. Many companies from developed countries have adopted global strategies and have been engaged in intra-firm trade, business tie-ups and technical cooperation, while governments have been constrained in their control of these companies beyond national borders. Such activities have to be covered in a trade policy study.

Fifthly, the GATT Uruguay Round is proceeding and efforts are being made to strengthen the multilateral free trade regime, which may modify trade policies of individual governments. These are the changes in the world trade environment in the last twenty years which the three sections of this book take into account.

For a full analysis of trade policies toward developing countries in Japan, the United States, and the European Community, the reader should refer to individual papers. Here, however, let me summarise the policies commonly observed in the three countries.

Firstly, individual country's trade policies towards developing countries have become so complicated that they can no longer be analysed simply in the context of North–South trade. Their stances to overall trade policies themselves, let alone those towards developing countries, differ significantly among the three. Japan's trade policy arguments focus on whether or not its imports have increased, since the beginning of the rapid yen appreciation, and how its trade policy has contributed to it.

Import promotion has been one of the major goals of Japan's trade policy since the early 1970s: tariffs have been reduced (by more than commitments at the Tokyo Round demanded), various non-tariff barriers abolished, import procedures simplified and market access improved for both developed and developing countries. Rapid appreciation of the yen on a few occasions (1973, 1978, 1985–87) triggered off import rushes of manufactured products. Especially noteworthy is the latest period, when the doubling of the yen rate, together with the stimulation of domestic demands, promoted industrial restructuring at home and relocation of production abroad. The value in US dollars of Japan's manufactured imports increased by 31.4 per cent in 1986, 25 per cent in 1987, and 25.3 per cent in 1988; 28.6 per cent of imports came from East and Southeast Asian developing countries.

The import of textiles from Asian neighbours has been one of the fastest-growing areas. There have been strong demands for import restrictions from domestic producers, but the Ministry of International Trade and Industry (MITI) has so far managed not to resort to the import control measures under the Multilateral Fiber Arrangement (MFA). Imports of beef and oranges, liberalised in 1991, leave rice as the only major farm product under strict import restriction. But Japan's trade partners have been watching closely to see whether it would become a major market for their exports, as presumably intended by its trade policies.

US trade policy has been significantly affected by concern about the persistent current account deficit and the ensuing accumulated external debt. International competitiveness has been eroded in such manufacturing sectors as textiles, iron and steel, and electronic products, and imports from the NICs of Asia, Latin America, and

Europe have been progressively regulated by the MFA and VERs. On the other hand, at both the Uruguay Round and various bilateral negotiations, the United States has demanded of NICs, Japan and the EC improvement in market access and export expansion in high-tech industries and services, where it is comparatively strong. The present GATT multilateral negotiation is trying to deal with the NTBs as one of the issues, but its success may depend on the success in the latter group of issues.

The EC's trade policy is directly affected by its need to produce a common external trade policy for the twelve member countries whose internal policies regarding agriculture and textiles are diverse. It is never easy to harmonise their internal policies and establish a common external policy. The EC Commission has been determined to move toward the irreversible formation of 'Single European Market by 1992'. It may well be that the integrated European Market itself will stimulate internal competition and lead to economies of scale, thereby increasing the purchasing power of the EC member countries as a whole and providing a greater market for exporters outside the region. Outside exporters are still concerned, however, that internal producers' requests for restrictions on external competition during the transition period may eventually lead to 'Fortress Europe'.

Secondly, authors of the three country papers are nevertheless positive toward the NICs. In 1978 the OECD published the so-called 'NICs Report' (*The Impact of Newly Industrializing Countries on the Pattern of World Trade and Production in Manufacturing*, OECD, Paris). Eleven developing countries were designated as NICs which had reached the exporting stage of industrialisation, and the report warned of their possible catching-up and rapidly increasing market shares in the member countries. At the same time, it pointed out that the imports of NICs from the OECD member countries were far larger than their exports; thus they supported economic growth of member countries. The report suggested that member countries should not restrict imports from NICs, but take advantage of their growth potential. This positive attitude is shared in the three papers, in describing restrictive measures taken by Japan, the United States and EC with critical reservations. In principle, the three papers search for the direction of 'live and let live' or 'prosper and let prosper' between developed and developing countries.

Thirdly, the future prospects in each paper are affected by the probable outcome of the ongoing Uruguay Round multilateral trade negotiations. None of the three major trading countries wishes to see it fail; to be more exact, none of them wishes to be criticised for its failure to contribute to the success of the Uruguay Round. Thus they will conclude the Uruguay Round with some concessions. But what matters is to what degree the present agenda for strengthening the multilateral free trading regime will be realised. How far will agricultural protection be removed? How quickly will the MFA be integrated into the GATT rules? How effectively will the voluntary export restraints be prevented under the new rules?

The UNCTAD used to be the major stage for the North–South trade negotiations, but it has lost its significance substantially. The GSP, the star proposal and achievement of the UNCTAD, is not highly evaluated here. The main stage of trade policy negotiations has moved to the GATT, and many developing countries participate in the Uruguay Round. They are also expected to make their own contributions.

As one of the interim, early harvest achievements of the Uruguay Round, trade policies of major countries are being reviewed jointly by the GATT Secretariat and government officials of individual member countries. United States, Japanese and EC policies are all under review. The reports will eventually be published and will stimulate lively discussion on this matter. This volume is an attempt to review trade policies of Japan, the United States and the EC by non-partisan economist groups. We hope it will contribute to the ongoing discussion of this important subject.

IPPEI YAMAZAWA

Part I

Japan's Trade Policies towards Developing Countries

1 Japan's Trade Imbalance and Policy Response to it

Ippei Yamazawa and Akira Hirata

1.1 SCOPE OF THE STUDY

Part I of this book aims to review and assess the impact of Japan's trade policies on developing countries. A wider than conventional approach has been chosen because of the recent economic transformation that has taken place in Japan. The 1970s and 1980s saw extensive changes in the industrial structure of Japan, and trade represented a major factor in this, although trade policies followed rather than led the general trend. An understanding of the factors lying behind Japan's conventional trade policies is necessary when dealing with the theme of this section.

Recently one of the major economic issues in Japan has been in large trade and current account surpluses and the trade frictions these have given rise to. This chapter gives an overview of the trade imbalance. The trade situation with developing countries is also touched upon, followed by a comment on the way in which developed and developing countries have affected Japan's trade and other economic policies vis-à-vis trade fictions.

Chapter 2 deals with relationship between trade and structural transformation, and its main focus is the rapid appreciation of the yen since the Plaza Agreement. The level of imports for Japan is still low (as has been pointed out in many works) in comparison with other developed countries. This situation has however started to change, and this is reflected by an increase in imports in real terms. The ratio in nominal terms has not changed significantly, but the argument here is that the trend in real terms indicates future import expansion. The rapid expansion of foreign direct investment since the appreciation of the yen receives some attention, since this has been instrumental in the expansion of imports.

Chapter 3 describes recent developments in Japan's trade policies, emphasising the revised import policies which have provided improved access to the Japanese market. Such conventional policy

measures as tariff reductions and the removal of import licenses were
the main revisions to take place in the 1970s. In the 1980s macroeconomic and other measures were given greater emphasis and a
number of action programmes were implemented in an attempt to
reduce the trade surplus. That trade became the focus of multifaceted
economic policies demonstrates the seriousness of the trade situation.

In the course of many trade negotiations Japan's trading partners,
especially the US, drew attention to Japan's various import barriers.
Many of these are institutional barriers, which are the topic of Chapter 4. Some of the barriers concern sensitive products and are clearly
policy-induced, but others are outside government control. Following
an overview, two sectors – agriculture and domestic distribution – are
evaluated.

Chapter 5 deals with the trade policies that are aimed specifically at
developing countries. Without any bilateral or regional preferential
arrangements, Japan's only trade promotion measure to favour developing countries is the generalised system of preferences (GSP).
Some positive impact has come from this scheme, but it is far from
ideal because of its complicated procedures and nontransparency.
Concentrating the scheme's benefits on Asian newly industrialised
countries appears to be central to its problems, and now may be the
time to reallocate the benefits. Asian newly industrialised countries
have had an additional impact on the rising demand for protectionism, especially in textiles. This also needs some attention, although
the Japanese government has so far thwarted any action, except on
one occasion regarding knitted imports from Korea.

1.2   THE EXPANDING TRADE SURPLUS

Trade policies reflect general economic trends. In recent years
Japan's main economic issue has been its large trade surplus, and
macroeconomic and conventional trade policy measures have been
implemented to tackle the problem. There have been some positive
effects from these measures, but there still remains substantial room
for improvement.

Japan's trade surplus started in the late 1960s, when exports caught
up with imports. In the next decade, and in spite of serious disturbances from the two oil price increases, exports exceeded imports by
about 1 per cent of GNP, save for two short periods immediately
after the oil price rises. This shows that the Japanese economy had

achieved a high degree of resilience to external disturbances. Individual producers also merit a mention as they managed to improve their productivity in the face of higher energy costs.

The situation however became serious in the early 1980s, when the surplus rapidly expanded to exceed 3 per cent of GNP. The reasons for this were manifold. Divergent growth rates with major trading partners, especially the US, were partly to blame, and the undervaluation of the Japanese yen, or the overvaluation of the US dollar, made the problem even more acute. Exports continued to expand relatively rapidly, while imports were discouraged.

The Plaza Agreement of September 1985 corrected the exchange rate disequilibrium by allowing the US dollar to fall sharply. Before the agreement the yen had stood at around 240 to the dollar, but immediately after the agreement it rose to less than 200 to the dollar, representing a rise in the yen of around 20 per cent. Within two years further appreciation had brought the yen to 120–130 to the dollar. Naturally this almost 100 per cent currency appreciation had a profound impact on the economy, and one of its effects was a shift of Japanese products away from the export market towards the domestic market. At the same time the inflow of imports had increased, so the trade surplus started to show signs of diminishing in 1988 and 1989.

1.3   THE DEPENDENCE OF DEVELOPING COUNTRIES ON JAPAN

For Japan, trade with developing countries is of greater importance than is the case for other industrial countries. As much as 34 per cent of exports and 42 per cent of imports in 1988 were with developing countries – about twice the industrial-country average. East and Southeast Asian countries are the major partners, accounting for almost all of Japan's exports and three-quarters of imports with developing countries (Table 1.1). Japan's greater reliance on trade with developing countries can be explained in two ways. First, Japan's lack of natural resources had led to the so-called 'processing type of trade structure', under which materials are imported for processing in exchange for finished-product exports. 62 per cent of Japan's imports in 1987 were primary commodities, compared with the 29 per cent OECD average. Secondly, geographical location has retarded a closer relationship with the world trade centres. These two factors were also responsible for Japan's reliance on domestic sources where-ever possible, especially as until recently its neighbouring countries had weak industrial bases, prohibiting the development of intra-industry trade.

The above factors started to lose significance in the 1960s, but the process was a gradual one. The importance of the former declined with the upgrading of Japan's industrial structure, which was accompanied by reduced reliance on natural resources. Even the two oil price increases in the 1970s served to promote the process by encouraging the development of energy-saving technology, although the short-term effect was in the opposite direction.

With rapid industrial development in East and Southeast Asian countries, the second factor also changed. Japan's neighbouring countries are now in a position to provide a variety of manufactures, and intra-industry trade has been on the rise. The import structure of Japan has however been relatively slow to change, as shown by the much lower market penetration of imports from developing countries compared with the US and the EC. Industrialisation in developing countries on the other hand boosted their import demands, especially for capital and intermediate goods, some of which were necessary inputs for their exports. Geographical proximity helped Japan to obtain a large share in these imports, and thus a one-way dependence developed.

As a consequence of the divergent import expansion rates, Asian countries developed sizable trade deficits with Japan. Among the nine developing countries in Table 1.1, only Malaysia and Indonesia had trade surpluses with Japan, and this was because of their primary exports. From the broad viewpoint, the situation was a natural result of their own development. The change in Japan's trade structure played only a passive role. In view of Japan's large overall surplus however, it is understandable ¡that the situation had become a source of tension. Here again, since the Plaza Agreement some improvement has already taken place. Asian newly industrialised countries followed by ASEAN are among the major beneficiaries of the yen appreciation. The rapid expansion of direct investment in ASEAN countries is expected to enhance intra-industry imports to Japan, thus creating a more balanced interdependence. But faster change in Japan may be necessary to maintain the pace of export expansion if US efforts to reduce the 'twin deficits' is not to damage export-led growth in these countries.

Table 1.1   Japan's trade with developing countries (millions of dollars)

	1980	1985	1988	1988 (%)
Exports:				
World	129 807	175 638	264 917	100.0
Developed countries	61 172	102 468	161 847	61.1
US	31 367	65 278	89 634	33.8
EC	16 650	20 016	46 873	17.7
Developing countries	59 480	56 978	89 250	33.7
Korea	5 368	7 097	15 441	5.8
Taiwan	5 146	5 030	14 354	5.4
Singapore	3 911	3 861	8 311	3.1
Hong Kong	4 761	6 509	11 706	4.4
Asian newly industrilised countries	19 186	22 492	49 813	18.8
Thailand	1 917	2 030	5 162	1.9
Malaysia	2 061	2 168	3 060	1.2
Philippines	1 683	937	1 740	0.7
Indonesia	3 458	2 173	3 054	1.2
ASEAN4	9 118	7 308	13 016	4.9
China	5 078	12 477	9 476	3.6
Imports:				
World	140 528	129 539	187 354	100.0
Developed countries	49 120	53 121	94 785	50.6
US	24 408	25 793	42 037	22.4
EC	7 842	8 893	24 071	12.8
Developing countries	84 733	67 936	78 704	42.0
Korea	2 996	4 092	11 811	6.3
Taiwan	2 293	3 386	8 744	4.7
Singapore	1 507	1 594	2 339	1.2
Hong Kong	569	767	2 109	1.1
Asian newly industrialised countries	7 366	9 839	25 002	13.3
Thailand	1 120	1 027	2 751	1.5
Malaysia	3 471	4 330	4 710	2.5
Philippines	1 951	1 243	2 044	1.1
Indonesia	13 167	10 119	9 497	5.1
ASEAN4	19 709	16 719	19 002	10.1
China	4 323	6 483	9 859	5.3

Source: Japan Tariff Association, Summary Report (1989).

1.4   JAPAN'S POLICY STANCE ON TRADE FRICTION

Much friction has resulted from the above situation, mainly with the major industrial countries but with developing countries too. Two types of demand have been made of Japan. First, a revision of Japan's macroeconomic management (such as boosting domestic demand and realigning the exchange rate) was pointed out as being necessary. Secondly, many of the demands were commodity- or industry-specific and were aimed at improving market access to Japan and limiting Japan's exports to the countries concerned. The orthodox answer that bilateral trade imbalances should be corrected within the framework of global free trade did not carry much force in the light of Japan's already large and still expanding surplus. As a consequence Japan had to give way, albeit grudgingly, in many cases.

In spite of the relatively low proportion of foreign trade in its gross national product, international transactions have been considered a vital element of Japan's economic wellbeing. The solution of the conflict with its trading partners therefore became the main concern of Japan's trade policies. On the macroeconomic level, fiscal measures were taken in the early 1980s to promote domestic demand and accelerate growth. There was little impact from these measures until the yen rapidly appreciated following the Plaza Agreement in September 1985.

On the individual commodity/industry level, traditional trade policies were not sufficient to remedy the situation. As a result of a series of liberalisation measures taken since the late 1960s, tariffs were in general already very low, especially in manufactures, and non-tariff barriers (NTBs) in the formal sense were relatively few, except in agriculture. The search for what was impeding imports therefore turned to informal, institutional, and structural aspects of the economy. Possible causes included the domestic distribution system, company groups (*keiretsu*), health and quarantine controls, the government procurement system, and R & D promotion policy, among other things.

Topics proposed at first by the US government for the recent structural impediments initiative (SII), which serves as a forum for identifying trade barriers in both countries, were reported to have numbered more than one hundred. Here the Japanese government faces serious problems. In many cases the 'impediments' are not under its direct authority. In others they are so structural that they would take a long time to remedy. In short, Japan now finds itself in a situation where trade issues cannot be approached with traditional trade policy instruments alone.

2 Recent Developments in Japan's Imports from Developing Countries

Shujiro Urata, Kazuhiko Yokota, Toru Nakakita, Hirokazu Kajiwara, Takashi Nohara, Hiroshi Osada and Satoru Okuda

2.1 RECENT CHANGES IN THE PATTERN OF JAPANESE IMPORTS

2.1.1 Overall imports

After a period of relatively slow growth in the first half of the 1980s, the volume of Japanese imports started to increase rapidly. This rapid expansion was led by manufactured imports – their volume increased by 80 per cent between 1985 and 1988, while the overall import volume increased by almost 40 per cent during the same period (Figure 2.1). The magnitude of this increase is even more remarkable when compared with the figures for 1980–5, when the volume of manufactured imports and overall imports increased by 42 per cent and 9.6 per cent respectively. The rate of increase was most spectacular in 1988, when the volume of manufactured imports and overall imports increased by 28 per cent and 17 per cent respectively. Among manufactured imports, particularly notable were electrical machinery and clothing which increased by 120 per cent and 98 per cent respectively from 1985 to 1988.

The rapid increase since 1985 can be attributed to a number of factors, one of the most important of which may be the decline in import prices which resulted mainly from the substantial appreciation of the yen from 1985. Indeed the unit price indices for overall imports and manufacturing imports declined by as much as 45 per cent and 30 per cent respectively between 1985 and 1988. In addition to the price effect, the effects exerted by income and wealth should be pointed out as important factors in the expansion of imports. Following a decrease in 1985 and 1986, the growth of real GNP accelerated in

9

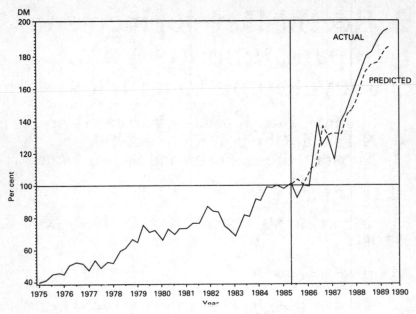

Figure 2.1   Manufactured imports

1987, when it recorded an annual growth of 4.5 per cent. The even higher rate of 5.7 per cent was recorded for 1988.

Japan's favourable economic performance in 1987 and 1988 can be attributed to the expansion of private consumption and investment which resulted from not only the higher income gained from greater production, but also from the increase in the value of assets. Indeed between 1985 and 1988 land prices in the Tokyo area more than doubled, and the stock price index of the Tokyo stock exchange increased by 230 per cent while there was virtually no increase in overall prices. It should be noted that the expansionary monetary policy of the Japanese government also contributed substantially to the expansion of economic activities as well as to the value of assets.

It is possible to argue that the rapid expansion in imports resulted from substantial changes in the magnitude of the above three factors without changing the underlying structural relationship between each one of these variables and imports. However we argue that the yen appreciation was so substantial that it led to a change in the Japanese import pattern. To test this hypothesis a statistical analysis is presented in Table 2.1.

Table 2.1 Estimates of Japanese import demand function for manufactures

Period	Const.	D×Const	PMD(-1)	D×PMD(-1)	GNP(-1)	D×GNP(-1)	M(-1)	D×M(-1)	R^2	F	DW
1975/1–1989/2	-2.09[a] (-3.62)		-0.41[a] (-4.32)		1.05[a] (4.58)		0.42[a] (3.71)		0.974	673.5[a]	-0.406
1975/1–1985/1	-2.05[a] (-2.90)		-0.28[b] (-2.10)		1.01[a] (3.53)		0.45[a] (3.22)		0.944	201.8[a]	-0.259
1985/2–1989/2	-10.03[b] (-2.52)		-0.64[b] (-2.68)		3.32[a] (3.11)		-0.12 (-0.47)		0.930	57.9[a]	-0.049
1975/1–2 1989/2	-2.05[a] (-2.75)	-7.98[b] (-2.23)	-0.28[c] (-1.99)	-0.35 (-1.40)	1.01[a] (3.31)	2.31[b] (2.34)	0.45[a] (3.04)	-0.58[b] (-2.10)	0.978	317.5[a]	-0.309

Notes: OLS with all the variables in logarithms. The figures in the parentheses are t-statistics.
Dependent variable is import volume taken from *The Summary Report on Trade of Japan* (Japan Tariff Association) various issues.

PMD=Import Price(PM)/Domestic Wholesale Price(PD). PM is taken from *The Summary Report on Trade of Japan* and PD is taken from *Price Indices Annual* (Bank of Japan), various issues.

GNP=GNP in constant prices, taken from *IFS*.

M=volume of import

(-1)=one period lag

D=a dummy whose value is 0 for 1975/1–1985/1 and 1 for 1985/2–1989/2.

a=1%, b=5%, c=10% level of significance.

The results of this econometric analysis indicate that Japanese imports became more sensitive to relative prices (import price/domestic price) and to income. In order to see if the Japanese import pattern changed significantly in 1985, we applied a Chow test and detected the presence of a structural shift in 1985.[1] The estimates on dummy variables indicate that the income elasticity of demand for imports increased significantly, implying that Japanese consumers' attitude towards imports became more favourable after 1985. This observation is consistent with the findings of a survey conducted by the Manufactured Imports Promotion Organization (1988). According to the survey, the proportion of consumers who would not discriminate between imports and domestic products increased from 66.3 per cent in 1982 to 74.8 per cent in 1988. We argue that the change in consumers' tastes was one of the reasons behind the opening up of new channels for imports, as will be discussed in Chapter 4. Inexpensive foreign products imported through the new channels whetted the Japanese appetite for foreign products, and therefore the rapid expansion in imports arose through an interaction between demand and supply.

The above discussion shows that the volume of imports increased rapidly after 1985 partly as a result of the decline in import prices in terms of the yen. As one of the reasons why policymakers and economists are interested in the Japanese import performance is to see whether Japanese import expansion has contributed to reducing the Japanese trade surplus, it is also worthwhile examining its import performance in terms of US dollars. As could be expected, the dollar value of Japanese imports increased by a substantial 45 per cent between 1985 and 1988 following a slight decline between 1980 and 1985. The rate of increase however fluctuated between 1985 and 1988 – the value of imports declining in 1986 before increasing in 1987 and accelerating in 1988.[2] Over the same period the value of exports increased steadily. Consequently the Japanese trade surplus increased in 1986, but started to decline in 1987 and continued to do so in 1988.

2.1.2 Imports from developing countries

The value of imports from developing countries fluctuated in the 1980s, declining from $89 billion in 1980 to $80 billion in 1985, and then increasing to $88.6 billion in 1988. The large decline in the value of imports between 1980 and 1985 was due mainly to the low price of oil and other raw materials – Japan's major imports from developing countries. During the same period the value of imports from developing countries increased more slowly than these from developed countries, again due largely to the declining price of primary commodities, especially that of crude oil. As a consequence the share of imports from developing countries in total imports declined from 62 per cent to 47 per cent.

Despite the overall decline in imports from developing countries, a number of East and Southeast Asian countries increased their shares over the same period, most notably Korea and Taiwan whose respective shares in total Japanese imports rose from 3.2 per cent and 2.6 per cent in 1985 to 6.3 per cent and 4.7 per cent in 1988 (Table 2.2). Indeed Korea and Taiwan contributed to the increase in Japanese imports from developing countries over the period by 95 per cent and 66 per cent respectively. In contrast Indonesia and Malaysia, whose exports to Japan consist mainly of primary commodities, lost their shares during the same period.

In comparison with non-Asian developing countries Asian developing countries fared better in the Japanese market. From 1985 to 1988 their share in total imports from developing countries rose from 50 per cent in 1985 to over 65 per cent in 1988. Their importance as suppliers of imports becomes even greater when only manufactured imports are considered: the share of Asian countries among all developing countries increased from 79 per cent in 1985 to 83 per cent in 1988.

As a large proportion of Japanese imports from developing countries, especially manufactured products, is held by East and Southeast Asian countries, we will examine the pattern of imports from them and the changes which took place in the second half of the 1980s. Focusing on the three groups of countries in East and Southeast Asia – Asian NICs, ASEAN4, and China – there are apparent differences in the composition of Japanese imports from each group (Table 2.2). Dividing the total imports into manufactured and nonmanufactured products, the share of manufactured products was high for the NICs (73 per cent in 1988), while the corresponding share was low for ASEAN4 (18 per cent). China was located in between at 47 per cent. In spite of the large differences there was a steady increase in the share of manufactured goods for all the groups over time, and an especially rapid increase from 1985.

Inspection of the changes at a more disaggregate level reveals that a large part of the share increase for manufactures from 1985–8 is

Table 2.2 Japanese imports from developing Asia (percentages)

		Non-Manufactures				Manufactures							
Country		Subtotal	Food	Raw Materials	Fossil Fuels	Subtotal	Chemicals	Machinery	Iron and steel	Textiles	Non-ferrous metals	Others	Totals
Commodity composition of Japanese imports:													
NIEs	1980	42.0	20.3	6.5	15.3	58.0	6.2	11.8	4.1	18.7	0.7	16.5	100.0
	1985	42.2	20.6	4.9	16.7	57.8	5.1	12.9	5.7	15.9	0.5	17.7	100.0
	1988	27.1	17.4	4.2	5.5	72.9	4.7	17.7	6.8	19.4	1.3	23.1	100.0
ASEAN4	1980	94.1	6.4	26.4	61.4	5.9	0.5	0.8	0.2	0.4	2.7	1.2	100.0
	1985	85.7	7.5	17.1	61.1	14.3	0.9	0.9	0.4	0.5	3.6	8.1	100.0
	1988	82.1	13.9	25.7	42.5	17.9	1.5	2.1	1.0	1.4	3.3	8.7	100.0
China	1980	77.4	10.9	11.6	55.0	22.6	4.6	0.1	0.8	12.3	0.3	4.4	100.0
	1985	73.0	14.4	12.8	45.9	27.0	4.7	0.3	0.1	14.8	1.3	5.9	100.0
	1988	52.9	18.1	13.4	21.5	47.1	6.3	1.5	4.5	24.7	2.4	7.6	100.0
World	1980	77.2	10.4	16.9	49.8	22.8	4.4	7.0	0.6	2.3	3.2	5.4	100.0
	1985	69.0	12.0	13.9	43.1	31.0	6.2	9.6	1.1	3.0	3.1	8.0	100.0
	1988	51.0	15.5	15.0	20.5	49.0	7.9	14.2	2.5	5.7	5.0	13.8	100.0
Share of developing Asia in overall Japanese imports:													
NIEs	1980	2.9	10.2	2.0	1.6	13.3	7.3	8.9	33.7	43.3	1.1	16.2	5.2
	1985	4.6	13.0	2.7	2.9	14.2	6.2	10.3	38.1	40.2	1.3	16.9	7.6
	1988	7.1	14.9	3.7	3.6	19.9	8.0	16.6	36.6	45.5	3.5	22.4	13.3
ASEAN4	1980	17.1	8.6	21.9	17.3	3.6	1.6	1.5	3.9	2.6	12.0	3.4	14.0
	1985	16.0	8.1	15.8	18.3	6.0	1.9	1.2	4.2	2.0	14.8	13.2	12.9
	1988	16.3	9.1	17.4	21.1	3.7	1.9	1.5	4.0	2.5	6.6	6.4	10.1
China	1980	3.1	3.2	2.1	3.4	3.0	3.2	0.1	4.0	16.8	0.3	2.5	3.1
	1985	5.3	6.0	4.6	5.3	4.4	3.7	0.2	0.3	24.6	2.1	3.7	5.0
	1988	5.5	6.1	4.7	5.5	5.1	4.2	0.6	9.7	22.9	2.5	2.9	5.3
World	1980	100.0	100.0	100.0	100.0	100.0	100.0	100.0	100.0	100.0	100.0	100.0	100.0
	1985	100.0	100.0	100.0	100.0	100.0	100.0	100.0	100.0	100.0	100.0	100.0	100.0
	1988	100.0	100.0	100.0	100.0	100.0	100.0	100.0	100.0	100.0	100.0	100.0	100.0

attributable to an increase in imports of machinery, iron and steel, and textiles. Again the three groups have substantially different individual shares of total imports. For machinery and iron and steel, shares in total imports were highest for the newly industrialised countries and lowest for ASEAN4, with China in the middle. China had the largest share of textiles, followed closely by the newly industrialised countries – ASEAN4 had a very small share. It is also interesting to note that China's share of food in total imports increased rapidly throughout the 1980s. The same applies to ASEAN4 during the second half of the decade.

The differences in the patterns of the three groups reflect the differences in their comparative advantage, which in turn are due largely to their factor endowments. The newly industrialised countries, which are highly successful developing countries lacking rich natural resources, tend to have comparative advantage in labour-intensive products such as textiles, as well as physical capital-intensive products such as iron and steel. They are currently improving their comparative advantage in capital-intensive products through active R&D policies and promotion of foreign direct investment. Their successful industrial development is likely to lead to an increase in intra-industry trade with Japan.[3]

China has a relatively well-developed industrial sector, although it is classified as a 'low income' economy in the World Bank's world development report. Industrialisation has been achieved mainly by active government policy which has focused on heavy industry throughout China's post-war history.[4] However excessively aggressive industrialisation policies have resulted in inefficiency in the heavy industry sector. China therefore appears to have a comparative advantage in labour-intensive light industries because of its vast workforce. Although China is richly endowed with mineral resources their potential has not been realised, mainly because of inadequacies in the Chinese infrastructure – such as an efficient transportation system to deliver mineral resources to the location where they are to be utilised.

The countries of ASEAN4, being richly endowed with natural resources, have a comparative advantage in primary products. During the 1970s and 1980s they acquired comparative advantage in labour-intensive light manufactured products such as textiles, and they are now attempting to move into more physical and human capital-intensive lines of production by pursuing outward-oriented trade policies.

The above findings indicate that the increase in Japanese imports of manufactured products from Asian developing countries is partly attributable to their successful industrialisation, without which they could not have responded to the increased Japanese demand for their products. It is also important to note that industrialisation in this region has been achieved mainly through export promotion policies which obviously facilitated the expansion of their exports to Japan. Finally, the globalisation of Japanese firms should be mentioned as a contributing factor to the expansion of Japanese imports from the region by opening up new channels for imports, as will be discussed in Chapter 4.

2.2   AN INTERNATIONAL COMPARISON OF IMPORT PATTERNS

We have seen that Japanese imports have been rapidly increasing since the mid-1980s in terms of both volume and US dollars. But the question still remains as to whether Japan imports as much as other developed countries. This question is often raised in the US and the EC, who have both been irritated by the fact that their bilateral trade deficits with Japan persist despite the substantial appreciation of the yen.

Interestingly enough, a similar complaint is often raised by consumers in Japan. Their complaint stems from disappointment that they are not gaining sufficient benefit from the appreciation of the yen as the prices of foreign products have not come down as much as had been expected. Some of the consumers accuse import firms of enjoying increased profits by selling imports at excessively high prices. Regardless of the motivation, it is important to examine the pattern of Japanese imports from an international perspective in order to see if Japan is indeed importing less than other countries.

There are a number of indicators which could be used to compare the importance of import activities in the domestic markets of different countries. Here we use the ratio of the value of imports to GDP. From Table 2.3 it can be seen clearly that the role of imports in Japanese economic activity is very limited in comparison with other countries. For example in 1988, if we use the ratio of total imports to GDP in nominal prices, the ratio for Japan was 6.6 per cent, substantially smaller than the average of 22.2 per cent for OECD countries. The US ranks second lowest at 9.5 per cent. The Japanese market

Table 2.3   Import pattern of selected industrial countries

Country	1970	1980	1985	1986	1987	1988
Total imports/GDP in current prices:						
Japan	9.3	13.3	9.8	6.5	6.3	6.6
France	13.4	20.3	20.6	17.7	17.9	18.8
W. Germany	16.3	23.1	25.3	21.4	20.4	20.8
UK	17.5	21.5	23.9	22.6	22.5	23.0
US	4.2	9.0	8.9	9.1	9.4	9.5
OECD average	21.6	26.7	26.8	24.0	23.6	22.2
Total imports/GDP in constant prices:						
Japan	11.1	11.4	9.8	11.0	11.4	12.6
France	14.5	21.1	20.6	21.9	23.1	–
W. Germany	19.8	24.9	25.2	26.1	27.0	28.0
UK	19.0	22.3	23.9	24.4	25.0	27.2
US	6.1	7.2	8.8	9.5	9.6	9.4
OECD average	22.9	25.9	26.8	27.7	28.9	–
Manufactured imports/GDP in current prices:						
Japan	2.3	2.6	2.6	2.3	2.5	2.9
France	7.8	11.1	12.3	12.1	12.8	–
W. Germany	8.9	12.8	15.1	14.5	14.4	–
UK	7.9	13.3	16.3	16.5	16.8	–
US	2.7	5.0	6.4	7.0	7.3	–
OECD average	14.4	16.3	17.6	17.5	17.6	–
Manufactured imports/GDP in constant prices:						
Japan	2.8	2.2	2.6	3.9	4.4	5.5
France	8.5	11.5	12.3	15.1	16.5	–
W. Germany	10.8	13.4	15.0	17.7	19.1	–
UK	8.6	13.8	16.3	17.8	18.7	–
US	3.9	3.7	6.4	7.4	7.4	–
OECD average	15.2	15.7	17.7	20.1	21.5	–

Note: Constant (1985) prices.
OECD average is computed for 20 OECD member countries for all years
except 1987 and 1988, for which 18 and 15 member countries are respectively
included.

Source: Computed from IMF. *International Financial Statistics*, various
issues and IDE, AIDXT.

would appear to be relatively closed to foreign products if manufactured products only are taken into account, because of their low share
of total imports. In 1987, the most recent year for which such comparison can be made, the ratio of manufactured imports to GDP for
Japan was a meagre 2.5 per cent, while the average for OECD

countries was 17.6 per cent. Lack of information has precluded us from making an international comparison for more recent years, but the total Japanese imports/GDP ratio and the manufactured imports/GDP ratio increased to 7.6 per cent and 3.6 per cent respectively in 1989.

What is notable about the changes in the import/GDP ratio for Japan over time is its rapid decline in the early 1980s before rising again the latter half of the decade: the overall import ratio to GDP declined from 13.3 per cent in 1980 to 6.3 per cent in 1987, and then climbed to 7.6 per cent in 1989. Several causal factors may be identified for this decline. Among these – for the period between 1985 and 1987 – the appreciation of the yen and the decline in the price of such raw materials as oil appear to be very important. The appreciation at first tended to reduce the value of imports in terms of the yen as the prices of a large number of Japanese imports are quoted in US dollars, while the reduction in the price of raw materials, which account for more than one-third of Japanese imports, lowered the import bill.

If these two possible sources of decline are taken into account, the trend of the import/GDP ratio is reversed: the ratio of manufactured imports to GDP in constant (1985) prices increasing from 2.2 per cent in 1980 to 2.6 per cent in 1985, and then to 5.8 per cent in 1989 (not shown in the Table 2.3). Although the increase in this ratio may be worth emphasising, it is still clear that the importance of imports, especially manufactured imports, in Japanese economic activity is still limited.

Looking at the share of imports from developing countries in overall manufactured imports, Japan had a higher share than both the EC and the US. In 1986 Japan's share was 31.6 per cent, whilst that of the EC was 10.1 per cent (24.9 per cent excluding intra-EC trade) and the US 28.6 per cent (Takeuchi, 1989). Japan's relatively high share of imports from developing countries may be attributable to its geographical proximity and close social and economic ties with dynamic Asian developing countries. The findings here appear to indicate that the problem of limited access to the Japanese market is not associated solely with imports from developing countries, but with imports from all sources (Takeuchi, 1989).

We have seen above that the importance of imports in the Japanese market is limited. A number of studies have been undertaken to assess whether the Japanese import pattern is statistically different from those of other countries. These studies may be classified into three types.[5] The first attempts to examine import patterns from the supply side by focusing on factor endowments (the Heckscher–Ohlin type). The second incorporates both demand and supply factors, without formal modelling, in the determination of import patterns. In this type of study the size of the market (population) and the level of economic development (per capita GNP) are usually included as explanatory variables. Both these types assume perfect competition and inter-industry trade as the underlying pattern of international trade. Unlike these, the third type of study assumes imperfect competition and intra-industry trade as the main form of international trade.

Consensus has not yet been reached regarding the normality or abnormality of the Japanese pattern of imports, but roughly speaking those studies that used factor endowments as explanatory variables did not find the Japanese import pattern to be significantly different from the average pattern, or the norm. In contrast those that used the level of per capita GNP and size of population found the Japanese import pattern to vary significantly from the norm. These conflicting conclusions appear to indicate that the pattern of factor endowments in Japan is quite different from the average pattern. Specifically, Japan appears to be unusually rich in physical and human capital in relation to labour for the level of its economic development.

One may speculate on the possible reasons behind Japan's abundance of physical and human capital. First, government policies, especially industrial policies, appear to have promoted fixed investment as well as R&D investment, thereby increasing the endowment of physical and human capital. Secondly, the strongly competitive market structure of the Japanese manufacturing industry appears to have encouraged firms to invest aggressively in physical as well as human capital. Indeed the problem of over-investment, resulting in an excess of capacity, has been frequently observed in a number of Japanese manufacturing industries.

Although the results from the third approach are mixed, and therefore no conclusive evidence can be derived from it, these studies point out that compared with other developed countries the share of intra-industry imports in total imports for Japan is very small. Some argue that the limited amount of intra-industry trade in Japan is due to its geographical location. According to this argument Japan, being geographically remote from the other developed countries, is likely to engage in inter-industry trade rather than intra-industry trade with neighbouring developing countries. Others ascribe the low level of intra-industry imports to a myriad of non-tariff barriers raised both intentionally and unintentionally in Japan.

2.3   THE IMPACT OF IMPORT EXPANSION ON JAPANESE PRODUCTION

We have seen that imports by Japan increased rapidly from the mid-1980s, mainly because of the substantial appreciation of the yen and buoyant domestic economic activities. This expansion has caused concern among both producers and workers in that it may lead to a reduction in production and employment. It is therefore worthwhile examining the impact of this recent import expansion since the imports, which consist largely of labour-intensive products, are likely to affect unfavourably the employment situation in Japan.

Levels of production are determined by supply-side and demand-side factors. Supply-side factors include factors of production such as labour and capital as well as technology, while demand-side factors include both final demand and intermediate demand. In this section we examine the impact of imports on production from the demand side. In addition to import demand, we analyse the impact of the following demand-side factors: domestic demand (consumption and investment demand), export demand, and intermediate demand. Increases in all three types contribute to output expansion, while increases in import demand have a negative effect.

In order to examine the magnitude of the contribution of each of the above demands to output expansion, we undertake a breakdown analysis à la Chenery–Syrquin (1980).[6] One of the notable features of this model is that it captures not only the direct effects of the changes in demand factors on output changes, but also the indirect effects that arise from inter-industry commodity flows. In other words the output change in one industry, say iron and steel, is attributable not only to changes in the import demand for iron and steel but also to changes in the import demand for automobiles, whose production requires iron and steel as intermediate inputs. Since this methodology performs an ex-post breakdown of the changes in output into various factors, one should not interpret the results as reflecting a causal relationship. The analysis is undertaken at an aggregate level as well as at a disaggregate level. The results from the disaggregate analysis should shed light on structural changes in the Japanese economy. Moreover Japan's trading partners are divided into three groups – developed countries, developing countries, and socialist countries – to shed some light on the importance of each region in affecting the Japanese production structure.

Before analysing the results of the exercise, we shall examine briefly the changes in the level of production and exports and imports over the 1985–7 period (Table 2.4).[7] During the period in question, overall production grew at an average annual rate of 2.02 per cent. At the aggregate industry level, the rate of increase was relatively high for both manufacturing and services – 2.14 per cent and 2.05 per cent respectively. Among manufactures, technology-intensive manufactures grew very rapidly, registering a 4.73 per cent growth rate. There are wider variations in the rate of output growth for manufacturing subsectors under finer groupings however, as the annual rate of output growth was particularly high for clothing (7.66 per cent) and electrical machinery (10.72 per cent), but that of iron and steel declined significantly (−5.34 per cent). Agricultural production grew by a meagre 0.34 per cent, while the level of mining production declined substantially at −8.29 per cent per annum. In spite of slow growth in agricultural production and a substantial decline in mining production, these two sectors did not significantly affect the growth rate of Japanese production as a whole as their shares in overall production in Japan were very small for the period under study. As a result of the differences in the magnitude of the changes in the level of production among different sectors, Japanese production shifted away from agriculture and mining toward manufacturing and services between 1985 and 1987.

The annual volume of total exports declined at the rate of 2.4 per cent from 1985 to 1987. Most sectors suffered a decline in exports, the notable exceptions being the chemical, plastics, electrical and electronics industries. The increase in the volume of exports of these industries' products, despite the substantial yen appreciation, reflects the fact that their competitiveness had increased substantially.

In contrast to exports, the volume of overall imports increased significantly at an annual growth rate of 4.8 per cent over the same period. In particular the increase was remarkably large for the following industries; fishing, alcohol and tobacco, clothing, paper (pulp and printing), chemicals, iron and steel, industrial machinery, electrical machinery and automobiles. As will be shown later, the increase in the volume of imports for some of these sectors is attributable to the opening up of new channels for imports. The rapid increase in imports led to an increase in the import ratio, defined as the ratio of imports to apparent consumption, which increased from 5.6 per cent to 6.1 per cent during the period under study. As for individual industries, the pattern of the changes in import ratios is similar to that observed for the change in import volume. Some of the sectors that recorded a large change were fishing (from 19.6 per cent to 28.6 per cent), clothing (6.2 per cent to 8.1 per cent), and toys and sporting goods (9.8 per cent to 15.5 per cent).

A breakdown of this is given in Tables 2.4 and 2.5. According to the results, of the 2.02 per cent growth in production between 1985 and 1987, 3.55 per cent was due to growth in domestic demand, while the contributions from export expansion, import expansion, and intermediate demand (expressed in the changes in input/output coefficients) were negative at −0.37 per cent, −0.73 per cent, and −0.23 per cent respectively. These findings indicate that output growth during the period was sustained solely by the increase in domestic demand, which completely offset the negative impact of the other factors. The magnitude of negative contribution was largest for the changes in import demand, followed by those in intermediate demand and then by those in export demand.

The result of the impact of the changes in final demand (domestic demand, import demand and export demand) show that the Japanese economy had become oriented toward the domestic market, and that of the impact of changes in intermediate demand appear to reflect cost-reducing efforts through rationalisation and/or the ability of Japanese producers to cope with the cost disadvantage imposed on them by the yen appreciation.

An examination of the magnitude of the contributions from various demand factors at the broad industrial level reveals interesting differences in their patterns. As with the contributions from expansion in domestic demand, the differences in their magnitude are small among the sectors. The only sector to experience a relatively small increase was services, while the growth rate was relatively high for technology-intensive manufacturing. Since the differences between the growth rates in domestic demand for the sectors other than services were not significant, the differences in the growth rates of production among them are due to differences in the contributions from demand factors other than domestic demand.

The low growth rate for agricultural products was due mainly to a decline in demand for them as intermediate goods, and in turn this was due partly to the substitution of agricultural products by manufactured goods. A similar pattern is observed for material-intensive

Table 2.4 Sources of output change in 1985–7 (average annual growth rate in per cent)

| | Mining and Agriculture | | | | Light industry | | Heavy industry | | | |
	Total	Fishing	Manufac-turing	Mining	Manufac-turing	Manufac-turing	Manufac-turing	Material-intensive	Technology-intensive	Services
Changes in output	2.02	0.34	2.08	−8.29	2.14	2.38	2.05	−0.80	4.73	2.05
Due to changes in:										
Domestic demand	3.35	4.58	4.68	4.30	4.69	4.25	4.86	4.42	5.26	2.24
Exports	−0.37	−0.16	−0.39	−0.73	−0.39	−0.39	−0.41	−0.49	−0.34	−0.36
DC	0.10	−0.03	0.19	−0.20	0.19	−0.03	0.28	0.04	0.50	0.04
LDC	−0.23	−0.08	−0.44	−0.37	−0.44	−0.20	−0.54	−0.36	−0.70	−0.06
SC	−0.02	−0.01	−0.04	−0.04	−0.04	−0.03	−0.05	−0.05	−0.06	−0.01
Services	−0.22	−0.04	−0.10	−0.12	−0.10	−0.07	−0.11	−0.13	−0.09	−0.33
Imports	−0.73	−1.71	−1.21	−11.29	−1.14	−1.16	−1.14	−1.78	−0.53	−0.30
DC	−0.33	−0.26	−0.61	−2.38	−0.60	−0.66	−0.58	−0.67	−0.50	−0.11
LDC	−0.34	−1.53	−0.55	−2.00	−0.54	−0.60	−0.52	−0.84	−0.23	−0.11
SC	−0.02	−0.04	−0.03	−0.09	−0.03	−0.01	−0.04	−0.08	−0.00	−0.01
Services	−0.06	−0.02	−0.02	0.00	−0.02	−0.02	−0.02	−0.02	−0.01	−0.09
Technology	−0.23	−2.37	−1.00	−0.57	−1.01	−0.37	−1.25	−2.95	0.35	0.48

Notes: DC, LDC, and SC respectively developed countries, developing countries and socialist countries.

Source: Authors' calculations.

Table 2.5   Sources of output change for selected manufacturing sectors: 1985–7 (average annual growth rate in per cent)

	Clothing	Leather and footwear	Iron and steel	Electrical machinery	Automobiles
Changes in output	7.66	3.91	–5.34	10.72	4.08
Due to changes in:					
Domestic Demand	8.41	4.84	3.13	7.31	3.53
Exports	–0.41	–0.82	–2.97	1.56	–0.91
DC	–0.25	–0.01	–0.77	1.18	0.53
LDC	–0.10	–0.63	–2.11	0.39	–1.18
SC	–0.03	–0.11	–0.04	0.01	–0.07
Services	–0.04	–0.07	–0.05	–0.02	–0.19
Imports	–1.27	–1.68	–1.00	–0.49	–0.76
DC	–0.24	–0.58	–0.07	–0.62	–0.73
LDC	–1.50	–1.37	–0.54	–0.56	–0.02
SC	0.00	–0.02	–0.11	0.00	0.00
Services	–0.01	–0.01	–0.01	–0.01	–0.03
Technology	0.93	1.58	–4.49	2.33	2.28

Notes: DC, LDC, and SC respectively indicate developed countries, developing countries and socialist countries.

Source: Authors' calculations.

manufacturing, especially iron and steel. These patterns reflect cost reduction efforts by producers through rationalisation and innovation. In contrast to these sectors, which experienced a negative contribution from intermediate demand, the contribution from the increase in intermediate demand was positive for electrical equipment and automobiles (including automotive parts). This observation indicates that on average the use of electrical components in the production of manufactured products increased over time and that the use of automotive parts in the production of automobiles also increased.

Import expansion was a major cause of the decline in mining production between 1985 and 1987, and the negative contribution of import changes was as large as 11.2 per cent a year. Although to a lesser extent, import expansion also contributed negatively to the output of agriculture and material-intensive heavy manufacturing. Among the imports from different regions, the expansion of imports from developing countries was the major negative contributer to output in these sectors. Although the magnitude of the negative contribution from import expansion to light manufacturing was not so different from that for overall manufacturing, there are some sectors in light manufacturing that experienced a sizable negative contribution. According to Table 2.5, output of clothing, leather and footwear were substantially affected. In particular, increased importation of these goods from developing countries led to a reduction in demand for domestically produced products.

As the volume of exports declined during the period under study, the contribution of export expansion to output growth was negative, −0.37 per cent for overall exports. Among the sectors the magnitude of the negative contribution from export expansion was quite large for mining. In manufacturing, material-intensive heavy manufacturing suffered greatly – particularly iron and steel. A major part of the decline in export expansion came from those exports destined for developing countries, and the decline in automobiles was substantial. These findings indicate that there was a significant decline in the export of material-intensive products.

In contrast to the above, export growth was observed for electrical equipment, parts and components. When coupled with the observation that import expansion contributed negatively to the output of electrical machinery, this indicates that intra-industry trade had increased for these products.

The breakdown of the increase in output over the 1985–7 period into demand factors revealed a number of interesting features. First, unlike in the 1980–5 period when both domestic demand expansion and export expansion provided impetus to economic growth, after 1985 the Japanese production moved away from exports towards the domestic market. This shift was mainly attributable to the following two factors: substantial increase in domestic prices relative to foreign ones following the appreciation of the yen; and buoyant economic activity in Japan – conducive monetary policies had resulted in capital accumulation and active private consumption.

Secondly, we observed that emphasis had shifted away from the primary sectors towards manufacturing and services. Among the manufacturing subsectors, technology-intensive heavy manufacturing had expanded rapidly. These changes were due largely to a shift in the pattern of comparative advantage between Japan and its trading partners. The relative decline in the shares of the primary sectors, light manufacturing, and material-intensive manufacturing was attributable largely to an increase in imports from developing countries and a decline in exports to them, indicating that for these sectors developing countries had gained comparative advantage vis-à-vis Japan. It was also found that for electrical machinery, which had experienced a sizable increase in production, intra-industry trade had increased.

Finally, we found that demand for material-intensive heavy manufactured products as inputs for the production of other products had declined significantly over time, whereas the demand for electrical equipment for that purpose had increased. Such a shift reflects a change in production technology from one that used intensively such materials as iron and steel to one that uses electrical components such as semi-conductors.

These structural shifts in the Japanese economy are likely to continue and will probably intensify. This is because the Japanese economy has already adjusted well to the new economic environment. More specifically, Japan has invested heavily in industries oriented towards the domestic market, such as services, and it has also invested significantly in new channels for imports, as will be discussed in Chapter 4. Therefore the reversal of these trends is unlikely.

Notes and references

1. An F-statistic for the Chow test is computed to be 2.25, while 10 per cent significant of $F(4.49)$ is 2.07. The Economic Planning Agency (1989) obtains a similar observation of the presence of the structural change without a formal structural change test. Corker (1989) on the other hand did not find any structural shift in the pattern of Japanese imports.
2. The value of overall imports in terms of the yen declined by about one-third from 1985 to 1986, before increasing slowly in 1987 and 1988. Despite the increase in two consecutive years, the value of imports in yen in 1988 stood at only about three quarters of the value recorded in 1985. These developments may be explained mainly by the fact that more than 80 per cent of Japanese import transactions were conducted in US dollars, and thus the price of imports in yen declined substantially because of the yen appreciation.
3. The Export-Import Bank of Japan (1989) shows that by 1987 intra-industry trade between Asian newly industrialised countries and Japan did not increase noticeably.
4. See Urata (1987) for heavy industrialisation policies in China.
5. Takeuchi (1990) provides a comprehensive survey of empirical studies regarding the Japanese import pattern.
6. The following methodology is used for the analysis. The idea of breaking down the production increase into several factors follows Chenery and Syrquin (1980). Their model compares I/0 tables of two different periods

at constant prices, and breaks down the factors contributing to the production increase of each sector. In our case, the latest I/0 tables of Japan is for 1985, and our intention is to look into the changes after that time which were caused by the yen appreciation. Modification of the Chenery–Syrquin model is therefore necessary. The year for comparison with 1985 is set at 1987, due to the availability of industrial surveys. It was also the year when imports from Asian newly industrialised countries increased to a large extent.

The following convention is adopted: X = output vector; A = input coefficient matrix; D = domestic final demand matrix; E = export vector; and M = import coefficient diagonal matrix where the coefficient is defined as the ratio of imports to total domestic demand.

Also, Δ signifies the change between the two periods, and subscripts 0 and t show 1985 and 1987 respectively. Since the 1987 I/0 table is not available, we allowed only the import coefficient (M) to change over time, and fixed A at A_0. Then the output change induced by the change in domestic demand (ΔD) is given by

$$\Delta Xd = [I - (I - M_0)A_0]^{-1} [(I - M_0)\Delta D] \tag{2.1}$$

Exports (ΔE) is

$$\Delta Xe = [I - (I - M_0)A_0]^{-1} \Delta E \tag{2.2}$$

When all the variables except A are allowed to change, the hypothetical output in 1987 is described as

$$X'_t = [I - (I - M_t)A_0]^{-1} [(I - M_t)D_t + E_t] \tag{2.3}$$

Then the pure and cross effects (ΔXm) of the change in the import structure is calculated as

$$\Delta Xm = (X'_t - X_0) - \Delta Xd - \Delta Xe \tag{2.4}$$

Moreover if X_t is available from other sources, then the effects of technology change (ΔXa), again including both pure and cross effects, is given by

$$\Delta Xa = X_0 - X'_t \tag{2.5}$$

As for the data for the exercise, the following procedure was used. First the sectors in the 1985 I/0 table of Japan were aggregated into 42 sectors for the industrial level analysis, then these sectors were aggregated further into nine sectors for observation at the macro-level. To estimate the output in 1987, the growth of output for each sector was calculated using the industrial survey. These growth rates were applied to the 1985 I/0 figures, and then deflated by the general domestic prices. Control totals of the domestic demand in 1987 were estimated using the growth rates of expenditure items in the national accounts, then converted to 1985 constant prices. The export and import vectors in 1987 at I/0 basis were estimated first by multiplying the 1985 totals by the growth rate (in terms of the yen) obtained from the national accounts; secondly by applying the commodity composition of 1987 in dollar terms to the control total; and thirdly, deflating each figure by the actual export or import price index. The import coefficient of each sector was also calculated in real terms.

7. The analysis is performed at the level of 42 sectors and the results are aggregated to the levels shown in Tables 2.4 and 2.5. The results for the 42 sector disaggregation are available from the authors on request.

3 General Measures toward Import Promotion in Japan

Kinya Onoda

3.1 TARIFF REDUCTION IN THE 1970s AND 1980s

After the compensatory rise in association with import liberalisation during 1960 and 1964, Japan's tariff level has continually reduced. 1972 marked a break from the traditional trade policy package. Pressures arising from Japan's trade surplus had been felt for some time and this led to the government making a major revision to Japan's tariff structure. The main points were: (1) a reduction in the escalating structure of tariffs; (2) a general reduction in tariff levels in accordance with the level of industrial development; (3) the abolition of the category of luxury goods; and (4) a reduction in the high tariff on agricultural goods.

It should be added that export encouragement in the form of low-interest export credit was terminated in the same year. Industry-specific promotion policies with an emphasis on achieving international competitiveness had on the whole already been dismantled. Thus Japan's trade policy took its first positive steps toward import promotion.

This revision was in accordance with the Kennedy round of the multilateral trade negotiation talks, (1962–7), the first trade talks in which Japan had actively participated. The main logic behind Japan's participation was seemingly a recognition that it should share the responsibility for promoting freer trade, but there also was a feeling that the Japanese economy had become mature enough to benefit from trade liberalisation. Its success encouraged Japan to propose that the next round (1973–9) should be held in Tokyo.

Tariff levels went down as a result of the agreements achieved at both rounds. For a number of tariff items, reduction was implemented earlier than scheduled as part of an import promotion policy. As is shown in Table 3.1, by 1980 Japan's effective tariff rates

29

Table 3.1   Average tariff rates of developed countries[1] (percentages)

Year	Japan	US	EC[2]
1981	2.5	3.2	2.5
1982	2.6	3.6	2.7
1983	2.5	3.5	2.7
1984	2.5	3.4	2.8
1985	2.6	3.3	2.7
1986	3.3	3.7	3.1

Notes: 1. Average tariff rate = tariff revenue/total imports.
2. Tariff revenue for the EC includes import surcharges on agricultural commodities.

Source: Japan Tariff Association, *Trade Yearbook*, 1989.

(the ratio of paid customs duties to total imports) declined to roughly the same level as those in the US and the EC.

Table 3.1 shows that the tariff rates were stable between 1980 and 1985, but underwent a small rise in 1986. In Japan's case this seeming stability hides an increase in the share of processed products – which are subject to higher tariff rates – in total imports. The share of processed products rose from 22.9 per cent of the total in 1980 to 31 per cent in 1985. The rise in 1986 resulted from the decrease in the price of oil. The lower value of imports used as a denominator naturally served to raise the average tariff rate. In addition, the tariff rate on crude oil actually went up since it was a specific duty, that is fixed duty on volume (Japan Tariff Association, 1988 version). Tariffs on individual commodities therefore kept reducing.

In spite of the overall reduction in tariff levels, the escalating structure was maintained, although to a lesser degree. Japan's post-Tokyo round average tariff on materials was estimated at 0.4 per cent (0.2 per cent when petroleum and gold are excluded), while those on semi-processed and processed goods were 4.5 per cent and 5.9 per cent respectively (4.0 per cent and 5.8 per cent when petroleum and gold are excluded). Effective protection in 1984 was still high – as shown in Table 3.2 – in metals, textiles, paper and forestry products (Yamazawa, 1986).

There is a discernible link between industrial development and tariff levels. Tariffs on mining and manufactures have in general been reduced, but those items with rising self-sufficiency and increasing export ratios have tended to receive higher cuts. Automobiles, elec-

Table 3.2 Escalating tariff structure by industry, 1984 (percentages)

Product	Nominal tariff rate	Effective tariff rate
Iron and Steel:		
Mining	–	–0.4
Crude steel	2.8	3.2
Cast steel	4.4	4.7
Rolled steel	5.0	8.9
Forestry products:		
Forestry	0.2	–
Timbers, wood products	1.9	3.6
Furniture	6.0	7.9
Textiles:		
Spinning and weaving	4.8	6.2
Fabrics	9.0	12.3
Other textiles	9.6	12.3
Knitted products	14.8	24.9
Garments	15.2	20.7
Paper products:		
Pulp and paper	1.6	1.4
Paper products	4.8	8.6

Source: Ministry of Finance, quoted in Yamazawa (1986).

trical and industrial machinery are among these. In contrast those products which were losing their international competitiveness and were experiencing decreasing self-sufficiency rates, such as textiles, processed food and some chemicals, lagged behind in the tariff reduction. For some of the products which have relatively recently become exports, such as synthetic fibres and office machinery, the tariff rates have remained stable and are now in the higher-rate category. In the second and third groups there still remains room for further tariff reduction.

Agricultural and fishery products are however the leaders in the tariff levels. For example, the tariff rates on dextrine (25 per cent), dextrose (35 per cent), beef (25 per cent), biscuits (24 per cent), oranges (20–40 per cent), juices (35 per cent), dairy products (25–35 per cent), and wine (45 per cent) far exceed the average industrial tariffs of 5–10 per cent. For these commodities there are also non-tariff barriers – these will be discussed later.

General tariffs decreased further as a part of action programmes to ease the tension arising from the trade imbalance. The main recent changes, excluding those items subject to GSP which will be discussed later, include the following. In 1986 there was a total withdrawal of tariff, or a uniform reduction in the tariff rates by 20 per cent, for 1853 items, and a total withdrawal of the tariff on computers, peripheral equipment, and parts thereof. In 1987 there was a 30 per cent reduction in the tariff on alcoholic beverages, a total withdrawal of the tariff on cigarettes, and a reduction from 20 per cent to 10 per cent for the tariff on chocolate confectionery. In 1989 the tariff was reduced on 131 tropical items, including bananas, rattan furniture, and so forth, and in 1990 it was announced that all tariffs of less than 5 per cent would be withdrawn.[1]

3.2 RELAXATION OF QUANTITATIVE RESTRICTIONS

The process of import liberalisation in Japan started in 1960, when the government announced its intention to remove most of import controls. Commodities were classified – according to the period required for liberalisation – into four categories: (1) those to be liberalised almost immediately, (2) in the near future (in around three years), (3) after a necessary period, and (4) those which would be difficult to liberalise for a considerable period. Category (3) included industries in the process of technological development, and those which were to be promoted as core sectors of the machinery industry, such as machine tools, automobiles, and heavy electrical machinery Category 4 consisted mainly of agricultural commodities.

In the space of four years, liberalisation of categories 1 and 2 had been completed, and 92 per cent of imports were outside the quota system. Since then the remaining sensitive items have been gradually liberalised. The liberalisation rate reached 95 per cent in 1970, most of category 3 having been released from restriction. This also meant that the promotion of specific industries through protectionism had in the main been halted.

Progress has been slow since then, for the remaining restrictions were on sensitive items. In April 1986 however, quantitative restrictions on four items, including leather and leather footwear, were abolished and the import liberalisation of industrial products was completed. As of March 1989 there were 23 items which remained subject to residual quantitative restriction (22 agricultural products plus coal). In addition there were 54 items subject to non-residual restriction. Thus the total number of restricted items was 76, as processed milk and cream were counted in both categories.

The quantitative restrictions had been a target of attack for a long time. The US led the attack, demanding better market access. Inside Japan the Ministry of Agriculture, Forestry and Fishery (MAFF) had remained adamant about maintaining agricultural protection on the grounds of food security and farm income maintenance. As a result relatively few products were released from quantitative restriction, although many quota increases were made.

A breakthrough was however made in February 1988 by the GATT panel on Japanese agricultural protection. The US appealed against twelve cases of import restriction, and ten of these were judged as violating GATT rules. Japan accordingly agreed that the import of ten items would be liberalised.[2] In the same year, at the Japan–US negotiation on beef and oranges, it was agreed that these imports also would be liberalised by 1991. Other items were placed on the liberalisation schedule, albeit grudgingly, and the number of restricted items continued to decrease. One notable exception, rice, is still under heavy protection – this will be discussed in Chapter 4.

3.3 ACTION PROGRAMME

In spite of the tariff reduction and trade liberalisation, Japan's trade surplus gave rise to much friction. In the 1970s the dispute was mainly over individual products – either over the rapid expansion of particular exports from Japan or over the lack of access for certain imports into the Japanese market. Japan's increased trade surplus in the 1980s however exacerbated the situation and the trade imbalance began to be more widely debated. Japan was called upon to improve access to its market by boosting domestic demand, improving import inspection, liberalising its financial and services markets, and so on, in addition to the commodity-specific issues. In short, structural aspects of the economy were now being targeted and revision of these was being demanded.

A series of measures were adopted by the government to reduce the trade surplus and help ease the tension. On 16 December 1981 a new external economic policy was announced which committed Japan to reviewing its residual quantitative import restrictions, examining its industrial standards and certificate system, and bringing forward by two years the implementation of the tariff reductions agreed at the Tokyo round. On 30 January 1982 another revision was made which aimed at improving the import inspection procedure and announcing Japan's intention to establish an Office of Trade and Investment Ombudsman. Both measures were in response to foreign criticism that Japan's procedural protectionism was discouraging imports. The former simplified the import procedure, while the latter was designed to act as a complaint-processing body. In its eight years of existence, the office received and processed more than 400 complaints.

On 28 May of the same year tariffs on 215 items were either withdrawn or reduced. Also the import inspection procedure for specific commodities was further improved – that for metal baseball bats was a prominent example. 1983 saw two more such concessions. On 13 January in yet another revision of Japan's external economic policy, tariffs were withdrawn or reduced on another 86 items, and a commitment was made to improve access by foreign producers to government procurement. In this context, sales to the newly privatised Nippon Telegram and Telephone Company (NTT) was regarded as a part of the package. Import restrictions on some agricultural products were also relaxed. On 21 October another tariff reduction/withdrawal on 44 items was implemented. The government also designated November as 'product import promotion month'.

Two further import promotion packages were made in 1984. On 27 April another revision of the external economic policy was announced. As well as tariff adjustment on 76 items, inspection of exports to Japan by foreign institutions were accorded wider acceptance. The 'specific products trade expansion programme' (STEP) – which was designed to provide specific foreign products with access to the Japanese market – was initiated, and exhibitions featuring foreign products (such as the German Exhibition and the French Fair) were accorded government assistance. Market liberalisation for advanced technology (communications satellites, telecommunications business, and so forth) was also provided. Later that year eleven tariff items were made free of duty or had their tariff rates reduced.

In spite of the wide coverage of these measures, they were obviously ad hoc and piecemeal. The trade surplus continued to increase and the demands from abroad intensified. A more radical and comprehensive approach was needed, and in July 1985 the 'outline of the action programme for improved market access' was announced. This was a joint undertaking by the government ministries and the ruling party. The headquarters for the programme had been established in April, the prime minister had been appointed chairman and officials of both the Liberal Democratic Party and the ministries had been elected as members. Thus the programme had a strong political backing.[3]

The programme specified that six issues be dealt with: (1) tariffs, (2) import restrictions, (3) standards, certification systems and import procedures, (4) government procurement, (5) financial and capital markets, (6) services and promotion of imports.

With regard to tariff reductions, in addition to the measures already mentioned it was proposed that all tariffs on industrial goods from developed countries should be abolished. The programme also aimed at the withdrawal of tariffs on high-technology products, and it was intended that escalating tariffs should be relaxed. With import restrictions there was a commitment to negotiate the agricultural protection issue at the GATT talks, thus opening the way for the abovementioned liberalisations at the Uruguay round.

On the issue of standards, certification systems and import procedures, the position of 'free in principle, restriction as exception' was clarified. A review of more than 40 existing acts and regulations found 88 (three more were added later) necessary improvements to make the system compatible with international standards. So far 89 of the 91 measures have been implemented. In government procurement, the contract procedure for the 67 organisations subject to the programme was revised to offer increased opportunities to foreign suppliers. This included an extension of the application period from 30 to 40 days. The value of foreign procurement increased from 43.5 billion yen in 1986 to 54.8 billion yen the following year, amounting to 19 per cent of total government procurement. Government-related organisations and local public bodies were also requested to cooperate in the programme. Later on 16 special corporations were added to the list.

Liberalisation measures were also implemented in financial and capital markets. There had been partial deregulation of bank deposit rates for some time, and there was a commitment to further liberalisation . This however took some time to materialise. Only in October 1989 was the minimum amount for the interest-deregulated accounts lowered to ten million yen, although accounts bearing slightly lower interest started in June 1989 with a minimum amount of three million yen. Bond markets moved more rapidly toward deregulation. The forward bond market was created in October 1985, and issues of variable interest-bearing Euro Yen bonds were liberalised, together with other measures to promote financial market diversification, in April 1986.

In services the status of foreign lawyers, which had been a source of conflict for some time, underwent major reform. The Special Foreign Lawyers Act was introduced in May 1986, opening up the way for foreign lawyers to engage in business concerning foreign laws. As of June 1989 there were 47 such lawyers practising in Japan. Foreigners were also given access to the national health insurance service. In import promotion, large companies were requested to take steps to increase their imports, and the number of such companies increased from 134 in 1985 to 302 in 1988. An import promotion taxation system was created to take effect from 1980 – this will be described in the next section. Measures to promote investment were also taken, including an expansion of the credit facilities offered by the Japan Development Bank for investment coming into Japan.

To what extent the action programme succeeded in its aim to increase imports is difficult to judge. In quantitative terms, the simultaneous yen appreciation probably had a far greater effect. The programme nevertheless made visible the government's seriousness about settling trade conflicts. There was an educational effect too in that the increasing interdependence of the world economy necessitated bringing traditional domestic policies into the realm of international negotiations. On the other hand there was growing irritation at being subjected to foreign demands, especially with the threats from Section 301 and Super 301. Later on this sentiment intensified with the market oriented sector specific (MOSS) talks and the structural impediments initiative (SII).

3.4   MORE ACTIVE IMPORT PROMOTION MEASURES

The import promotion policies described so far in this chapter have dealt with lowering and dismantling trade barriers. Recently more unorthodox measures have been taken to increase imports. Various financial measures include preferential taxation and low interest loans on certain types of imports. Information and other services are also used extensively. An import expansion effect can be expected, for example, from information on foreign products being made available to prospective importers in Japan and on information on market conditions inside Japan being made available to foreign exporters.

These active policies are worth noting, and are described in some detail in this section.

3.4.1 Preferential taxation and financial measures

In 1986 a new preferential taxation system was introduced to promote imports of machinery, mainly in response to strong pressure from foreign exporting countries. This measure provides an extra 20 per cent tax deduction on that specified in two promotional taxation schemes.[4] One is a preferential taxation system to promote investment in new technologies (applies to equipment for productivity improvement and managerial modernisation) by small and medium enterprises, and the other relates to promoting investment in social, economic and energy infrastructure (applies to equipment for improving energy efficiency and industrial upgrading). The total tax deduction from the scheme was estimated at approximately two billion yen in 1988.[5]

The idea of an import taxation system covering a wider range of imports was first mooted around the time of the Arches summit meeting in the summer of 1989, and it took its concrete form in the general rules for the revised taxation system for 1990. Any person who imports finished products (parts 5 to 8 of the standard international trade classification: SITC) in excess of 10 per cent of the same products in the reference year (the year in which the highest value of a particular item is recorded) is eligible to benefit. The scheme is to run for three years, commencing in April 1990. Eligible manufacturers are allowed one of two benefits: a tax deduction of 5 per cent of the increased import amount (the maximum limit is 10 per cent, or 15 per cent in the case of small and medium enterprises, of the corporate tax), or an extra depreciation of 10 per cent (20 per cent for machinery) with the maximum limit set at 50 per cent of the increase of each type of import. Wholesalers and retailers can save up to 20 per cent of the increased amount of each type of import, depending on the reference year, as a tax-free 'market development reserve for imported products'. The products covered in the scheme total around 2300 items with a total import value of approximately five trillion yen.

It is estimated that annual tax reductions alone will amount to around 10 billion yen, and the overall tax savings will reach 85–90 billion yen. The effect on import expansion will be in the range of $3 billion in 1990.[6] The system is analogous to the now defunct export promotion measures of export income deduction and the export market development reserve system in the 1950s and 1960s, but on the reverse side.

There are also import credit schemes, such as sales-promotion credit on imported goods for small and medium retailers, a credit facility at the Bank of Japan, loans by the Export-Import Bank on manufactured imports, and loans to facilitate import expansion offered by the Development Bank of Japan.

The first measure is a loan towards shop refurbishment and working capital geared to facilitate the sale of imported goods by small and medium retailers. This credit first became available in 1986 with the establishment of the special credit fund for international trade arrangements for small and medium-scale enterprises. The second originated in 1978 when the yen was reaching its peak, but it was suspended at the end of 1979 as a result of Japan's current account deficit following the second oil price hike. However it was reinstated at the end of 1983 in view of the increasing trade surplus. In this scheme the Bank of Japan offers yen loans against import bills as collateral, and the exchange rate is taken into consideration.

The Export-Import Bank loan is a low-interest, medium-term (up to 10 years) credit to cover imports of manufactures (defined as SITC 5 to 8). This started in 1983, and subsequently dollar loans were added and the interest rate lowered. The Japan Development Bank provides long-term (up to 25 years) credit for the purchase of fixed assets such as warehouses and land for improving import facilities.

3.4.2 Information and other services

Trade missions were the major means of increasing imports during 1973 and 1983, when two large missions were sent abroad. Since then emphasis has shifted to more indirect means of providing information, both at home and abroad. For example, the promotion of imports by providing foreign producers with information on Japanese market trends and market requirements was stepped up. However trade missions have continued to be sent to such major trading partners as the US, Western Europe, Australia and China.

In addition STEP, which was discussed earlier, has been more closely linked to specific commodities. This scheme includes studies of sales promotion strategies to assist the sale of imported goods in Japan. The commodities selected so far have been Spanish wine and Chinese carpets in 1987, and Portuguese wine and Thai rubber gloves the following year. The Office of Trade and Investment Ombudsman, also described earlier, takes rapid action on concrete complaints from foreign exporters and Japanese importers about import inspection and other procedures.

Following the creation of 'import promotion month' in 1983, this became an annual undertaking to stimulate public awareness of foreign products and thereby increase their sales. JETRO (Japan External Trade Organisation, formerly Japan Export Trade Organisation) and other organisations, including large retailers, annually hold large exhibitions of imported products.[7] A special organisation, MIPRO (Manufactured Imports Promotion Organisation), was established in 1978 with an emphasis on promoting personal imports.

Import insurance is another scheme to enable small companies to import. The advance payment insurance scheme started in 1987 as a government undertaking to cover the risks involved in paying in advance for imports, including non-recovery due to bankruptcy or foreign exchange regulations in the exporting country. At first all imports from some 100 countries were excluded from the scheme because of political instability or bad debts, but the coverage was recently enlarged.[8]

The import-promotion information network is being so designed as to establish an on-line information network between the JETRO headquarters and the local terminals to be set up in all the prefectures in Japan. Its aim is to disseminate information on imported products to consumers and distributors. There is a plan to link the network with the US Department of Commerce data base on products available for export, their prices and the names of enterprises able to supply them. The Ministry of International Trade and Industry (MITI) hopes the network will also encourage non-agent and private imports, and will help break the exclusive distribution channels and trade customs through the freer flow of information.[9]

3.5 EVALUATION OF RECENT IMPORT PROMOTION MEASURES

While it is difficult to separate trade policies into those aimed at developed countries and those aimed at developing countries, Japan's recent import promotion measures have been mostly formulated with developed countries in mind. There are various reasons for this, among which are traditional and close trade ties and the serious friction caused by the trade imbalance. That the main thrust of import expansion has been oriented toward finished products also works in the favour of developed countries. In practice, neighbouring developing countries have also benefited from the measures, especially in recent times, and it is therefore incorrect to say that Japan's import promotion measures neglect developing countries.

Japan's import promotion efforts started in earnest in the early 1980s, but the action programme of 1985 was the first systematic and comprehensive measure to be implemented. Its launch coincided with the start of the rapid yen appreciation, and imports began to show a structural change toward more manufactured imports, which was the desired outcome of the scheme. However the liberalisation of the Japanese market still presents some problems. One is the efficiency of the measures employed. There is concern that strong measures such as tax reductions on import promotion are really import subsidies and that in the long term they will damage the efficiency of the Japanese economy. Also import expansion by means of administrative and political measures is inherently limited. The main impetus for import expansion may therefore have to come from economic efficiency. The importation of some intermediate products and parts, in particular, is looked upon as causing inefficiency, and any increase in such imports may harm Japan's future industrial structure.

The second problem is the possible emergence of protectionism if the economy were to be disrupted by external factors, including another oil shock. Larger imports then will become a heavy burden in economic management, and it is questionable whether the Japanese government will be able to ignore political pressure from industrial circles wishing to protect their industries.

The third problem relates to the fact that tax reduction on import promotion and other similar measures only provide incentives to import-related industries, and that they disrupt the distribution of income between industries and between the corporate and household sectors. In this context such measures as the import-promotion information network, which would create a greater degree of trade efficiency, are deemed more appropriate.

Notes and references

1. The Tariff Council, a consultative body for the Ministry of Finance, formulated a plan to abolish in principle all import duties on industrial products with less than a 5 per cent rate, to take effect in 1990. The number of those items is currently around 2700, of which 1300 are industrial products. Altogether 1400 items are listed, approximately 60 per cent of which are machinery. This will realise a zero-tariff on virtually all machinery. Of industrial imports, those with a zero-tariff will comprise some 80 per cent, twice the current proportion of 40 per cent. Another salient point in the plan is the creation of a tax refund system. Under this, and within a specified period, the import duties paid on imports would be refunded should they be re-exported because of non-sale and so forth. This is designed to reduce sales risks, especially for overseas exporters, and is therefore a part of import promotion. On the other hand the plan includes tariff rate increases for 19 processed agricultural products, such as tinned pineapple and apple juice, as compensation to domestic farmers for the proposed import liberalisation due in the same year (The *Nihon Keizai Shimbun*, 20 December 1989).
2. The 12 agricultural products are: (1) sugarless condensed milk, (2) processed cheese, (3) beef and pork-based products, (4) fruit puree or paste, (5) fruit pulp and tinned pineapple, (6) non-citrus fruit juice (such as tomato juice), (7) tomato ketchup and tomato sauce, (8) dextrine, (9) glucose, (10) miscellaneous beans, (11) peanuts, and (12) other processed foodstuffs. The GATT panel ruled that import restrictions on 10 of these (all but items 10 and 11 above) were in violation of the GATT articles. At the GATT council meeting in February 1988 Japan accepted the ruling, at first with reservations concerning items 1 and 8, and subsequently proposed a liberalisation schedule. In the case of the Japan–US dispute on beef and oranges, an agreement was reached at the ministerial meeting in June 1988.
3. The action programme is detailed in Japanese and English in: Cabinet Secretarial Special Mission Office and Coordination Bureau of the Economic Planning Agency (General Editorship), and the Working Group on Market Liberalization (Editor), *Action Program*, 1985.
4. The ordinary tax deduction rate was increased from 7 per cent to 8.4 per cent, while the special depreciation rate was increased from 30 per cent to 36 per cent.
5. The *Mainichi Shimbun*, 18 July 1989.
6. The *Nihon Keizai Shimbun*, 20 December 1989.
7. The Japan Tariff Association and the Ministry of International Trade and Industry report the following exhibitions. In 1984 – German Exhibition 84, French Exhibition 84, Made in USA Fair, and World Import Fair Nagoya 85; in 1985 – Second French Exhibition and Made in Europe Fair; in 1986 – Made in USA Fair (medical equipment exhibition); in 1987 – Made in Korea Fair, and Sport and Leisure 88.
8. The *Nihon Keizai Shimbun*, 22 July 1989.
9. The *Nihon Keizai Shimbun*, 8 December 1989.

4 Japan's Import Barriers – Agriculture and Distribution

Akira Hirata, Hirohisa Kohama, Shujiro Urata and Kazuhiko Yokota

4.1 NON-TARIFF BARRIERS

This chapter deals with institutional import-limiting factors in Japan. Under the present international arrangements, most trade policies are required to be applied equally to both developed and developing countries. Strictly speaking therefore, as in the case of the import promotion policies discussed in Chapter 3, there is no import-limiting policy designed specifically for developing countries. This fact also determines the approach taken in this chapter. Policies which specifically affect developing countries, either positively or negatively, are relatively few and these will be discussed in Chapter 5.

Since the late 1960s Japan's import policies have been continuously liberalised. This does not however mean that imports to Japan are free from artificial barriers. Although overt and formal quantitative restrictions are few, some individual sectors are still heavily protected – agriculture being the most important example.

More importantly, 'procedural' protection has often been pointed out as an effective deterrent to imports. These include government domestic regulations on hygiene, communication, and so forth. In Japan's case more subtle 'structural' aspects, such as firms relying mainly on domestic supplies and distribution channels, are also pointed out. Some of these are products of historical development or some government intervention. In some cases the two factors are intertwined.

The Office of United States Trade Representatives (USTR) for example stated in its 1989 report that as many as 29 barriers existed in Japan, and claimed that their removal or relaxation would substantially increase US exports to Japan.[1] Japan's agricultural protectionism and its distribution system received the most attention. This

42

chapter will likewise, and will work on the two sectors in some detail. Before going into individual cases however, an overview of Japan's institutional non-tariff barriers would be useful.

Domestic industrial regulations are the grey areas of import barriers. They do not necessarily violate GATT rules, although efforts are being made at the Uruguay round to tighten the reins on them. From an individual country's viewpoint, they bring about possible encouragement to domestic production as well as preventing welfare losses. The degree of protection afforded by these measures has not been directly worked out, but price differences in Japan and abroad provide an important indication. Table 4.1 gives details of an international price comparison of selected commodities, including manufactures and services, made recently by the Japanese government. It shows that prices are generally higher in Tokyo than in other major cities. For example the Minolta Maxxum 7000i camera is reported to be cheaper in New York than at discount shops in Shinjuku, Tokyo. This would not be possible without either dumping/discriminatory pricing practices or distribution inefficiency.[2] The following factors are among the possible reasons for the discrepancy between prices in Japan and abroad: (1) government regulations, (2) distribution systems, (3) the pricing policies of Japanese producers, and (4) consumers' brand-oriented tastes.

Government regulations have a visible effect on agricultural products. Rice, wheat, beef, sugar and dairy products are among the most prominent, as can be seen from the large international price differences in agricultural products in the table – this subject will be dealt with in section 4.2. Manufacturing and other industries are also tightly controlled by industry-specific laws, including those on price and entry control for electricity (Electric Power Industry Law) and gas (Gas Industry Law), on railways (Railway Industry Law), on buses and taxis (Land Transportation Law), and on air transportation (Air Transportation Law).

The telecommunications industry is also subject to price and entry controls (Telecommunication Industry Law), but following the privatisation of Nippon Telegraph and Telephone Company (NTT) the regulations were relaxed somewhat. A similar deregulation process has been taking place in the tobacco industry (Tobacco Industry Law), with privatisation and easier access to the Japanese market. The production and sale of alcoholic beverages is under license, which limits entry. The Large-Scale Retail Store Law requires coordination with and consent from local business associations on the

Table 4.1   Price comparison of selected commodities (Tokyo = 100)

	New York	Hamburg	London	Paris
Rice	36	123	48	43
Bread	91	84	48	136
Beef	31	35	28	35
Beef (Imported)	96	109	88	107
Ham	42	47	40	37
Milk	50	44	53	55
Sugar	53	43	48	47
Chocolate	84	70	78	74
Butter	44	44	36	37
Egg	76	126	129	144
Onion	65	54	99	38
Cabbage	35	27	75	51
Banana	59	59	120	113
Tea	71	80	22	39
Spaghetti	92	67	33	38
Suit	63	63	68	69
Shirt	102	56	79	78
Skirt	96	97	72	94
Shoes	100	139	89	88
TV	56	112	98	135
VCR	93	135	118	135
Film	78	101	98	120
Petrol	30	57	73	89
Hair Cut (Man)	46	84	47	91
Hair Cut (Woman)	133	120	166	137
Movie	60	49	71	53
Laundry	111	105	124	136

Source: Economic Planning Agency (1989).

establishment, enlargement and business practices (opening date, store size, business hours, number of closing days a year) of large retail outlets, and, as will be discussed later, this is often used to block new entries. This law has also been central to the distribution controversy. Many of these government regulations are among the issues being discussed with the US at the Structural Impediments Initiative (SII) talks.

The pricing policy of producers needs some scrutiny here in connection with the drastic shift in the terms of trade caused by the appreciation of the yen. Price disparities can come about in one of two ways. First, taking the abovementioned case of the camera as an example, one possible reason for the difference between the New York price and the Japanese price is that, following the very rapid yen appreciation, the producer did not increase the camera's dollar-term export price quickly enough from fear of losing a valuable export market. This fear would be acute in industries that are highly dependant on the export market. From a managerial viewpoint this decision is understandable, but it does open the way to charges of dumping.

The second reason for price disparities is failure to reduce the price of imported commodities. Complaints have been made by Japanese consumers that the benefits from the yen appreciation have not been passed on to them. A recent report by the Economic Planning Agency (EPA) revealed that on average only half of the gains have been used to lower prices – the other half has been absorbed by importers/ distributors. Undoubtedly such practice has retarded an increase in consumption, thereby diluting the import expansion effect.

4.2 AGRICULTURAL PROTECTIONISM[3]

The core of Japanese protectionism lies in agriculture. Japan's formal NTBs, or quantitative restrictions, are relatively few, perhaps even fewer than in most other industrial countries. But these formal NTBs still remain high in agriculture. According to Saxonhouse and Stern (1989), the estimated *ad valorem* equivalent of Japan's NTBs for agriculture is as high as 48.5 per cent, which is higher than in the other major industrial countries, except for the NTBs on petroleum and related products in France.

The imposition of these barriers is probably the largest single practice to negatively affect the market opportunities of developing countries. Although Japan does not subsidise major agricultural commodities for export, extensive domestic protectionism seriously reduces or denies their importation, thereby contributing to the decline in international food prices.

The purposes of such action are threefold: 'food security',[4] fairer rural-urban income distribution, and to help the sectoral adjustment process. Whether these are justifiable as policy goals is a potent question, especially when judged in terms of the cost-effectiveness of such measures. In addition questions have been raised recently on the safety of the herbicides and pesticides used in exporting countries. This issue is however political rather than economic.

4.2.1   Structure of the agricultural sector

In 1985, 4.6 million people, or 8 per cent of the total Japanese labour force, were engaged in farming, contributing only 3 per cent of GNP. It should also be added that 85 per cent of farmers' incomes derive from non-agricultural activities. Full-time farming and part-time but mainly farming households number only 600 000 and 800 000 respectively, leaving three million households relying mainly on non-farming incomes. Most farms are smallholding – the number of farms with more than two hectares is only 370 000, or slightly more than 8 per cent of the total. There are 1.7 million farms of less than half a hectare, where only 2 per cent of household income comes from agriculture.

The major crop is rice (2.3 million hectares, or 40 per cent of total farmland), which is the main recipient of government protection. Rice is the principal staple in the Japanese diet and is thus the main focus of 'food security'. Yet the demand for it is declining – the average consumption of rice per capita dropped sharply from the prewar 150 kg to 112 kg in 1965 and to only 75 kg in 1985. Against this drop, since a reduction in the price paid to producers was politically not possible, the paddy field reorientation programme was introduced to match supply and demand, which expanded the scope of agricultural protectionism.

4.2.2   Rice Policies

Two historical events appear to have dominated Japan's postwar rice policies. The first was the land reform, under which most sharecropping ceased to exist. The idea of 'land to the tiller' still prevails, making buying and renting farmland very difficult. Thus Japan's rice production is characterised by very small farming plots. Together with Japan's rapid economic growth, the smallness of their holdings encouraged farmers to seek temporary or permanent off-farm employment while keeping the land for part-time farming. This is changing only slowly. The other event was the acute food shortage experienced immediately after the Second World War which emphasised the importance of maintaining adequate supplies, or self-sufficiency as the policymakers saw it. Price support has been the main means of achieving self-sufficiency in rice, which was reached around 1960. Even then the cost-plus basis for fixing the price of rice was strengthened on the grounds of preventing shortages and attaining urban–

rural income parity. The paddy field reorientation programme somewhat reduced the relative importance of rice as a major crop, but in 1985 it still accounted for one-third of total agricultural income.

The Food Agency, which administers production and both the domestic and international trade in rice, consistently allowed higher than national average price increase for rice. This swung the intersectoral terms of trade in favour of farmers, in contrast with the reverse trend in the international and US markets. As a result the price of rice in Japan became four to twelve times higher than the international price. Early research estimated Japan's nominal rice protection in 1980–2 at 235 per cent. Since then the yen appreciation has made the price disparity even larger, although an exact comparison is difficult because of rice's large price fluctuations in the international market due to its relatively small share.

Higher prices encouraged rice production to such an extent that in the late 1960s overproduction became a problem. In response to this the government started the paddy field reorientation programme, under which farmers were encouraged (and subsidised) to cease production in a certain portion of their paddy fields or to use the land for other purposes. Early in the 1970s the partial liberalisation of rice sales was allowed as an incentive to produce better-selling varieties. Since then the price of rice has continued to rise, although more slowly. Only in 1987 did the Food Agency for the first time reduce the price paid to producers by about 6 per cent.[5]

The rice policies certainly did achieve self-sufficiency, and also contributed much to the urban–rural income parity. The cost however was enormous. Financially it has been a cause of budget deficits, although gradual increases in the selling price have recently narrowed the gap. Also the policies may have helped maintain inefficient producers and retarded structural change in agriculture. Table 4.2 indicates that rice sales in 1985 accounted for only 17 per cent of total income for full-time farming households, 26 per cent for part-time with mainly farming income, and 53 per cent for part-time with mainly non-farming income. For the last group, farming generated only a small proportion of total income – 7 per cent on average. Therefore if they ceased to cultivate rice this group would lose only 3.5 per cent of their income. And yet they are the major beneficiaries of rice price support (Fitchett, 1988).

Table 4.2   The importance of rice in farm income in 1985

Type	Farm households Number	Gross agricultural income (thousands of yen) Rice	Total	%	Group's share in gross income from rice (%)
Full-time	626 143	1152.6	6694.8	17	16
Part-time mainly farming income	775 308	2319.9	9006.4	26	32
Part-time mainly non-farming income	2 974 562	810.7	1541.1	53	52
Total	4 376 013	956.4	2896.8	33	100

Source: The Ministry of Agriculture, Forestry and Fisheries, *Statistical Year-book*, 1986. Quoted in Fitchett (1988).

4.2.3   Protectionism in other agricultural products

Other agricultural protectionist measures in Japan are often related to rice policies. Wheat and barley, for example, are substitutes for rice and are also under control of the Food Agency. They are also the main substitute crops in the paddy field reorientation programme, and they receive government-fixed prices which are much higher than the international ones. Some vegetables and other agricultural products share the same benefit. Citrus fruits (tangerines) have received protection, but are to be liberalised.

Sugar and beef are accorded independent protection. Both cane and beet sugar are produced in relatively poor regions of Japan. Minimum prices are guaranteed by a statutory body, which also administers the stabilisation of the price of imported raw sugar. Beef was under strict quantitative restriction until recently, but the government is committed to liberalising this within a short period.

The protection of milk had some effect on beef. Milk production was encouraged to diversify and modernise the national diet and production expanded rapidly. This however caused overproduction in Hokkaido and elsewhere and surplus milk had to be sold for processing at cheaper price, which was put under a deficiency payment scheme. The increased number of milking cows, which also account for one-half of beef production in Japan, was translated into beef production after a time lag, and made the situation even more complex.

Agricultural products under NTBs also include dairy products (cheese and curd), leguminous vegetables, flour, dextrine, fruit juice, and tomato sauce.[6]

4.2.4 Agricultural subsidies

Import restrictions are only one aspect of agricultural protectionism. The other is the massive provision of direct and indirect subsidies. Of these market price support, for rice in particular, is the main means. Other types of subsidies – including direct payment, input cost reduction and general services – are however by no means insignificant.

The budget allocation to MAFF in 1988 was 3171 billion yen, or 9.6 per cent of total central government expenditure. Of this some 80 per cent was spent on agriculture to improve productivity and expand production; to provide structural improvement, price stability and income support; to rationalise distribution channels; to improve farmers' welfare and regional development; to assist agricultural associations; and to make provisions against natural disasters. In addition local governments also provide a significant sum for agriculture, mostly in the form of subsidies. It is not easy to work out the total amount of these, but the total expenditure at the end of 1989 was around 4–5 trillion yen. Table 4.3 provides a breakdown of central and local government expenditure – although the information is a little dated it does provide some idea of the current situation.

Table 4.3 is almost self-explanatory. Government expenditure per agricultural household in 1983 stood at slightly more than one million yen. In the same year, agricultural income per household was only 989 600 yen, 5 per cent lower than government expenditure. This fact alone is more than enough to question seriously the efficiency of these measures in supporting farmers' incomes.

4.2.5 Political and economic aspects of agricultural protection

Although the cost-effectiveness of Japan's agricultural protectionism is questionable, even on purely domestic grounds, the political situation makes its reform very difficult. Agricultural cooperatives and their national organisations are a huge pressure group lobbying for the continuation of the present measures. Their campaign was so successful that it even persuaded some consumer groups to accept their views. Especially effective in this was the emphasis they placed on the use of chemicals, insecticides and herbicides, which are

Table 4.3   Evolution of agricultural expenditure by central and local governments

	1960	1970	1980	1983
Total expenditure (billions of yen)	212.0	1348.8	4833.3	4695.6
Central gov't (%)	64.1	69.5	65.7	63.4
Proportion to govt expenditure (%)	7.4	9.4	6.7	5.5
Proportion to gross agricultural product (%)	14.6	41.5	79.2	76.2
Expenditure per agricultural household (thousands of yen)	35.0	249.7	1036.9	1038.4
Expenditure per hectare (thousands of yen)	34.9	232.7	886.1	867.8
Proportion of agricultural product to GDP (%)	9.4	4.4	2.6	2.4

Source: Australian Bureau of Agricultural and Resource Economics (1988).

prohibited in Japan but are widely used in some other countries. The soybean embargo by the US in the early 1970s was also often cited as a reason for continuing to offer protection to Japanese agriculture.

No political party can afford to ignore the importance of the lobby group. This is underlined by the present constituency system, which was based on population distribution immediately after the Second World War, under which rural votes are disproportionately powerful. The ruling Liberal Democratic Party has benefited much from this situation. Although the system shows signs of changing, this may take a long time.

The strongest countervailing force comes from abroad. With trade surplus growing, the 1980s saw ever-increasing pressure from foreign agricultural producers, particularly those in the US. The liberalisation of citrus fruit and beef was very much an outcome of this. In Japan events like this generated resentment and some felt that Japan's agricultural policies were being shaped over the trade nego-tiating tables, although it was well-received in certain other quarters.

One unfortunate point in this context is that the products nego-tiated were very often the same crops which were being encouraged in the paddy field reorientation scheme. In many cases substantial loans had been taken out, though at a preferential low interest rate, to facilitate the shift. Farmers therefore often found themselves with large debts and a threatened market. This has made their reactions even sharper, with the important side-effect that they have soured to the MAFF policies. This could result in demands for deregulation of the agricultural sector, or even for its total restructuring, which perhaps is inevitable anyway. It most certainly could work against the vested interests of MAFF and many farmers.

Between the two forces, future agricultural protectionism is hard to predict. Since the decision to liberalise beef and oranges, the main issue has been the liberalisation of rice. The outcome of this is hard to predict. In 1989 the minister for agriculture was quoted as saying that not a grain of rice would be imported, while newspapers and other media have gradually come to favour more liberal policies. It is possible that liberalisation will proceed slowly. Very possibly, however, protectionist measures will take more subtle forms, including more use of direct subsidies. The overall result may not be very different.

Agricultural liberalisation by the back door has been observed recently. The price disparity between domestic and international markets became so large for processed food manufacturers, who have no effective protection, that they started to import processed agricultural materials in large quantities. Imports of half-processed rice crackers (*sembei* and *arare*) for example have increased enormously. Similarly imports of rice mixed with sugar and other additives for food processing reportedly reached the 30 000 ton mark recently. This alone represents 0.3 per cent of rice consumption in Japan. Importation of precooked rice (pilaff) has also taken place. Therefore, although rice is still subject to strict import restrictions, de facto liberalisation for inputs is proceeding rapidly. A similar method is used to import sugar-based cakes from Korea, which are used as sweeteners. If this can be used as an indicator, economic forces prevail in Japanese trade even under a regime of intense protectionism.

4.3 JAPAN'S DISTRIBUTION SYSTEM[7]

The complexity and rigidity of Japan's distribution system has been a focus of attention for some time as a limiting factor in market access. The USTR, for example, in its 1989 report singled out Japan's distribution system, discussing in some detail how it reduces the access of US exports. The same has been said of exports from developing countries. In many industrial markets, large supermarkets and chain stores have been instrumental in promoting imports from developing countries, so the relative absence of the same imports in Japan, has been linked to Japan's distribution system. Also, as has already been noted, the bulk of the blame for the failure of prices to reduce following the yen appreciation has been directed at the distribution sector.

In this section some important features of the retail and wholesale structure of Japan's distribution system are reviewed, including *keiretsu* (business groups), marketing practices, the sole-agent system, and the Large-Scale Retail Store Law. The recent diversification of trading channels is also touched upon in order to look into changing business behaviour in the distribution sector. This change also has a bearing on the expansion of imports from developing countries.

4.3.1 Structure of the retail and wholesale sectors

There are 1.62 million retail stores in Japan, according to the preliminary result of the latest commerce census by the MITI. One salient point which can be picked up from the census is the large number of small retail shops. In 1988 93.3 per cent of the total number of shops had less than ten employees (54 per cent had one or two employees, 26.1 per cent had three or four employees, and 13.2 per cent had between five and nine employees). In comparison the corresponding figures for the US and West Germany were 80.5 per cent and 77.5 per cent respectively in 1982, although France stood slightly higher at 96.8 per cent. The average number of employees per retail store in Japan in 1985 was 3.9, with 8.1 in the US, 5.8 in West Germany (1984–5), 6.8 in the UK (1984), 4.3 in France (1985), and 1.99 in Italy (1981). Clearly Japanese retail stores are smaller than in most industrialised countries.

However Japan has a greater number of retail shops. Per 1000 residents there were 13.5 retail shops in Japan in 1985. In comparison the US had 8.3 (1982), West Germany 6.6 (1984–5), the UK 6.1 (1984), France 8.6 (1985), and Italy 17.5 (1981). The larger number of retail stores per capita of course reflects their small size.

These characteristics are rooted in such factors as population density, the pattern of urban development, and the level of development in transport and car ownership. There is also a policy-related aspect to this in the form of the Large-Scale Retail Store Law, which controls, or effectively limits, the establishment of new department stores and supermarkets, which will be discussed later in some detail.

In the wholesale sector similar characteristics are observed. The census reveals that there were 437 000 wholesale premises in Japan in 1988. Again the share of small wholesale premises with less than ten employees is higher in Japan (at 74.9 per cent) than in most industrialised countries. The numbers of these premises also show the same pattern. In 1985 Japan had 3.1 per 1000 residents. The corresponding numbers were 1.5 for the US (1982), 1.9 for West Germany (1984–5), 1.4 for France (1985), and 2.3 for Italy (1981).

These characteristics are translated into the multi-layered structure of the wholesale industry. In Japan it is not unusual for a commodity to pass through the hands of several wholesalers before reaching a retailer, although the extent to which this happens varies from commodity to commodity. The W/R ratio (the ratio of wholesale to retail sales values) shows that Japan has the highest figure among major industrialised countries: Japan (1985) 3.44; USA (1986) 0.97; West Germany (1984) 1.80; UK (1984) 2.09; France (1985) 1.18. The W/R ratio is admittedly a very crude indicator, and some sectoral investigation is desirable. In Japan, for example, large trading houses (*sogo shosha*) command a large part of international business, and this may have significantly distorted the W/R ratio. Still, the comparison gives a clear enough picture of the multi-layered nature of Japan's distribution system.

4.3.2 Productivity and efficiency of the Japanese distribution system

The smallness and the multi-layered nature of the Japanese distribution system could cast doubts on its efficiency. In order to check this, productivity, distribution margins and inventory ratios will be looked into here.

Relative productivity is the ratio of the value-added labour productivity of the distribution sector (including the retail and the wholesale sectors) to that of total industry (relative productivity 1), and manufacturing (relative productivity 2). Below is an international comparison of major industrialised economies for 1985, as estimated by Maruyama (1990).

In both cases Japan's distribution system shows roughly similar values to the US, West Germany and the UK, although France and Italy score better. Again much caution is needed regarding the aggregate nature of the indicator, but the comparison suggests that the Japanese distribution system is no less efficient than those of other developed countries.

Country	Relative Productivity 1	Relative Productivity 2
Japan	0.76	0.64
US	0.70	0.63
West Germany	0.68	0.71
UK	0.58	0.61
France	0.82	0.85
Italy	0.90	0.88

This good relative performance may well be the outcome of artificially high profit margins in distribution, therefore the gross margin rates for the wholesale and retail sectors need to be looked into (Maruyama, 1990).

	Japan (1986)	US (1986)	West Germany (1985)	UK (1984)
Mw/W	11.2	19.4	12.6	13.4
Mr/R	27.1	31.0	34.2	27.6
$(Mw + Mr)/R$	57.6	49.7	58.9	55.6

Here, Mw refers to the gross margin of the wholesale industry and W to the total sales of the wholesale industry. Mr is the gross margin of the retail sector and R its total sales. The bottom line therefore shows the gross margin rates of the distribution sector as a whole. The gross profit margin rates for both sectors in Japan are comparable to those in the two European countries, although slightly lower than those in the US, which indicates that the two sectors performanced competitively.

Nor are Japan's inventory ratios for the wholesale and retail sectors higher than those of the major industrialised countries. This together with the two previous indicators, seems to suggest that Japan's distribution system is as efficient as those of the other major countries.

4.3.3 Sole agent system

The sole agent system, under which many brand named goods are imported, is in part responsible for the price disparities between Japan and other countries which were discussed earlier. A recent government report revealed that the commodities under this system had had more or less stable retail prices in Japan in spite of their lower import costs since the start of the rapid yen appreciation. The quasi-monopoly position of the sole agents obviously made this situation possible, and their profit margins soared as a result. Yet the agents have been reluctant to increase import volumes lest this should damage the brand images and decrease their profitability. Thus the system serves to limit the import growth of the commodities concerned.

In 1987 there were 420 sole agents in Japan, and their number increased to 497 the following year. Since they deal mainly in such luxury goods as premier whiskies and brandies, sole agents have little effect on imports from developing countries. However the system may extend to these countries' exports in the future.

The sole agent system can play a positive role at the beginning of import market development. In Japan's case however, at least in the product groups with a high profit margin, many sole agents have tried to maintain their profit margin by jealously guarding their monopoly. With the recent rise of 'parallel' imports – one of the new import channels which will be discussed later – they are often in dispute with alternative importers. A well-known example was the case involving the Apple Computer in October 1989. The FTC (Fair Trade Commission) made a formal warning to the company that no illegal pressure should be applied on personal-computer shops to stop them from selling products not imported through the 'official' channel, nor to prevent personal-computer magazines from accepting advertisements for unofficially imported goods.

The FTC pointed out the following six actions as unfair trade practices: (1) preventing foreign producers from selling their products to 'direct' importers, (2) preventing wholesalers and retailers from handling directly (unofficially) imported goods, (3) asking wholesalers not to deal with retailers who sell directly imported goods, (4) labelling directly imported goods as counterfeit or substandard, (5) buying up all directly imported goods, and (6) refusing to service the products which had not been imported through 'official' channels.

4.3.4 Large-scale retail store law[8]

Since large supermarkets and chain stores are instrumental in promoting imports from developing countries, institutional regulations limiting their establishment has a large relevance. One such regulation in Japan is the Large-Scale Retail Store Law of 1974, which restricts the opening of new branches, the enlargement of existing branches, and other business practices of large stores (department stores and supermarkets). Its purpose is to protect small and medium-sized local retailers from the stronger competitiveness of large stores, and to help them adjust to new business environments.

The most controversial issue surrounding the law is not the law itself, but its application and transparency. According to the text of the law, opening a store should take one year at most after the first public announcement has been made. In practice however there are many cases in which it took more than five years, or even ten years. One reason for such delays was the insistence of local governments that applicants should seek consent from local business associations, which often is very difficult to obtain. This condition appears to help delaying actions taken by local retailers. Thus the law itself is sabotaged.

The law and its implementation were one of the important issues discussed at the SII. In April 1990, at an interim meeting, an agreement was reached and the Japanese government committed itself to taking deregulatory measures. The reform will follow the recommendations given in the report on the future of the distribution system announced in June 1989. More exact enforcement, a revision of the law, and a thorough assessment after three years were the report's main recommendations.

The follow-up measures toward more exact enforcement specified the following points:

1. A time limit should be set on public-hearing periods which have not been specified, limiting the whole period of adjustment to 18 months.
2. Minor increases in sales areas (up to 10 per cent or until the increase reaches 50 square meters), changes of shop tenants, and increases in sales areas devoted to imported goods, should be made exempt from adjustment procedures.
3. Shopping time not required to go through the adjustment procedure is extended by one hour so that large-scale shops can remain open until 7 o'clock in the evening without the consent of local business associations.
4. The transparency of the adjustment procedure should be increased by making public the proceedings of both the council for adjustment of commercial activities (the adjustment organisation

to consist of representatives from local merchants, learned people, and consumers), and the council for large-scale retail stores.

At the same time it was requested that the additional regulations adopted by one-third of local governments should conform with the general principles of the law.

Revision of the law itself was scheduled for the Diet meeting in 1990, with the following three aims:

1. To introduce preferential measures for sales areas for imported goods.
2. To reduce the processing period for the adjustment to new establishments to approximately one year.
3. To specify the maximum adjustment period.

Moreover, two years after the revision more fundamental deregulation should take place, including the abolition of regulatory measures in metropolitan areas.

The question here is whether or not such deregulation will be carried out. A repetition of the past practise of drafting measures that are rarely implemented will not do. Recovering the balance between production efficiency, equal opportunity, and freedom of choice should be the target for the future (Sakaiya, 1990).

4.3.5 *Keiretsu* and long-term intercompany relations

Very close intercompany business relationships, sometimes to the point of being exclusive, between the producers of parts and of finished products have developed over time in Japan. When this involves share ownership and/or substantial finance it is described as *keiretsu* (a business group). Associated with this kind of relationship are barriers to outside suppliers, including foreign companies. As such the practice has been criticised as an important import barrier.

Long-term intercompany relationships are not unique to the Japanese distribution system, but they appear to be stronger in Japan and among Japanese companies abroad. Part of the reason for this is the level of standardisation of traded goods (parts and components). When a commodity has been standardised, price is the most important factor when deciding where to purchase it. For non-standardised goods, the service content is more important.

The relationship between automobile assembler and parts producer is a good example. Their close business relationship has been extensively documented, especially in connection with the 'just-in-time' practice. Flexibility regarding the quantity and specification of the parts it requires makes even a standard part a special item in the assembler's eyes. As a result, the relationship is often carried over to abroad, and when an assembler makes a direct investment, very often some key parts producers follow suit.

Similar long-term relationships exist in the wholesale and retail distribution system, although to a lesser degree. Long-standing business relationships are perceived as reliable ones by business partners, and the practice is characterised by small production and sales units. With interlinked financial networks among distribution companies, this practise has effectively erected a high import barrier. There is a possibility, however, that foreign exporters could benefit by penetrating the Japanese distribution system – once inroads had been made it is likely that they would be accepted as partners. Such relationships could bridge national boundaries, open up import channels and revolutionise the domestic distribution system, as will be pointed out in the next section.

4.4　NEW CHANNELS FOR IMPORTS

The globalisation of Japanese manufacturing and retail firms, together with their greater awareness of the potential benefits to be gained from imports, has been gradually changing the traditional import system in Japan. Various new import channels have emerged in response to the radically changed price structure at home and abroad, and some of these are affecting the long-established business behaviour of the distribution sector. (It is noteworthy that imports from developing countries – Asian newly industrialised countries and ASEAN countries in particular – have benefited most from this. This assertion can be supported by the findings of the Japan Foreign Trade Council (1989) that the share of imports by the nine largest general trading companies, the traditional means of importing, declined from 40.4 per cent in 1985 to 34.9 per cent in 1987.

The following new import channels will now be looked at in turn: (1) reverse import, (2) development import, (3) direct import, and (4) parallel import.

4.4.1 Reverse import

Faced with unfavourable cost conditions at home, a number of manufacturing firms have undertaken foreign direct investment (FDI) in order to minimise their production costs. Through FDI, the firms relocate part of different production processes in different countries who can carry out particular processes at the least cost. Intra-firm division of production processes has led to an increase in intra-firm trade. For example, electronic components such as semiconductors are shipped from Japanese parent companies to their overseas affiliates, who use the components to produce household appliances such as microwave ovens and air conditioners. The final products are then sold in the host countries, or they are exported to other countries including Japan. Products coming back into Japan are often called 'reverse imports'. This type of production and trade arrangement tends to be more frequently undertaken for products whose production processes may be broken down into a number of sub-processes. Electrical machinery is a notable example.

As can be seen from Table 4.4, reverse imports from Asian countries increased rapidly from 252 billion yen in 1983 to 506 billion yen in 1986, with a near-stable period from 1980 to 1983. Because of the substantial yen appreciations in 1985 and 1986, the already large 1983–6 increase was even larger if measured in US dollars. Indeed the increase from Asia was so large that its contribution to the overall increase between 1983 and 1986 was 152 per cent, resulting in an increase in Asia's share in total reverse imports from 38.7 per cent in 1983 to 61.9 per cent in 1986.

The rapid increase in reverse imports from Asia reflects both increased affiliate activity and the increasing attractiveness of the Japanese market. Annual approval of Japanese foreign direct investment (FDI) in manufacturing in Asia increased rapidly from 1985 to 1988. As a result the total approved foreign direct investment in the 1985–8 period was greater than the cumulative approved foreign direct investment from 1951–84. Among developing countries, Asia received the largest share in manufacturing, amounting to 64 per cent of the total in 1988. Together with the yen appreciation, local foreign direct investment promotion policies in these countries and their favourable economic performance contributed to the increase.

The increased attractiveness of the Japanese market to Asia is evidenced by the sharp rise in the share of reverse imports in affiliates' overall sales (their degree of dependence on the Japanese

Table 4.4 Reverse imports of Japan from overseas affiliates (manufactured products)

Origin of import	Value of reverse imports (millions of yen)			Share of sales to Japan in total sales (%)			Share of intra-firm reverse imports in total reverse imports (%)		
	1980	1983	1986	1980	1983	1986	1980	1983	1986
Asia	244 917	251 907	506 039	9.8	10.8	15.8	89.2	74.4	76.5
ASEAN	–	82 166	130 932	–	6.5	10.0	–	63.7	78.5
Latin America	97 091	134 736	28 803	9.4	7.7	4.1	96.3	77.1	8.9
Middle East	167 345	141 932	89 039	72.3	73.0	79.1*	0.0	95.5	94.7
World Total	682 008	650 748	818 058	10.9	11.6	7.8	67.5	83.3	75.9

Notes: *79.1 per cent is the value of the share given in the source, but the computation from corresponding exports and sales figures give 51.7 per cent

Source: Ministry of International Trade and Industry, *Kaigai Toshi Tokei Soran* (A Comprehensive Survey of Foreign Investment Statistics) nos 1, 2, 3.

market) from 10.8 per cent in 1983 to 15.8 per cent in 1986. Rigorous export promotion in Asian countries may have contributed to this. In contrast Latin American affiliates' share of reverse imports in total sales declined over the same period.

Table 4.4 also shows that more than three-quarters of reverse imports from all sources has been conducted in the form of intra-firm trade. This probably reflects the development of an extensive network of processing linkages inside the firms.

An examination at the sectoral level reveals that electrical machinery accounted for the largest share of reverse imports – 27 per cent in 1986 – followed by other machinery subsectors such as general machinery and transport equipment (Urata, 1989). The machinery sectors outperformed other sectors not only in the value of reverse imports, but also in the degree of this dependence on the Japanese market and in their share of intra-firm trade in overall trade.

For ASEAN countries, in addition to machinery, textiles and non-ferrous metals are major reverse export items. The difference in the pattern of reverse exports between ASEAN and non-ASEAN (mainly Korea, Taiwan, Hong Kong and China) reflects the difference in their pattern of comparative advantage, which was discussed earlier.

4.4.2 Development imports

The term 'development imports' is used by importers as a synonym for consignment basis transactions when describing the following arrangement. To take advantage of low-cost processing, a firm consigns the manufacture of particular goods to overseas firms, providing them with such necessary information as the design and specifications of the products, as well as with intermediate goods such as fabric. The firm then imports the finished product. Large retailers, such as department stores and supermarkets, are among the main users of this practice. The Japan Department Stores Association (1989) found that in 1988 development imports had increased by 73.1 per cent over the previous year's total, faring better than the expansion of their total sales of imports at 17.7 per cent. As a result the share of the former to the latter rose from 3.7 per cent to 5.4 per cent.

Since labour-intensive products are the most suitable for this type of arrangement, a large share consists of clothing, as can be seen in Table 4.5(a). The share taken by houseware has been increasing rapidly, although from a low base. The combination of low wages and

Table 4.5   Development imports and direct imports.

(a) Composition of development imports

	Clothing	Houseware	Furniture	Food	Other	Total
1986	83.8	2.0	4.3	9.9	0.0	100
1988	87.6	3.6	4.6	4.0	0.2	100

Share of total (percentages):

	Europe	USA	East Asia	South-East Asia	Others	Total
1986	15.7	1.7	75.4	7.1	0.1	100
1988	16.7	3.7	67.9	9.9	1.8	100

(b) Composition of direct imports

	Clothing	Houseware	Furniture	Food	Other	Total
1984	38.4	21.2	13.7	13.2	13.5	100
1986	38.8	17.4	7.5	11.2	25.1	100
1988	35.8	11.2	7.2	7.8	38.0	100

Share of total (percentages):

	Europe	USA	East Asia	South-East Asia	Others	Total
1984	69.8	11.8	17.5	0.0	0.9	100
1986	68.2	16.3	9.8	0.0	5.7	100
1988	61.7	18.3	15.5	3.3	1.2	100

Source: Japan Department Stores Association, July 1989.

high labour standards in East Asia were the principal factors in development imports being largely negotiated with that region – 67.9 per cent of the total in 1988. Europe and Southeast Asia followed with shares of 16.7 per cent and 9.9 per cent respectively. The volume as well as the shares of East and Southeast Asia are likely to increase further in the future, as the large Japanese distributors have stepped up their efforts to establish overseas offices in these regions in order to collect information on their production capabilities.

In spite of the rapid expansion of development imports, it appears that further expansion will first require the overcoming of some problems. First, the interval between the development and final delivery of a product is often very long – in order to keep up with the changing needs of consumers this delay should be reduced. This is of particular importance with clothing, as consumers' demands change most quickly in this area. Secondly, customer service for development imports has been considered less than satisfactory. Thirdly, importing retailers run a greater risk of articles being rejected or left unsold when they rely on trading companies for their supply. Fourthly, the recent reversal from appreciation to depreciation of the yen and wage increases in Asian NICs have reduced the benefits to be gained from trading in development imports.

Importers have adopted various measures to overcome these problems. First, in order to take advantage of lower wages, they started to move their business from Asian newly industrialised countries to ASEAN countries. In response to the weaker yen and the rapid changes in consumers' tastes, large department stores initiated a more sophisticated production strategy, by which the materials and technology of more than one country are involved. For example, a department store purchases the cloth for men's suits from England and the design from Italy. The sewing is consigned to a firm in Korea. The final products are then imported into Japan and labelled with the importer's brand name for sale on the domestic market.

4.4.3 Direct imports

Direct imports are a form of import transaction by which large retailers bypass domestic wholesalers, including trading houses. By so doing retailers benefit by cutting out the wholesale margins – theoretically this enables them to charge lower prices to consumers. The room for reduction is considerable since the wholesale margin ratio (defined as the ratio of wholesale margins to retain margins) in Japan in 1986 stood at 57.6 per cent.

According to the Japan Department Stores Association (1989), direct imports have increased rapidly in recent years: 28.7 per cent in 1987 and 32.1 per cent in 1988. Sales of direct imports comprised 2.2 per cent in 1987 and 2.6 per cent in 1988 of the total sales of the department stores surveyed.

Imports comprising art objects and crafts (the main items included in the category 'other' in Table 4.5) expanded by a remarkable 64.5 per cent in 1988. This led to a relative decline in the shares of clothing, houseware, furniture and food, as can be seen from Table 4.5(b). In 1988 'others' captured a share of 38 per cent of total direct imports, while the shares of clothing (35.8 per cent), houseware (11.2 per cent), and furniture (7.2 per cent) all fell. Imports from Southeast Asia increased by a massive 76.4 per cent in 1988. Those from the US and East Asia also registered a rapid expansion at 57 per cent and 52.1 per cent respectively. European products lagged behind at 23.6 per cent, but Europe still remained the largest supplier with a share of 61.7 per cent of total direct imports by department stores in 1988.

Recently, medium and small retail chains have started developing direct import channels. As they lack the extensive overseas procurement network enjoyed by large retailers, they rely more on cooperative action by forming common direct import organisations. In addition central and local governments have made efforts to promote direct imports by hosting a variety of import fairs. Local governments and chambers of commerce have also sent missions to Korea, Thailand and other countries in a search for further direct imports.

4.4.4 Parallel import

'Parallel import' refers to imports of commodities under the sole agent system made by dealers other than sole agents. The practice therefore is unofficial in the sense that the importer cannot make purchases directly from the manufacturer. The transaction takes place when there is a wide gap in the price of a product in different countries, and the product goes through unauthorised channels such as overseas retail dealers or sole agents in a third country. Hence, the 'parallel' route of an import is created.

The price gap leading to this type of transaction may be attributable to a number of factors. First, price discrimination by suppliers increases the import cost of a product to the sole agent. Secondly, sole agents may pursue rigid pricing policies, which do not respond to exchange rate fluctuations. Thirdly, sole agents may set high prices in order to cover the cost of advertising, marketing and developing customer service systems. Their monopoly position associated with wellknown brand names is however the main contributor to making such a practice possible.

Parallel import came into existence in Japan in the early 1970s when people became angry that the yen appreciation had not brought down the prices of imported goods. A wide variety of products are now imported through such channels, including watches and clocks, jewelry, bags, whisky, automobiles, compact disks and personal computers. Indeed parallel imports have captured a large share of the import market for some products – 25 per cent of Scotch whisky imports arrived this way in 1987. The Fair Trade Commission (1987) found that 50.9 per cent of department stores and 44.4 per cent of chain stores used parallel import channels in 1987.

Faced with decreasing market shares, some sole agents have tried to interrupt parallel imports and their sale in Japan. The Fair Trade Commission however, as described in some detail in section 4.3.3 in connection with the case involving a personal computer company, has apparently been determined to take measures against such illegal practices.

Thus parallel import helps to reduce the price gap between Japan and abroad by preventing sole agents from setting artificially high prices. The practise is however not free from problems. Since parallel importers cannot rely on the original producers, they inevitably have to cope with an unstable supply, which may make it difficult for them to develop reliable customer service systems. Moreover, once the sole agents have reduced their prices to maintain their market shares, the incentive for undertaking parallel import may disappear.

4.5   RESPONSE TO INSTITUTIONAL BARRIERS

There exist various types of 'institutional' trade barriers in Japan. Some of these are simply business practices and systems of long historical development, which may be different from those found internationally. Sometime even cultural heritages, for example the Japanese language, and infrastructural environments are counted as institutional trade barriers as they are man-made. They may well be trade barriers in the sense that they make import penetration more difficult.

But they are not always as unfair as some foreign critics seem to suggest. For example, the height of railway fly-overs was once pointed out as a trade barrier on the ground that it makes the transport of large containers very difficult, or even impossible. This may be a fact, but even a very sincere will on the part of the Japanese government cannot easily remedy the situation. The *keiretsu* type of subcontracting is a more delicate case, but it can be explained by a natural inclination to trust in long-established and reliable relationships between firms, although some non-trasparency cannot be denied.

More problematic are the policy-induced or policy-supported

barriers. Although the overall direction of Japan's policy package is undeniably toward import promotion, there still remain large areas where other policy objectives prevail, sometimes very inward-looking ones.

Agriculture is certainly one such case. The days of food shortage are long gone, and the need for production enhancement has given way to production controls. Moreover income support for the farmers has already lost much of its significance, judging from farmers' average income on the one hand and the proliferation of part-time farming on the other. Yet traditional price supports are continuously resorted to, although revisions have become inevitable in view of the cost of this protection on the national economy and government finances.

Policies have their own inertia, and they produce factors to maintain and justify themselves, even when they have lost much of their significance. This is the case with Japan's traditional agricultural policy. When self-sufficiency in rice was reached, instead of reforming the price support system a new control on cultivated areas was introduced. Changing to crops other than rice was also encouraged by the granting of direct and indirect subsidies. The rationale behind maintaining price support was the need to achieve income parity between rural and urban areas. Later on, when the price disparity between Japan and abroad became too large, the concept of 'food security' was introduced, claiming that dietary staples should be produced domestically in view of the risks of possible embargoes. Thus economic logic was conveniently neglected. A recent addition to the protectionist's arsenal has been the danger of imported food being contaminated by chemical insecticides and herbicides, the use of which is not allowed in Japan.

Japan's distribution system also has policy-induced aspects which inhibit imports, although as a whole there is no evidence that these result in a systematic bias against imports or reduce overall inefficiency. The Large-Scale Retail Store Law is a salient case. Strict regulations on the opening of new establishments and the expansion of department stores and supermarket chain, which have shown increased willingness to sell imported goods, has clearly limited competition and reduced access to imports. This issue was discussed at the SII talks, and some reforms were promised.

The sole agent system is also a policy-related barrier, but to a lesser extent. It is basically a device to aid imports, but the position of monopoly it brings with it can serve to limit imports in certain cases.

Relatively weak enforcement of the Fair Trade Law appears to be the root cause of the failure of the sole agent system to expand imports.

Institutional barriers however can be circumvented. New import channels will provide the means to evade the rigidities in the distribution system. A sizable drop in recent years in the share of large trading companies in total imports indicates the ongoing proliferation of import business, which may well significantly affect the structure of Japan's domestic distribution. Stronger enforcement of the Fair Trade Law can contribute much to the progress of this process.

The circumvention of import regulation has been taking place in agriculture too. Food-processing industries have been disadvantaged by a lack of effective protection. In response to import liberalisation of processed food, they have started to import agricultural products, including slightly processed rice and sugar, on a large scale. Similar action has been observed among silk weavers, who have jointly filed a suit against the import quota on raw silk. Since the import of silk products such as neckties and scarves have been liberalised, the weavers have faced price disadvantages vis-à-vis foreign producers in materials procurement. Thus market forces are at work in reducing strict import restrictions.

Notes and references

1. The United States Trade Representatives Office (USTR) listed the following items as Japan's import barriers in its 1989 report: (1) Import policies: (a) tariffs, (b) cigarettes and tobacco products, (c) leather and leather footwear, (d) wood and paper products, (e) aluminum, (f) quantitative restrictions (agricultural protection, feedgrain, rice, and fish products). (2) Standards, testing, labelling, certification: (a) telecommunication terminals, radio equipment and systems, (b) pharmaceuticals/medical devices, (c) food activities. (3) Government procurement: (a) supercomputers, (b) satellites, (c) government procurement code implementation. (4) Barriers to intellectual property protection: (a) patents, (b) trademarks, (c) copyrights. (5) Service barriers: (a) construction, architectural and engineering services, (b) legal services, (c) insurance. (6) Investment Barriers: (a) direct investment. (7) Other Barriers: (a) semi-conductors, (b) tron (a new system of computer operation), (c) optical fibres, (d) aerospace, (e) auto parts, (f) soda ash, (g) distribution system, (h) restrictions on marketing practices, (i) law on large retail stores.
2. Cline (1990) however argues that the price disparity is statistically insignificant except for imported items and food.
3. Japan's agricultural protectionism is discussed extensively internationally.

Major literature includes OECD (1987), Australian Bureau of Agricultural and Resource Economics (1988), and Fitchett (1988). This section is based on these three volumes.

4. 'Food security' refers to the necessity to maintain reliable supply source of foodstuff. Its advocates claim that Japan's low overall food subsistency below 40 per cent makes it necessary to reduce vulnerability against possible worldwide harvest failure, and so on.

5. Reduction of the producers' price for rice was repeated in 1988 and 1989. It was likely that the reduction would again made in 1990.

6. A novel was written by a former secretary of the diet member on protectionism of the red bean, one of the crops under quantitative restriction. The political and non-transparent relationship between the importers and MAFF and MITI was severely criticised, although protectionism itself was not questioned. Y. Arikawa, *Agricultural Imports – A Novel* (in Japanese), Kodansha, 1987.

7. For a detailed discussion of Japan's distribution sector, see Maruyama (1989 and 1990), the MITI report, Tsusho Sangyo Chosakai, *The Vision for Distribution Industry in the 1990s* (1990, Tokyo) (in Japanese), and Motoshige Ito and Akihiko Matsui, 'Japanese Way of Transactions' (in Japanese)', in Motoshige Ito and Kazuo Nishimura, *Applied Microeconomics* (University of Tokyo Press, 1989).

8. Toshimasa Tsuruta 'The Large-Scale Retail Store Law in the Globalization Era', *Ekonomisuto*.

5 Trade Measures affecting Developing Countries

Ippei Yamazawa, Kinya Onoda and Hivohisha Kohama

5.1 TRADE FRICTIONS WITH DEVELOPING COUNTRIES

Some trade measures inevitably have a greater effect on developing countries because of their coverage or intention, although most of Japan's trade policy conforms with the GATT rule of non-discrimination. The General System of Preference (GSP), an internationally recognised exception to the general rule, is of course one such measure. Japan's stance on the Multi-Fiber Agreement (MFA) is unique among developed countries, and attention will be given to this in this chapter, as will tariff discrimination between imports from developed and developing countries, which has also given rise to trade friction.

Before going into individual issues it would be useful to have an overview of Japan's trade friction with developing countries. Although this is not as acute as the situation with developed countries, Japan's large trade surplus has given rise to demands for more imports from developing countries also. East and South-east Asian countries in particular have for a long time been voicing their dissatisfaction with the imbalance of their trade with Japan.

In 1988 Japan exported goods worth 89.3 billion dollars (33.7 per cent of the total) to developing countries, and imported goods worth 78.7 billion dollars (42.0 per cent of the total) from them, resulting in a trade surplus of 11.6 billion dollars. The export/import ratio for that year was therefore 100:88, a reversal of the 100:142 in 1980. The overall picture however can be very misleading where relationships with individual countries are concerned because of Japan's large imports of crude petroleum and other primary commodities. Nonetheless – apart from the major commodity exporters, Indonesia and Malaysia – all the Asian newly industrialised countries and ASEAN countries have been recording large trade deficits against Japan.

69

These countries are following export-led growth, in which the export of manufactures plays a pivotal role. This process can be seen as a cycle of export and investment. Increased exports mean increased foreign exchange earnings, which lead to increased import capabilities. Then increased imports of capital and intermediate goods are made possible, which in turn are translated into an increased production capacity. If a part of this increased production is exported, the cycle is complete.

In the course of export-led growth in East and South-east Asian countries, Japan's main contribution has been the provision of resources such as capital and intermediate goods, investment, and technology. Its role as an export market for manufactures has however been relatively limited, and the largest receiver of exports from developing countries has been the US, followed by European countries. This asymmetry is rooted in the different production structures, levels of industrial development and factor endowments between Japan and these countries. This one-sided dependence has nevertheless understandably been a source of frustration in Asian developing countries.

The expanding 'twin deficits' in the US in the 1980s, together with the European initiative toward stronger internal market integration, triggered anxiety in developing countries over creeping protectionism and led to another round of demands, or expectations, that Japan should import more manufactured goods. Since their rapid growth depends to a large degree on export expansion, Japan is expected to play a greater role in absorbing their exports. As discussed in Chapter 2, such import expansion has been taking place in Japan, but only gradually. At present however their imports from Japan are likely to continue to exceed their exports to Japan.[1]

In ratio terms some improvement has been observed. Table 5.1 shows Japan's trade balance ratio – the Japan/world ratio peaked in 1986, but has declined since then. With Asian newly industrialised countries and ASEAN, in addition to the recent drop, a longer-term decline has also been observed.

The decline in the ratio with Asian newly industrialised countries has been very sharp, from 0.602 in 1970 to 0.331 in 1988. That with Korea was especially remarkable, falling from 0.565 to 0.133 over the same period. This change reflects the progress of industrialisation in the Asian countries, as well as the gradual shift in Japan's industrial and import structures. The rapid decline after 1985 was caused by the appreciation of the yen. With ASEAN, Japan's trade balance ratio

Table 5.1   Japan's trade balance ratio, 1970–87

	1970	1975	1980	1985	1986	1987	1988
World	0.011	-0.019	-0.043	0.149	0.242	0.210	0.171
Asian NICs + ASEAN	0.247	0.131	0.019	0.058	0.171	0.164	0.176
Asian NICs	0.602	0.431	0.444	0.392	0.412	0.355	0.331
Hong Kong	0.768	0.697	0.786	0.791	0.740	0.700	0.695
Korea	0.565	0.263	0.285	0.268	0.331	0.243	0.133
Taiwan	0.474	0.384	0.383	0.195	0.250	0.228	0.243
Singapore	0.661	0.583	0.439	0.417	0.511	0.491	0.561
ASEAN	-0.124	-0.151	-0.371	-0.391	-0.305	-0.265	-0.187
Indonesia	-0.335	-0.300	-0.588	-0.648	-0.477	-0.476	-0.513
Malaysia	-0.431	-0.099	-0.260	-0.329	-0.392	-0.378	-0.212
Philippines	-0.082	-0.041	-0.076	-0.145	-0.061	-0.025	-0.080
Thailand	0.409	0.138	0.257	0.330	0.184	0.241	0.304

Note: Trade balance ratio = (Exports − Imports)/(Exports + Imports).

Source: Management and Coordination Agency, *Japan Statistical Yearbook*, 1989.

has been negative, reflecting ASEAN's export surplus with Japan for the last twenty years. Of the four ASEAN countries, only Thailand is suffering from a trade deficit. The Japan ASEAN ratios have tended to fluctuate widely, due mainly to commodity price fluctuations and investment booms.

Understandably Japan's trade conflicts have been more serious with Asian newly industrialised countries and Thailand. Korea's dissatisfaction is mainly over Japan's slowness in increasing manufactured imports. The speed with which Korea improved its balance of payments was very rapid, and it attained an overall surplus in both trade and current account in 1986. Bilaterally Korea's trade balance with the US, West Germany and the UK turned into surplus in 1982, 1974 and 1973 respectively.[2] That with Japan is still negative, although the situation has recently been much improved.

Korea's high degree of dependence on imported inputs from Japan, an example of one-way dependence, is the main cause of the deficit. One response by Korea to the situation was its import source diversification programme, under which imports from Japan were discouraged. However the real answer lies in promoting exports to Japan and making the one-way dependence into interdependence. In addition to improving Korea's access to the Japanese market, technology transfer would contribute to a positive solution, which is exactly what Korea has been requesting of Japan.

The recent rapid expansion of Korean exports to Japan has to some extent reduced Korean dissatisfaction. The same phenomenon has however led to a gradual build-up of protectionism in Japan. The most notable example of this was Korea's voluntary restraint in exporting knitted products to Japan. This topic will be looked into later.

For the Thailand–Japan conflict also, a large Thai trade deficit has been the main cause. The 1980s saw a rapid expansion of the deficit in spite of an overall improvement in Thailand's trade balance. In 1985 Thailand's trade deficit with Japan was as high as 70 per cent of this total deficit. In 1986 and 1987 the deficit exceeded one billion dollars. In response to this situation the Thai government established in 1984 a committee on the structural adjustment of Thai economic relations with Japan, chaired by the prime minister. A report was published the following year on the three issues of trade, investment, and economic cooperation. The report suggested that Japan should relax its import barriers to products from developing countries, as well as pointing out the weak competitiveness of Thai products.

One specific reason for Thailand's poor export performance pointed out in the report was the lack or underdevelopment of Thai trading companies and of Thailand's export marketing network.[3] A substantial part of Thai exports to Japan had been made through Japanese trading agents and companies, who were considered less eager to expand or develop new exports than indigenous ones would be. The underdevelopment of Thai trading firms cannot be blamed on Japan's import barriers, but it may be possible and desirable for Japan to extend export marketing knowhow to Thailand and other developing countries through technical cooperation schemes and other means. The report also blamed Thailand's low level of technology and packaging, and its inadequate ocean transportation system, for its weak export competitiveness. Whether Japan's import promotion policies should be expanded to counter those shortcomings is questionable, but a closer link between import promotion and official development aid policies is certainly desirable.[4]

The report presented the need for both short-term and long-term policies. The short-term policies relate mainly to Japan's import barriers, requesting (1) improvement of the tariff escalation structure, (2) expansion of import quotas, and (3) deregulation of import-restricting standards. In connection with the third point, the Thai government requested that Japan should send experts/officials on Japanese industrial and agricultural standards.

With regard to long-term policies, the following were listed:

1. Improvement of the quality and standard of Thai agricultural products (for example preventing carcinogens in Thai maize).
2. Improvement of the standard of agro-industrial and industrial products (establishing an export inspection system in accordance with Japanese standards, if possible with Japanese technical cooperation).
3. Improvement of the design and packaging of Thai products.
4. Diversification of the Thai economic structure.
5. Intensification of export marketing efforts.
6. Supplementary measures such as counter-trade and a buy-back system.

There is a need for more closely-linked import promotion and economic cooperation policies. The Thai case probably should be extended to many developing countries, but such a policy coordination would be most effective for such outward-looking economies as the ASEAN countries, whose rapid growth, through close cooperation on the level of industrial production, would have positive effects on the Japanese economy, making import promotion from these countries doubly desirable.

5.2 TARIFF DISCRIMINATION AGAINST DEVELOPING COUNTRIES

Trade conflicts with developing countries sometimes take a different form over specific products. Tariff discrimination favouring developed countries, especially the US, is a notable example. Very often this positive discrimination is little more than symbolic and has a limited effect in promoting exports. Nevertheless it is important in that developing countries may see themselves as being disadvantaged by the bilateral trade negotiations between Japan and the US.[5]

A well-known case was the conflict with Thailand over chicken imports. Boned chicken from the US and boneless chicken from Thailand – which started to be imported on a large scale in the 1980s – began to face different tariff rates in 1980, as can be seen in Table 5.2.

Table 5.2   Tariff rates – chicken, 1951–89 (percentages)

Year	Boned chicken	Boneless chicken	Difference
1951	10.0	10.0	0.0
1965	20.0	20.0	0.0
1980 (Jan.)	17.5	20.0	2.5
1982 (Jan.)	16.3	20.0	3.7
1982 (April)	13.8	20.0	6.2
1984 (April)	13.8	18.0	4.2
1985 (Jan.)	12.5	18.0	5.5
1985 (April)	11.3	18.0	6.7
1986 (Jan.)	11.3	14.0	2.7
1987 (Jan.)	10.0	14.0	4.0
1989 (April)	10.0	12.0	2.0

Source: The Japan Tariff Association

The difference between them was as high as 6.7 per cent from April 1985 to January 1986. Following negotiations between Japan and Thailand the gap was narrowed. In April 1989 however there still remained a tariff rate difference of 2 per cent.

The difference in tariff rates appears to correspond with the levels of processing, and thus is an example of tariff escalation. The imports of boneless chicken, usually on skewers (*yakitori* or chicken kebabs), started to increase in response to a labour shortage in Japan's processing industry which led to reduced domestic production. The rationale for tariff escalation, therefore, seems very slim.

Timber and wood products are also subject to tariff discrimination and the cause of trade friction. Coniferous timber is imported mainly from the US and Canada at tariff rates of between 4 per cent and 10 per cent. The GSP rates are either zero or 5 per cent, but this covers only a negligible quantity. The rate for tropical timber is 10 per cent, with a GSP rate of 5 per cent. For plywood the difference at one time was larger. Coniferous plywood in April 1986 had a tariff rate of 15 per cent, while tropical plywood was rated at 17 per cent (6 mm or more) and 20 per cent (less than 6 mm). Thus there was a difference of 2–5 per cent between the two products. In response to complaints from ASEAN countries, especially Indonesia, the difference was narrowed to 2.5 per cent and 1 per cent respectively in April 1987 and was removed entirely in April 1989.

5.3 CHANGES IN THE POLICY STANCE TOWARD TEXTILES

Japan's textiles policy is unique among industrial countries. Textiles are very often the first industry to be established when developing countries begin their industrialisation, and often they are the first commodity to be exported. In developed countries, where wages and therefore production costs are higher, locally-produced textiles face stiff competition from these imports. When automation and labour-saving innovations are difficult to obtain, especially among small and medium firms, demands for protection and import restrictions are very often made by domestic industries. At present the industry is under a very tightly managed trade regime in the form of the Multi-Fiber Arrangement (MFA). Naturally much discontent is expressed among exporters from developing countries, and the issue is attracting the largest attention from developing countries in the Uruguay round negotiations.

Japan's unique position in all this derives from its transformation in the last 30 years from being the largest textiles exporter to a net importer. Import controls on textiles started in the 1950s in the US and Europe, and Japan was the main target. As early as 1951 Japan's cotton exports to the UK became subject to import control, but the first managed trade regime was initiated with the Short-term Cotton Textile Agreement (STA) in 1962, by which the maximum annual export volume of cotton products was bilaterally specified between North American and European importers and Japanese and other exporters. This was extended into the Long-term Cotton Textile Agreement (LTA, 1963–73) the following year.

Throughout the 1960s Japan maintained its position as the largest textiles exporter to the US, but the end of the decade saw the development of the US–Japan textiles wrangle (1969–71), in which President Nixon proposed expanding the marketing agreement to include woollen and synthetic textiles, which Japan rigidly opposed. After Japan finally conceded to this as a political compromise, the US proceeded to conclude similar arrangements with Taiwan, Korea and Hong Kong. In 1974 this was extended to the MFA, and thus a large variety of textile products were drawn into the MFA's fold. Almost all the developed countries and the major textile-exporting developing countries participated in this arrangement. Importing countries came to bilateral agreements with individual exporting countries and set quota restrictions on a product-by-product basis.

Textile imports into Japan started on a large scale at the beginning of the 1970s. The international competitiveness of the Japanese textiles industry had already been in decline because of wage increases at home and because of the industrial progress of the Far-eastern newly industrialised countries. By the time the MFA was initiated, Japan had been replaced as the major exporter by these countries, who then started to export to Japan. The yen appreciation in 1973 and 1978 accelerated import expansion, but the really rapid expansion started after 1985 when the yen was revalued twice against the US dollar. Japan's total imports of textile products expanded by 27.4 per cent in 1986 over the previous year's figure, then by 49.9 per cent in 1987, 42.4 per cent in 1988, and 22.4 per cent in 1989. Textile imports were twice the volume of textile exports in 1987, and the import penetration rate (import divided by domestic demand) increased rapidly up to 38.7 per cent in 1989 (Figures 5.1 and 5.2).

The rapid increase in import penetration is more evident for individual products (Table 5.3). On average the ratio is 31–34 per cent for cotton yarn and fabric, but it amounts to 65 per cent for low-count yarn and 78 per cent for low-technology unbleached fabric with low value-added (1989). Clothing imports also increased rapidly, on average by over 50 per cent in recent years. The volume of imported sweaters for example increased for three consecutive years (1986–8) by 50 per cent, 51 per cent and 54 per cent respectively, and amounted to 69 per cent of total domestic consumption. The major suppliers of clothing are Far Eastern countries such as Korea (46.6 per cent in 1989), China (25.9 per cent), Taiwan (13.3 per cent) and Hong Kong (3.9 per cent).

With export reduction and rapid import expansion, domestic producers competing with imports started to demand the imposition of import restrictions to bring Japan's policy stance closer to that of other importing countries. Since 1983 the Textiles Manufacturers Association, the political arm of the business group, has been putting pressure on the Ministry of International Trade and Industry. MITI, despite its announcement that it would act on the MFA provisions, so as not to disrupt the surge in imports has so far refrained from doing so on the grounds of Japan's huge and persistent trade surplus and MITI's endeavour to promote imports.

Import restrictions extra to the MFA have however been imposed on a few products. Imports of silk yarn and fabric from Korea and China have been subject to a severe quota restriction since 1972. This is mainly to protect domestic sericulture. In 1983 the Japan Spinners'

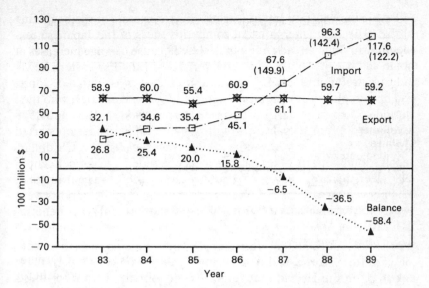

Figure 5.1 Exports and imports of textile products

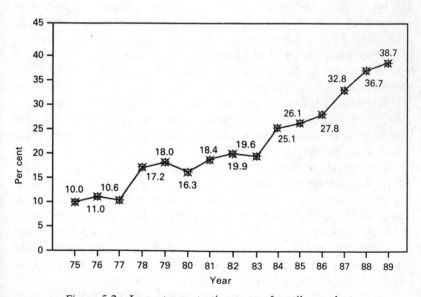

Figure 5.2 Import penetration rate of textile products

Source: Customs statistics (MOF) and textile statistics (MIT).

Table 5.3   Increase in import penetration (1984–9) (percentages)

Import	1984	1985	1986	1987	1988	1989
Yarns:						
Cotton	27.2	28.9	26.1	28.9	30.3	31.5
Fabrics:						
Cotton	22.1	22.1	24.9	28.8	31.3	34.2
Synthetic	10.2	15.1	15.3	8.0	4.7	11.7
Clothing:						
Knitted outerwear	26.7	27.4	34.8	46.3	53.2	55.0
Sweaters	44.7	42.2	49.0	54.8	65.9	69.0
Knitted underwear	21.0	23.0	25.4	36.2	44.2	50.8

Source: Customs statistics (MOF), and textile statistics (MITI).

Association petitioned for anti-dumping measures on imports of cotton yarn from Korea, and countervailing duties on cotton yarn from Pakistan, on the ground that imports of low-priced yarn from these countries were repressing the price of domestic products. The request for action against Korea was withdrawn following the announcement of a voluntary export restraint by the Korean Spinners' Association, and the request for protection against imports from Pakistan was dropped when its export subsidy was withdrawn by the Pakistan government. The Japan Weavers' Association has also been opposed to the rising import trend and has taken every opportunity to protest against imports of cotton fabrics from China, which accounts for three-quarters of Japan's cotton imports.

In October 1988 the Japan Knitters' Association petitioned for anti-dumping duties on imported sweaters from Korea. The association had earlier requested its Korean counterpart to restrain its export rush. In July 1988 the Korean side implemented a 'recommendation system' for exports to Japan, but this had little effect. Intergovernmental negotiations took place, and the Korean Ministry of Industry implemented the Voluntary Export Restraint (VER) in April 1989 and the check price system in July 1989. Imports of sweaters from Korea during the year commencing April 1989 decreased by 23.2 per cent in comparison with the previous year and the conflict with Korea eased. The Japan Knitters' Association is now concerned about the increase in imports from China.

It should be stressed however that Japan's import restrictions do not cover all textile products, and their restrictive impact cannot be compared with the one the MFA has had in North America and the

EC. Furthermore, both the US and the EC exclude textile products from their general system of preferences (GSP), while the Japanese scheme still covers textile imports, apart from the few products mentioned above. Textile products account for over 40 per cent of Japan's GSP imports, and China, Korea and Taiwan are the major beneficiaries.

Japan is participating as an importing country in the textile negotiations at the Uruguay round. But the Japanese government has so far managed to avoid resorting to MFA provisions in spite of its pledge to do so in the event of disruptive import surges. Japan had a hard time in Geneva, at the mid-term review in April 1989, when developing countries demanded a freeze on further import restrictions. Indeed it was very hard for the Japanese government to continue to go it alone in the midst of increasing pressure. It would help the government to continue its free import policy if the MFA could be phased out and there was a return to GATT rules.

How could the MFA be phased? At the mid-term review ministers agreed: (1) to reach an agreement within the duration of the Uruguay round on modalities for the integration of this sector into GATT, (2) such modalities should cover the phasing out of restrictions under the MFA and other restrictions on textiles not consistent with GATT rules and disciplines, and (3) the phasing out should be implemented in a progressive manner within a predetermined period of time, immediately following the conclusion of the Uruguay round. No matter what modality is agreed upon, there should be a definite time limit and no further extension, so the measures to be implemented during the transitional period have to be clearly defined and irreversible.

In accordance with the agreement at the mid-term review, there have been proposed such modalities as (1) tariffication, (2) tariff quotas, and (3) global quotas. Japan proposed a 'transitory safeguard' whereby MFA restrictions should be abolished in July 1991 when MFA4 is due, and be replaced by transitory safeguard measures. These will take the form of quota restriction on particular products and particular exporting countries, but they should only be triggered by objective and strict criteria under the surveillance of the Textile Surveillance Board (TSB). The criteria will be tightened and the quotas enlarged every year so that all transitory measures become integrated into the general safeguard of Article 19 by the year 2000. In this modality both the US and the EC will have to shift from the present restrictions under MFA Article 4 to the transitory safeguard measures, which will enable Japan to implement a new safeguard measure should disruptive import surges take place. But the advantages of dismantling the current MFA and an explicit pledge to adopt the general GATT safeguard measures will make it acceptable to developing countries. We wish Japan would take more advantage of its unique position by taking the initiative to persuade both importing and exporting countries to integrate the textile trade under GATT rules.

Nevertheless the MFA has already lasted for fifteen years and both importing and exporting countries have benefited from the economic rents brought about by MFA regulations. There is no clear sign of the arrangement being terminated, either by the US or by the EC, and there have been three consecutive extensions. In addition exporting countries such as Thailand are satisfied with the MFA because it has enabled them to increase their export shares by receiving quotas larger than their initial capacities. This view is of course short-sighted, and the MFA will eventually restrict the export growth of Thailand as it undergoes further industrialisation.

The critical issue of phasing out the MFA depends not so much upon how to compensate the loss of benefits as upon how to encourage individual governments to terminate the MFA within a definite deadline. The rent aspect of the MFA was not articulated at the beginning of the arrangement. Its supposed purpose was to give import-competing firms a clearly defined period in which to adjust. The need for a period of adjustment cannot be questioned, but fifteen years is too long a breathing space. The textile industry itself has changed much during these years. Many incompetent firms have already quit, either by switching to other areas of interest or simply by ageing of owners/workers. The protection afforded by the MFA has tended to prolong the adjustment of incompetent firms, but quite a few have adjusted and become competent producers.

5.4   JAPAN'S GENERAL SYSTEM OF PREFERENCE

The general system of preference (GSP) was introduced in Japan on 1 August 1971 following UNCTAD and GATT negotiations. Its duration was intended to be limited to ten years, but it was extended for a further ten years in 1981. The scheme was extended again in 1991. At first there were 96 beneficiary countries and areas, but the number gradually increased to 154 in 1989. Special preferences to the least developed countries (LDC special preference), offering in principle zero import duties, started in 1980 with 29 beneficiaries and expanding to 38 countries and areas in 1989.

Japan's GSP scheme is fairly complex. The positive list method is used for agricultural and fishery commodities (CCCN 1–24), reducing tariffs by 10 per cent to 100 per cent. A very low reduction of 10 per cent was made on bananas, but a recent revision took this to 50 per cent. There is also an escape clause, but this has never been invoked. There were originally 59 agricultural and fishery commodities under the GSP, but this number gradually increased to the present 77.

Mining and manufacturing commodities (CCCN 25–98) have been subject to the negative list method, under which 10 items (now 27) were specified as exception items outside the scheme. In addition there was a special measure to exclude certain imports, mainly textiles from Hong Kong, from GSP benefits. This was abolished in 1985 but some items were moved to the exception category. The rest in principle receive a 100 per cent tariff exemption. The selected products however are accorded only 50 per cent tariff cuts in order to protect domestic producers. There were 57 such items at the beginning of the scheme, decreasing gradually to 30 in 1987, but jumping again to 67 in 1988 in response to the change of classification from CCCN to HS.

Mining and manufacturing commodities are subject to GSP ceilings, which specify annually the maximum amount of preferential imports for each of the GSP items. At the beginning, the ceilings were the sum of two parts: the basic quotas (imports from GSP beneficiaries in the base year 1968) and the supplementary quotas (10 per cent of non-GSP imports in 1968). Base years were later changed several times to increase the ceilings. Since 1985 four types of calculation have been used to set the ceilings: (1) the sum of the 1982 base plus 10 per cent of non-GSP imports of the same item two years previously; (2) a 6 per cent increase of the quota of the previous year; (3) a 3 per cent increase; (4) no increase. The total ceiling in 1971 was 117 billion yen, but this increased to 1164 billion in 1989.

The ceilings are monitored and controlled using three methods: monthly administration, daily administration, and prior allotment. The first is a mechanism by which provision of references in the year is stopped on the first day of the second month after the ceiling has been reached. Daily administration is a stricter control method, and stops the GSP provision on the second day after the ceiling has been reached. It is possible therefore for a product to face GSP suspension on the third day after the start of the fiscal year (April 3), and such

Table 5.4   Evolution of Japan's general system of preference, 1971–89

	1971 *(from August)*	1977	1984	1988	1989
Beneficiaries:					
Countries (no.)	96	117	122	129	129
Areas (no.)	–	24	24	25	25
LDCs (no.)	–	–	34	37	38
Agriculture and fisheries:					
Items (no.)	59	77	75	77	77
GSP imports (billions of yen)	8.5	132	301	326	
Mining and manufacturing:					
Exceptions (no.)	10	12	20	27	27
Selected products (no.)	57	46	41	67	67
Ceilings (billions of yen):	117	640	1217	1146	1164
Base year	1968	1975	1982	1982	1982
Total items (no.)	214	189	201	146	145
Daily (no.)	95	42	41	41	40
Monthly (no.)	108	135	141	82	82
Prior allocation (no.)	11	12	19	23	23
Flexible items (no.)					
Global quota		108	110	51	51
One-half clause		121	134	78	78

Notes: Year refers to fiscal year. The one-half clause was replaced by one-third and one-quarter clauses in 1984 and 1987 respectively.

Source: The Japan Tariff Association (1985, 1985–9).

cases are common. Prior allotment is the strictest control, and is actually an advance quota allocation for specific importers.

The one-half clause was part of the scheme from the beginning, whereby importation of an item from any specific beneficiary was suspended from preference upon reaching half of the total ceiling. This was changed to a one-third clause in 1984 and a one-quarter clause in 1987. The stated purpose of such a clause is to provide GSP opportunities to a larger number of beneficiaries. There is a danger however that the clause can be used to aid protectionism.

Flexible administration – which was added to the scheme in 1973 and is an interesting way of increasing GSP imports – allows certain products duty-free entry after their ceilings have been reached. Originally it covered 110 items of global quota, and 85 items subject to the one-half clause. Table 5.4 demonstrates the evolution of Japan's GSP scheme over time.

Table 5.5 GSP imports and total imports, 1971–88

Year	GSP imports (billions of yen)	Total imports (billions of yen)	Ratio (%)
1971 (from August)	44	4 421	1.0
1972	110	7 659	1.4
1973	267	12 369	2.2
1974	380	18 276	2.1
1975	386	17 396	2.2
1976	526	19 717	2.7
1977	600	18 509	3.2
1978	639	17 057	3.7
1979	979	27 384	3.6
1980	1104	31 138	3.5
1981	1224	31 899	3.8
1982	1311	31 432	4.2
1983	1260	30 301	4.2
1984	1448	32 657	4.4
1985	1334	40 731	3.3
1986	1106	34 576	3.2
1987	1346	33 068	4.1
1988	1809	34 933	5.2

Source: The Japan Tariff Association (1985, 1985–9).

The effect of GSP appears to be mildly positive. Imports increased markedly immediately after the introduction of the GSP in 1971 – thereafter expansion continued, but more gradually. The annual rate of GSP import expansion was 30.7 per cent from 1972 to 1980, and 6.4 per cent from 1981 to 1988. This compares favourably with the annual expansion rates of total imports of 22.7 per cent and 3.2 per cent, respectively, for the same years, but the difference may be considered only marginal.

Table 5.5 compares GSP imports with total imports. Reflecting the faster growth of GSP imports, the share of GSP imports in total imports grew from an insignificant 1 per cent in 1971 to 4.2 per cent in 1983, then to 5.2 per cent in 1988. These figures can be translated into 2.5 per cent and 7.5 per cent of total imports from developing countries in 1972 and 1983.

The following breakdown reveals the shortcomings of Japan's GSP scheme. The low value for B may well have been caused partly by a large share of duty-free resource imports. But the low value for C in mining and manufactures, though rising, indicates there is much room for improvement.

	A (%)	B (%)	C (%)
Agriculture and fisheries:			
1972	3.6	4.1	89.6
1976	9.1	9.7	93.5
1983	16.1	16.8	95.9
Mining and manufactures:			
1972	2.5	12.2	29.1
1976	5.3	9.4	46.7
1983	6.3	11.6	54.4

Note: GSP Imports/Imports from Developing Countries (A) = GSP Covered Imports/Imports from Developing Countries (B) multiplied by GSP Imports/GSP Covered Imports (C).

Source: The Japan Tariff Association (1985).

The low utilisation rate of the GSP highlights the scheme's short-comings. First the system has grown evermore complex and harmful effects have resulted from control on individual items. With the expansion of the GSP, a number of carefully arranged protective and regulatory measures have been introduced and revised, making full understanding of the system by developing countries more and more difficult. Uncertainty over whether or not particular imports are granted GSP benefits – because of the ceiling administration – has also undermined the effectiveness of the scheme. Also, a measure to withdraw GSP benefits from products of specific beneficiary countries (partial graduation) was introduced in 1981 to protect domestic industries. An escape clause for mining and manufactured products was also added to the system in 1987. Although these have not yet been utilised, they increased further the complexity of the system. Product classification adds to this complexity. The scheme basically uses the CCCN (HS from 1988) classification, but for certain items much more detailed classification is used. Again, this is to protect domestic industries.

Secondly, Japan's GSP does not cover such major products of developing countries as dairy products, vegetables, fruit and grain. Even for manufactures the GSP on commodities in which developing countries have competitiveness, such as textiles and footwear, tends to be strictly administered. In contrast conditions are more lenient for the products in which developing countries are less competitive, such as machinery. Such practice of course limits seriously the significance of the GSP scheme.

Thirdly, there is a tendency for small groups of developing countries to monopolise the benefits. Korea, Taiwan and China in particular account for some 50 per cent of Japan's total GSP imports. The one-half (later one-third and one-quarter) clause was devised to prevent such monopolies, but the clause may lead to the creation of segmented markets where competition is restricted.

All three of these points are closely related to the strong competitiveness of Asian newly industrialised countries. One possible option would be the introduction of a 'graduation clause', and moving the whole system back to the original purpose of promoting exports from poor countries. Such action would certainly enable Japan to abolish most of the ceilings and to streamline the whole GSP system. When the US withdrew its GSP benefits from Asian newly industrialised countries, the Japanese government was reluctant to follow suit because of its large bilateral trade surplus with them. But it may have to seriously consider that option now.

As a part of the recent series of import promotion measures discussed in Chapter 3, several revisions were made to the GSP scheme. The most important of these revisions were as follows. In 1985, an increase in the ceiling for mining and manufactured products by some 100 billion yen, and withdrawal of the exception items vis-à-vis Hong Kong. In 1986, the withdrawal of GSP benefits for Spain and Portugal with their entry into the EC, the addition of Hungary as a GSP beneficiary, and a reduction in the GSP rates on 15 agricultural and fisheries products in accordance with the action programme. In 1987, the transfer of 59 out of 199 items subject to the ceilings to the escape clause category, an increase in the ceilings by approximately 30 per cent, reclassification of exception items and eight SP items, and introduction of the one-quarter clause. In 1988, an increase in the ceilings on 62 items by approximately 25 per cent, and abolition of the last two exception items in the LDC special preference system (beeswax and jute yarn).

Notes and references

1. For example in 1986 and 1987, in spite of the large appreciation of the Japanese yen and the resultant improvement in Korea's price competitiveness with Japan, the Korean bilateral trade deficit with Japan increased

rather than decreased, due mainly to increased importation of parts and components from Japan. Their exports to Japan increased rapidly, as did those to the rest of the world, but imports from Japan, due to structural reasons, increased even faster.

2. Economic Planning Board of Korea (1989).
3. On the development of Thai trading companies, see Yamazawa and Kohama (1985).
4. The new AID (Asian Industrial Development) plan, undertaken by the Ministry of International Trade and Industry, has the stated objective of promoting exporting industries in ASEAN countries by supporting intitiatives by private exporters in these countries. Its impact on local exporters however is too early to judge.
5. Bilateral trade dispute settlements between Japan and the US have raised suspicions in other countries. Australia, for example, once pointed out the possible harmful effects on Australian beef exports to Japan as a result of the US–Japan beef talks.
6. For the Japanese GSP scheme, see Japan Tariff Association (1985); ibid., *Trade Yearbook* (various issues); and I. Yamazawa (1988).
7. The criteria for the special preferences are those adopted by the twenty-third UNDP Committee meeting in 1987, and beneficiary countries must satisfy one of the two sets of conditions: (1) an average annual GDP per capita between 1983 and 1985 of $427 or less, a ratio of manufacturing output in GDP of 10 per cent or less, and an illiteracy rate of 80 per cent or more; (2) a GDP per capita of $356 or less, and a manufacturing output ratio of 10 per cent or less.

6 Japan's Trade Policies and Developing Countries

Ippei Yamazawa and Akira Hirata

Developing countries have attracted only minor attention in Japan's trade policies. The main preoccupation, especially in the 1980s, has been with evading or relaxing Japan's trade conflicts with developed countries. The US, Japan's largest trading partner, has had special leverage in this. The development of the large trade surplus in Japan on the one hand, and the 'twin deficits' in the US on the other, have been the important underlying factors. Also important has been the magnitude of the US bilateral trade deficit with Japan. Thus emerged a series of lengthy trade conflicts.

In dealing with these conflicts, the stance of Japanese government appears to have fluctuated between being bilateral and multilateral, perhaps in response to the negotiation stances of the US. In the various voluntary export restraint negotiations, for example, the agreements which were reached were clearly bilateral, although they did not openly violate GATT rules. The semi-conductor arrangement under the market-oriented sector-specific (MOSS) talks is an interesting example, in which the Japanese government is believed to have conceded a share of 20 per cent of the domestic market to the US.

Japan's main measures to cope with the situation have been increased import liberalisation and improved market access under the most favoured nation (MFN) principle. Liberalisation efforts, through the reduction of tariffs and relaxation of import controls including import procedures, have been by no means meagre. Together with the rapid and large appreciation of the yen since 1985, imports, especially manufactured imports, started to grow faster than exports.

Structural changes in the Japanese economy have also helped reduce the trade imbalance. A clear shift toward greater emphasis on domestic consumption has been observed. This shift was naturally most prominent in the period after 1985, as was shown in Chapter 2, but the long-term transformation of Japan's industrial structure has also played a role.

The substantial increase in imports, however, has so far had little effect on Japan's import ratio. In nominal terms the import/GDP ratio actually dropped from 9.8 per cent in 1985 to 6.3 per cent in 1988. The price effect and the reducing cost of importing petroleum are the main reasons for this. The import/GDP ratio in constant prices however shows a steady increase, indicating that import volume is growing faster than GDP. This may point to the future trend. The low level of the ratio is often taken as a sign of Japan's protectionism, although empirical tests are not conclusive as to whether or not Japan's import structure differs from the norm in industrial countries.

Japan's import regime in the formal sense, however, is one of the most open among industrial countries. There are few quantitative restrictions, and even these are being reduced, although there still remains tight control on some agricultural commodities. Tariff rates are also generally low, especially on manufactured imports. In both areas further liberalisation and import promotion measures were taken in the 1980s to help alleviate trade conflicts. These measures often appear ad hoc and piecemeal, but taken as a whole their effect is by no means small. Measures have been also taken to improve market access, import procedures, certificates, and industrial standards. Indeed Japan's import promotion policy has gone so far as to start a tax reduction scheme under which a proportion of increased imports would be exempt from corporate tax.

Other policy objectives, as in other countries, often conflict with import promotion. Agriculture is clearly such a case. Price support on rice and other agricultural products is linked with tight controls on imports of the commodities concerned, which reduces market opportunities for foreign farmers and – although Japan does not engage in subsidised export of agricultural products – may well negatively affect the world price. The rationale for such a policy has been the narrowing of the income gap between urban and rural areas. Its cost effectiveness is however questionable. Moreover the policy itself is likely to have hindered improvement in agricultural productivity by enabling relatively inefficient farmers to continue farming their small plots.

The distribution system in Japan is also often pointed out as an impediment to imports. Statistical evidence suggests that the productivity and efficiency of Japan's wholesale and retail industries are comparable to those of most industrial countries in spite of their multi-layered nature.

Nonetheless some aspects of the distribution system undoubtedly limit imports. One of these is *keiretsu* or company groups, who prefer local producers of parts and components to overseas ones. In some way this makes sound economic sense. The close link between the final manufacturers and the parts manufacturers makes it possible to develop, for example, tailor-made parts. Flexibility with regard to the volume and delivery time of parts, and firm orders covering a long enough timespan to enable new investment, benefits both parties. In a sense, these are non-standard goods. Also not to be overlooked is the fact that there are often financial ties between such firms.

The Large-Scale Retail Store Law is a clearer example of an institutional trade barrier, by which the establishment and enlargement of department stores and supermarkets are controlled. Since large stores are instrumental in increasing imports of consumer goods, the tight control on them inevitably works against import promotion. The purpose of the law, again, is the protection of small and medium sized local retail outlets. This issue was taken up at the SII talks, and there have since emerged signs of improvement.

In both agriculture and distribution there have been moves to circumvent import barriers – for example a substantial volume of rice is now imported in a slightly processed form. There has also been a rapid development of new import channels, showing that the market can prevail over institutions.

General import policies are not necessarily formulated with developing countries in mind. Rather, they often arise from trade conflicts with developed countries, especially the US. They nevertheless do affect developing countries. Among the largest beneficiaries of the recent import promotion policies, for example, are Asian newly industrialised countries, Korea and Taiwan in particular, and ASEAN countries.

Trade policies aimed specifically at developing countries are few in Japan, the GSP being the only major exception. Japan does not participate in any regional free trade areas, or extend special trade preferences to any group of countries. Strong economic ties with East and Southeast Asian countries have developed for economic and geographical reasons. Some policies, by their nature or coverage, affect developing countries more than others. Tariff discrimination, for example between boned and boneless chicken and between coniferous and tropical plywood, has sometimes become a sore point and has led to trade conflicts. The continuance of this escalating tariff structure, and the sometimes justifiable anxiety on the part of developing countries that they may be disadvantaged by the Japan–US bilateral trade talks, are part of the cause of developing countries' discontent.

However trade friction with developing countries is mainly due to the one-way dependence of Asian developing countries on imports of capital and intermediate goods from Japan. Production increases in these countries tend to induce imports from Japan, while Japan depends on them only for natural resources. As a consequence economic growth in developing countries is likely to bring about larger imports from Japan than exports to Japan. For example, Korea's bilateral trade deficit with Japan increased rather than decreased following the start of the rapid yen appreciation, although this had contributed to Korea's export expansion by strengthening Korea's price competitiveness. One-way dependence is structural in the sense that it plays a role in production and in that different levels of development between the two groups of countries are its root cause. In view of the export-led growth strategy adopted by developing countries, it is not difficult to understand their irritation.

Another type of trade conflict is emerging. Industries with declining competitiveness, textiles in particular, have been feeling the pressure from imports from developing countries, which is bringing about increased demands to the government for industrial protection. Quantitative import restriction under the MFA, for example, has been strongly advocated. The Japanese government, up to the present, has only conceded minimum protection of the textile industry, but the voluntary export restraint agreement on knitwear with Korea may prove to be the forerunner of further protectionist moves.

Stronger competition from developing countries however does show that a more balanced trade interdependence has been gradually developing. In ratio terms the trade imbalance, including trade imbalance in manufactures, has been decreasing for a long time. The yen appreciation helped promote the process, but the initial gap was so large that there still remains much room for improvement.

The GSP should be an instrument to aid improvement. Japan's GSP scheme however appears to be a conflicting mixture of genuine promotional measures and various safeguards – such as ceilings and administration methods – to check imports. The latter became 'necessary' to cope with the rapid increase in imports from Asian newly industrialised countries, who have monopolised GSP benefits. As a result the whole scheme has become too complicated to be very effective. One possible solution would be to separate the two aspects. The adoption of some sort of 'graduation' clause in association with the abolition – or radical expansion – of ceilings would make the GSP scheme simpler and more transparent, and so able to better serve its original purpose.

Developing countries are now engaging more actively in the GATT negotiations than they have in the past. Behind this is the recognition by at least some of them that maintaining a global free-trade regime is of critical importance to themselves. Some have started to accept a positive role by, for example, unilaterally liberalising imports. Broadly Japan has adopted the same position as them, although interests may differ on specific issues.

In summary Japan's trade policies toward developing countries are on the whole generally liberal – albeit with some shortcomings in a few areas – and do not appear to overly restrict imports from developing countries. However this may not be sufficient to ease the tension arising from trade conflicts. Import promotion using more active and positive measures, which may go beyond the narrow definition of trade policies, may be necessary. Such measures would have to be based primarily on industrial adjustment at home. Direct and indirect assistance to strengthen the export capacity of developing countries would also be helpful. After all, rapid economic growth in East and Southeast Asia would benefit Japan through trade and industrial links. It is in Japan's long-term interest to support their export-led growth. In view of the anticipated slowdown in import growth in the US, Japan will have to play a more active role as an absorber of their exports.

Part II

US Trade Policy towards Developing Countries

7 The Force of the Economic Winds

Stuart K. Tucker

Throughout the post-war era, US trade policy has been determined by a number of factors. Faith in free trade and markets has been one guiding principle. Industry-specific concerns have also driven policy at times. More often, national welfare considerations have pushed presidential action in other directions. The checks and balances of the US governing system have reduced the possibilities for consensus, but they have also allowed new initiatives to burst forth from unexpected origins.

However if there was one overriding element behind US trade policy until the mid-1970s, it was that US business ought to be able to succeed internationally as long as the US government used its world leadership position to create fairly-applied rules for international trade. In short, if the 'playing field was level', then US products would win a more fair share of the market because of the US's overarching competitiveness.

In the 1980s not only was that confidence in US supremacy shaken, but US policymakers were confronted with an international system where fair merchandise trade rules were no longer sufficient to foster US exports. Imbalanced macroeconomic policies in the 1980s left the US with a large and unsustainable trade deficit. The growth of the deficit in the mid-1980s was accompanied by the growing political strength of those who would restrain trade in the name of shielding weak US industries or fostering strong ones behind protectionism. General Congressional criticism of President Reagan's handling of the trade crisis has pushed the executive branch to find policies to address the imbalance, allay the concerns of damaged domestic export and import-competing industries, and meet US multilateral obligations. That response in the 1980s was in itself more protectionist and antagonistic toward US partners than policies in previous decades.

Meanwhile the international economic environment changed dramatically. With the explosion of the Third World debt crisis in the early 1980s, US trade potential took a dramatic turn for the worse. Significant markets for US exports disappeared. In fact many debtor countries turned into export competitors. The ensuing international trade imbalances left their biggest mark on the US due to the fact that the US had emerged from the recession as the strongest growing industrial-country market for internationally traded goods. The resolution of these dramatic imbalances (given the current political context) will inevitably involve dramatic changes in current US policy toward developing countries.

7.1   THE TRADE DEFICIT

The US trade deficit hit an historic high in 1987, both in absolute terms and as a percentage of national production (Table 7.1, 2 and 3). Rising from a moderate level in 1980 of $32 billion, the merchandise trade deficit hit $171 billion in 1987, amounting to nearly 4 per cent of the US gross national product.[1] During the period 1980–6 the sectoral trade balances in such mainstays of US competitiveness as agricultural goods, services and high technology goods deteriorated dramatically. The trade balance in machine and transport equipment went from a $24 billion surplus in 1981 to a $74 billion deficit in 1987. This trend continued in 1987 despite a large depreciation of the dollar and a 16 per cent growth in merchandise exports in 1987. By the end of 1987 the real value of US exports was less than it had been at the beginning of the decade. Meanwhile imports had grown fairly steadily since 1982, thereby swamping exports. Thus the US trade deficit could only reduce if export growth continued to outpace considerably the growth of the much larger value of imports.

At the beginning of 1988 most analysts held the view that the deficit would shrink significantly within a few years if the dollar depreciated to a more appropriate (lower) value and if the economies in Europe and Japan grew rapidly. Conventional wisdom said that these factors alone would be sufficient to boost US exports and reduce the deficit in the early 1990s. If this happened as hoped, then the US debt would be manageable and an import-contracting recession unnecessary.

The prognosis seemed correct as exports jumped 27 per cent in 1988 and the deficit fell by $31 billion to $140 billion. Yet this appears to have been largely the one-time result of the currency correction of the previous two years. Though many advocated a continued dollar

Table 7.1   Trade balances, 1980–9 (billions of dollars)

	US trade with:		Japan's trade with:	
	World	Developing countries	World	Developing countries
1980	−32	−37	−11	−28
1981	−40	−30	8	−19
1982	−30	−21	7	−16
1983	−69	−36	21	−9
1984	−123	−53	34	−10
1985	−148	−53	47	−6
1986	−170	−58	83	11
1987	−171	−72	80	8
1988	−140	−60	78	11
1989 (est.)	−130	−54	NA	NA

Note: Imports are c.i.f. value.

Sources: US data from US Dept of Commerce, *Highlights of U.S. Export and Import Trade*. Japanese data from IMF, *Direction of Trade Statistics Yearbooks*.

depreciation, the magnitude was not expected to be anything like the steep drop from the 1985 peak.

In 1989 the improvement of the US merchandise trade deficit slowed considerably. A safe estimate is that the deficit will be only about $10 billion smaller than in 1988. Some estimates indicate no improvement or even deterioration in 1990. Furthermore the current account appears to be again heading in a negative direction. Because the US is now the world's largest debtor (foreign liabilities exceeded overseas assets by about $533 billion in 1988), the debt service payments are making a large dent in the current account balance. This will necessitate not just a trade balance, but also large trade surpluses sometime in the near future.

The slowdown of trade progress in 1989 led to a splintering of economic opinion. The mainstream believed that the trade effect of the dollar depreciation of 1985–7 had run its course and consequently no further trade improvement was likely without further depreciation.[2] This opinion meshed well with the general belief that the economies of Europe and Japan had grown about as rapidly as could be expected without risking substantial inflation. Opposing minority views argued that the dollar needed only to slide a little

The Force of the Economic Winds

Table 7.2   Exports, 1980–9 (billions of dollars)

| | US to: | | | Japan to: | | |
	World	Developing countries		World	Developing countries	
1980	221	88	(40%)	130	61	(47%)
1981	234	97	(41%)	151	70	(46%)
1982	212	88	(42%)	138	67	(49%)
1983	201	77	(38%)	147	68	(46%)
1984	218	80	(37%)	170	72	(42%)
1985	213	77	(36%)	177	71	(40%)
1986	217	75	(35%)	211	76	(36%)
1987	253	87	(34%)	231	86	(37%)
1988	320	114	(36%)	265	102	(38%)
1989 (est.)	370	130	(35%)	NA	NA	(NA)

Export growth rates (average annual percentages):

1986–7	16	15		9	13	
1987–8	27	31		15	19	
1988–9	15	14		NA	NA	
1980–8	5	3		9	7	
1980–9	6	4		NA	NA	
1980–6	0	–3		8	4	
1986–9	19	20		NA	NA	

Sources: US data from US Dept of Commerce, *Highlights of U.S. Export and Import Trade*. Japanese data from IMF *Direction of Trade Statistics Yearbooks*.

because the full effects had not yet been felt. In short, these analysts believe that the J-curve effect of depreciation had become elongated beyond the more typical one or two year lags. Whether this was wishful thinking or solidly based, the latter opinion gathered many adherents within the Bush Administration.

Though both camps saw no reason for the dollar to rise in value, the market for dollars at the end of 1989 continued to defy the predictions of competent economists. Indeed in 1989 a new stream of thought began to gain advocates in the US business community. This point of view argued that the deficit did not matter since there was so much capital flowing into the booming US economy. So long as financing is abundant, US growth is rapid, and the debt remains small (now only slightly above 10 per cent of GNP), then the US trade deficit is an indication of wise investment in long-term US competitiveness, so the argument goes. This phenomenon may be what is

Table 7.3   Imports, 1980–9 (billions of dollars)

| | US from: | | | Japan from: | |
	World	Developing countries	World	Developing countries	
1980	253	125	(49%)	141	89	(63%)
1981	273	127	(47%)	143	89	(62%)
1982	255	109	(43%)	131	83	(63%)
1983	270	113	(42%)	126	77	(61%)
1984	341	133	(39%)	136	82	(60%)
1985	362	130	(36%)	130	77	(59%)
1986	387	133	(34%)	128	65	(51%)
1987	424	159	(37%)	151	78	(52%)
1988	460	174	(38%)	187	91	(49%)
1989 (est.)	500	184	(37%)	NA	NA	NA

Import growth rates (average annual percentages):

1986–7	10	19		18	20
1987–8	8	9		24	17
1988–9	9	6		NA	NA
1980–8	8	4		4	0
1980–9	8	4		NA	NA
1980–6	7	1		–2	–5
1986–9	9	11		NA	NA

Note: Imports are c.i.f. values.

Sources: US data from US Dept of Commerce, *Highlights of U.S. Export and Import Trade*. Japanese data from IMF, *Direction of Trade Statistics Yearbook*.

keeping the US economy from entering a recession. Indeed business cycle theorists have been confounded by the length and strength of the US recovery since 1982. As appealing as this line of thought may be, it has the troubling echo of the argument made in 1984–5 that the US dollar should be strong, reflecting confidence in the US economy. In retrospect the dollar was clearly overvalued in those years.

If the 'dollar pessimists' are correct, then the 15–20 per cent US export growth in recent years is not likely to be sustained much longer. Income growth in industrial countries cannot be reasonably increased. Growth in developing countries is still restricted by the Third World debt (more on this below). Trade liberalisation efforts, both bilateral and multilateral, will be small and too slow to take effect in comparison with the US trade imbalances now faced.

Therefore the US trade balance can only worsen and a great deal must happen with macroeconomic, debt, investment, and trade policies before a significant improvement can take place in the US trade accounts.

Consequently the US economy remains critically dependent upon the inflow of foreign capital. Without this capital or rapid export growth the US cannot finance its imports. Of course the recent inflows of investment capital have been used to create export capacity and to replace imports in some sectors. However this investment has not been sufficiently widespread to put a dent in the import figures, and major export markets in the Third World remain weak.

In short, unless a major US recession takes place, the high trade deficits of the 1980s cannot be expected to disappear quickly in the early 1990s.[3] This will probably have rather substantial political ramifications for US trade policy, as did the deficits of the mid-1980s.

To fully understand how these economic winds have pushed around US trade policy, it must be realised that many analysts misread the underlying causes of the problem and underestimated its force, leading the US government to move ponderously on the issues that mattered most to US trade, especially trade with developing countries.

7.2 CAUSES OF THE TRADE DEFICIT

In the aftermath of the 1980–3 global economic recession, it was commonly hoped that worldwide economic recovery would wipe away the economic ills caused by the severely contractive macroeconomic policies of the early 1980s. When the US was the first to recover this hope was modified to the expectation that the US economy would be the engine of growth pulling along the rest of the world. To some extent this happened. Strong US import growth acted positively in the adjustment process of other economies. However global recovery was imbalanced and the pattern of the recovery had a significant impact on the US trade deficit.

The US has pursued a highly expansionary growth policy since 1982 through large budget deficits. Meanwhile the rest of the world – especially developing countries burdened by debt and low commodity prices – remained in recession longer and then only slowly began to recover. Many parts of the Third World have still not attained their prerecession growth rates.

US imports as a percentage of GNP quickly rebounded to prerecession levels, while US exports, hindered by stagnant markets abroad, remained low. By 1984, and ever since, the US was buying a substantial majority of Third World manufactured exports. Low rates of income growth in Europe and low import rates (despite strong income growth) in Japan contributed to this massive shift of Third World manufactured exports to the US.

In those same early post-recession years the perceived US economic strength, combined with high real interest rates, swiftly drove up the value of the dollar. Between 1980 and the first quarter of 1985 the dollar appreciated 60 per cent against the trade-weighted average of the currencies of seventeen other industrial countries. Not only did this boost US imports from, and hurt US exports to, those industrial countries, but it also damaged trade with the Third World by making US goods relatively more expensive for Third World buyers compared with goods from other industrial countries.[4]

As a consequence of 'dollar bravura' – bragging that it was good for America to have a strong dollar – the executive branch did little to adjust the misaligned macroeconomic policies. Politicians began to feel the pressure being exerted by their manufacturing constituents – most of whom were suffering heavy losses in profits and jobs. When the US trade deficit doubled in 1984 and then redoubled in 1985, US politicians began to fear a permanent loss of trade competitiveness, especially in the manufacturing sector. Charges of unfair foreign trade practices abounded as attempts were made to displace the blame.

In fact economists underestimated the damage that would be caused by the macroeconomic imbalances and relied upon market adjustments to work for them. Although many decried the huge budget deficits, few made the evident connection that the budget deficits were linked to the trade deficits until after Congress had reached a budgetary deadlock and opted for the slowly progressing Gramm–Rudman–Hollings budget cuts. On the other hand politicians looked for foreign devils where none existed. Most economists consider unfair foreign trade practices to have had a relatively minor role in the ballooning of the US trade deficit. Although the worldwide level of trade restriction increased during the 1980s, the shift was dramatic.

By the mid-1980s and thereafter the US had a trade deficit with seventeen of its top twenty trading partners, who accounted for over 80 per cent of US trade. Moreover the US also has a negative trade balance with many other nations. If unfair practices were at the root of the deficit, then the deficit would be more concentrated than it is in the countries where unfair trade is practised most intensively. Therefore unfair trade practices cannot explain the sudden and large increase in the US trade deficit in 1980s.

Of course, many Third World countries have reduced imports and promoted exports by using barriers and subsidies, but for the most part these are debtor countries which would have foregone trade intervention in the absence of a debt burden. As a matter of debt policy, the US has encouraged these countries to apply measures that have led them to have trade surpluses in order to repay their debt. But these barriers and subsidies should more properly be cited as being in the 'debt crisis' explanation of the US trade deficit.

7.3   THE THIRD WORLD DEBT CRISIS

Perhaps the biggest analytical oversight by economists was the impact of the Third World debt crisis. At first (in late 1982) mainstream economists were concerned about the liquidity of developing countries (which suffered during the global recession), but denigrated the notion that a real solvency crisis was at hand. Hence policy discussions centred around temporary, stop-gap measures to prop up the banking system through the worst moments of the crisis. Moreover the effects on trade balances and US employment were conveniently forgotten until the mid-1980s, when much of the damage had already been done to the US manufacturing sector.

For some countries, including the US, the recovery of 1984–5 was rapid and the effects of the recession largely disappeared. Income grew in the mid-1980s faster than the average for the years since the Second World War. However many countries, particularly the heavily-indebted developing countries, achieved only modest growth for a few 'recovery' years. This was followed by continued stagnation or even a decline in their income. Furthermore the probability of vibrant income growth in the near future is slim. Though economic mismanagement has played a role, for the most part these poor economic performances and prospects are due to the debt crisis.

7.3.1   Successes prior to the debt crisis

The continuing economic malaise stands in stark contrast to the prerecession record of the income growth of developing countries. During the period 1965–80 the combined gross domestic product

(GDP) of developing countries grew at an average annual rate of 6.1 per cent. Although performance varied from country to country, this growth was fairly widespread. Sub-Saharan Africa's GDP grew 5.6 per cent, while a group of seventeen now heavily indebted countries (mostly in Latin America) grew at the rate of 6.6 per cent per year.[5] Latin America as a whole grew 6.1 per cent annually. Despite the growing Third World population, the generally high growth rates in this pre-debt crisis era provided much of the impetus for development progress and rapidly expanding world trade. The mutual gains from global interdependence were widely felt.

During 1965–80 world trade more than quadrupled in real terms. In the 1970s the exports of industrial countries grew in volume by 6.3 per cent per year. This growth was based largely upon the import growth of developing countries (8.1 per cent per year). At the same time world financial relations become more intertwined, with industrial countries as well as developing countries profiting from high rates of return on investments in the Third World.

7.3.2 Impact of the crisis

This era came to an abrupt end in 1981–3. Not only did incomes decline precipitously, but international financial and trade flows swung dramatically. By 1983 international lending to developing countries had been surpassed by debt servicing repayments of principal and interest which resulted in a negative net resource transfer to the developing countries. The resulting financial crunch caused debtor countries to rapidly constrict imports and redirect production toward exports, leading to a shift from trade deficit to surplus. Even this did not completely compensate for the rapid rise of debt service payment obligations relative to export earnings. Consequently debtor countries began to fall into arrears in their payments. Involuntary lending by private commercial banks, and rescue packages by governments and international organisations, continue to feed the growing debt. Many countries in Africa and some in Latin America now owe more money than they produce in annual income. In some parts of Africa, where exists the highest debt burden relative to capacity to pay, the debt is as large as three years' income.

7.3.3 Income declines

One major effect of the recession and the lingering debt crisis is the dramatic decline in income in the highly-indebted countries (HICs) and Sub-Saharan Africa. For the seventeen HICs, GDP per capita declined at an average annual rate of 1.7 per cent during 1980–6. Average income in these countries was $1540 per person in 1980, but by the end of 1988 it was $1400 (in constant 1986 dollars) – 10 per cent below the 1980 level and about 33 per cent below the level that would have been reached had the 1965–80 growth trend continued through to 1988. Income growth in Sub-Saharan Africa came to a halt, and no new income existed to accommodate the growing population. During 1980–6, per capita GDP declined at an average of 3 per cent per year, and by 1988 income per capita was only $360 – 81 per cent of the 1980 level. During the course of 1980–8, the seventeen HICs lost over $2 trillion (in constant 1986 values) in foregone income – nearly four times the amount of their payments to creditors.

Asia alone prospered during the global recession, with a per capita GDP growth of 3.5 per cent annually during 1980–5. The per capita GDP of the People's Republic of China is estimated to have grown a dramatic 9 per cent annually during 1980–6. The other low-income countries of the region were able to keep their GDP per capita above the 1980 level.

The aggregate 1.8 per cent annual growth of the per capita GDP of developing countries during 1980–6 is somewhat misleading as it masks the tremendous divergence of the paths of the most heavily debt-burdened countries and the remainder of the Third World. According to UNICEF, during the recession of the 1980s average living standards fell in countries that are home to 29 per cent (719 million) of the developing world's population (UNICEF, 1988).

7.3.4 Social crisis

During the last two decades developing countries have made tremendous progress in raising their physical standard of living. Since 1965 infant mortality rates have been reduced by nearly a half, life expectancy has increased by more than ten years, and daily caloric intake has increased 15 per cent. On average, people in developing countries are better educated than they were in the 1960s or 1970s. Yet aggregate social indicators for developing countries tend to obscure the development reversals experienced by selected population groups in the 1980s. Most indicators mix rich populations with poor ones and there are significant time lags between economic recession and the measurement of social effects.

Child mortality figures provide one useful means of assessing the impact of debt and recession. UNICEF recently reported that although the mortality rate among children under five years of age (U5MR) did fall during 1980–5, it did so at a much slower rate than during the period 1950–80. Much of this slowdown was concentrated among the poorest populations within developing countries.

Slower progress among the poor can also be seen in data on access to safe drinking water. Thirteen per cent of rural populations in developing countries had access to safe water in 1970, 32 per cent in 1980, and 43 per cent in 1985. Thus the proportion of rural populations with access to safe water more than doubled in the 1970s but increased only one-third in the succeeding five years. In Mexico the rural population's access to safe water actually worsened from 49 per cent in 1975 to 40 per cent, by the most recent estimate, in the 1980s. In Cote d'Ivoire, the urban population's access to safe water declined from 50 per cent in 1975 to 30 per cent by the most recent estimate (UNICEF, 1989; World Bank, 1988).

These conditions are likely to be aggravated in the long term by the reduction of public spending on social programmes such as education, health, housing, welfare and social security. As income in debtor countries declined, overall government revenue and spending declined by nearly the same proportion. Furthermore large public sector debts required ever-increasing amounts of money to cover interest and principal payments. Thus the proportion of developing countries' aggregate central government expenditure devoted to interest payments grew from 7 per cent in 1980 to 16 per cent in 1985. Consequently a lower proportion of government spending was devoted to social programmes, falling from 32 per cent of total expenditure in 1980 to 29 per cent of total expenditure in 1985 (IMF, 1987).

The shifts in public spending were more dramatic in debtor countries. Latin America devoted 27 per cent of central government spending to interest payments in 1985, as opposed to 9 per cent in 1980. Consequently public spending on social programmes contracted from 44 per cent of spending in 1980 to 36 per cent in 1985. This reduced social spending is today creating a growing 'social debt'. The failure to invest in educational training, health standards and other improvements in living conditions will reduce the development potential of Third World populations in coming years and thereby increase the future costs of development.

7.3.5　Regaining lost ground

The debt crisis has left a painful legacy – relieving the resultant economic stagnation will not be easy, and the time lost during the 1980s may not be recoverable. For Third World income growth, and perhaps for development in general, the 1980s represent a decade of lost opportunity.

Estimates of short- and long-term growth prospects differ, but analysts generally agree that it will not be easy for policymakers to create the economic climate necessary to increase the incomes of developing countries at the same pace as before the debt crisis. In fact most estimates for the next several years project growth rates that are generally about 1.5 percentage points below the rate achieved in 1965–80. If these projections are correct, many countries will still be poorer in 1992 than they were in 1980. Sub-Saharan Africa, for example, would not recover its 1980 per capita GDP level until the year 2005 if it grew at a rate of 1.5 per cent below the prerecession growth rate (that is at 1.3 per cent instead of 2.8 per cent).

Of course policymakers are trying to find ways of boosting income growth back towards its previous rates. But even in the unlikely event that growth were to immediately resume at the 1965–80 rates, then highly-indebted countries would not recover to the 1980 per capita GDP level until 1991. In short, even under optimistic conditions the major debtors have lost at least a full decade of income growth. Sub-Saharan Africa has lost at least 16 years. Even if per capita GDP were to rise at 4.5 per cent (0.5 per cent faster than in the 'golden years'), the income of the highly indebted countries would not catch up to the extension of that 1965–80 trend line (4 per cent growth from 1980) until the year 2077. So even under optimistic scenarios the effects of the debt crisis will linger for at least a lifetime.

7.4　IMPACT OF DEBT ON US TRADE AND JOBS

By treating the debt crisis, in its early stages, as a temporary liquidity problem, policymakers avoided contemplation of drastic debt relief action. The burden of the debt was assumed to rest mostly on the banks and the debtor countries themselves. As the previous section suggests, the burden has indeed been large – and will continue to be so even if the Brady Plan works. However the burden of the debt has not rested solely on the creditors and debtors. US businesses and workers have also suffered severely during the course of the crisis. This is especially true for business related to US exports to Latin America.

In order to continue to service their debts while the private banking system ceased voluntary new lending, Latin American countries slashed imports from $121 billion in 1981 to $70 billion in 1983. Since then imports have grown slightly, but remain about one-third less than the peak in 1981. Although Latin America has maintained its share of world exports, essentially all the adjustment to the debt crisis has taken place on the import side. The import compression has been so severe that many countries have postponed vital capital projects, thus impairing their long-term growth prospects. Between 1980 and 1985 Latin America shifted its trade balance from a deficit of $12 billion to a surplus of $25 billion. All of these earnings went to cover the net resource transfer gap created by the withdrawal of commercial lenders and the maturation of past debt. Now Latin America is transferring about $20 billion per year to its creditors (over and above new lending). To compound the difficulties, the slight slowdown of the income growth of industrial countries in 1986 led to a $9 billion contraction of Latin American exports to industrial countries.

The first evidence of the impact of debt on US trade was how the share of US exports to developing countries in total US exports had generally declined since 1982. Thus exports to other parts of the world at the end of the global recession of 1980–3 grew faster than exports to developing countries. The Third World share of US exports dropped from 42 per cent in 1982 to about 35 per cent in 1989.

Although all industrial countries have experienced lost export opportunities, the large US trade share made the costs of the debt crisis particularly high for the US. Furthermore the marginal changes in Latin American imports affected US exports slightly more than other industrial countries. Between 1981 and 1987 the US trade balance with Latin America shifted from a surplus of $2 billion to a deficit of $14 billion, making the deficit in 1987 equal to two-fifths of US exports to Latin America ($35 billion). My estimates show that US exports to Latin America in 1987 could have been about twice their actual size in the absence of the recession and debt crisis of the 1980s. US export industries have lost well over $30 billion of potential exports. Consequently the share of Latin American trade in overall US exports dropped from 18.4 per cent in 1981 to 13.8 per cent in 1987.

These lost exports also had a severe impact on employment in the

US – by 1987 an estimated 860 000 jobs had been lost.[6] Only approximately half of these jobs did actually exist in 1980, but the other half could have been created had US exports continued to grow at the same pace as they had in the 1970s. About three-quarters of the jobs were lost due to the poor performance of manufacturing industries, especially the capital goods industries. However agricultural exports to Latin America also suffered, being 42 per cent lower in 1987 than in 1981. Lost sales to Mexico (which ranked as the third largest US trading partner in 1980) cost over 300 000 US jobs, lost exports to Venezuela cost over 100 000 jobs, and lost sales to Brazil and Argentina each cost the US 90 000 jobs.

The 1987–9 recovery in US exports to Latin America holds out some hope for a better future. However much of this rise in absolute terms is less significant because of the very low level of exports in 1986. In fact the increases in absolute export value in the late 1980s did not make up much of the ground lost earlier – the 1965–80 trend line, when extended beyond 1980, remains far above current export levels. Moreover these increases relate largely to rapidly shifting currency values which are not likely to be repeated. Future export growth will have to be based on strong Latin American income growth rather than currency depreciation.

Although the debt crisis has centred on Latin America, the debt burden has been large for other Third World countries as well. Furthermore the dampened global economic climate has also restricted the successes of the fast-growing East Asian countries, thereby curtailing US exports to Asia.

As a result of the decline in exports to the Third World, as well as the failure to grow in line with historic trends, in 1987 the US had an estimated 1 774 000 jobs fewer than it could have expected in the absence of the recession and debt crisis. The most important export sector to the US economy is that which produces machine and transport equipment. Lost Third World export sales in this sector had cost 731 000 jobs in manufacturing and supporting service industries by 1987. A substantial portion of these largely 'capital goods' exports were non-electrical machinery (424 000 jobs lost). The most concentrated losses (in terms of job losses relative to number of producing companies) came in the transport equipment sector (267 000 jobs lost). Another important export sector is agriculture, where the export collapse caused the loss of about 470 000 jobs in farm and farm-related industries, services, and communities in 1987.

In short, the impact on employment and production in the US as a result of lost trade due to the debt crisis has been substantial. Any effort to correct the US trade deficit will therefore be only partially successful in the absence of more effective debt relief measures. Conventional wisdom holds that the trade imbalance can be largely corrected by depreciation of the dollar and by rapid growth in other industrial countries, especially Japan and Germany. This perspective ignores the very important role that must be played by growth in the middle-income developing countries.[7]

7.5 POLITICAL RAMIFICATIONS

In Washington, where *budget* deficits seem habitually to go un-noticed, the record *trade* deficits and the attendant job losses caused a widespread outcry and quite a number of legislative and executive branch actions were implemented to remedy the situation. In general the gravity of the impact of the debt crisis and the need for US fiscal and monetary policy adjustment were ignored. The more 'macro-minded' trade deficit solutions emphasised dollar depreciation combined with fiscal stimulus by major industrial trading partners. However quite a number of 'micro-management' solutions were proposed during the mid-1980s – most of which sought to solve the symptoms rather than the root-causes of the problem.

Discussions on direct policy intervention through trade legislation began with the battle over what became the Trade and Tariff Act of 1984. The extraordinary efforts of the executive branch led to the removal of protectionist clauses in the proposed law, but Congress then began to scrutinise more closely executive branch administrative measures in the hope of pushing President Reagan to take direct action on the deficit. As most politicians were concerned about the unfair trade practices of other countries, President Reagan announced an aggressive new bilateral negotiation policy at the end of 1985 in the hope of staving off legislative efforts.

Despite a marked increase in executive branch-initiated trade restrictions after September 1985, Congress moved ahead with its consideration of major pieces of trade legislation, many of which were branded as protectionist by observers. After three long years of discussions, numerous administration trade actions, and quite a bit of editing, the omnibus trade legislation was finally passed in August 1988. Thus the succeeding Bush Administration had to implement trade policy with a number of significant changes in its policy tools.

Furthermore it inherited a US trade regime which was more protectionist than it had been in 1980 as a result of the efforts of the Reagan administration to avert Congressionally-mandated protectionism by implementing its own brand of trade intervention.

The result of the large US trade shifts in the 1980s has been a marked increase in Congressional concern about sectoral competitiveness problems. Thus US trade policy in the 1980s can be typified as driven by sectoral responses to what for the most part was a broader macroeconomic problem. These sectoral efforts have helped but a few by strengthening their lobbying position. Of course many of the trade restrictions preceded the 1980s – being long-lasting residuals of past political fights over trade. However the macroeconomic environment in the 1990s created a new and strong political pressure which forced executive branch responses. A pivotal issue for the 1990s is whether these economic and political forces have created a dynamic of trade concern that will lead to long-lasting trade protectionism.

On the other hand the post-recession period has witnessed a renewal of the increasing and positive interdependency that typified US economic relations at the end of the 1970s. Considerable pro-trade sectors of the US economy have gathered political weight as a result of the Uruguay round of multilateral trade negotiations. If this can be sustained until the trade deficit falls into a more reasonable range, then the worst impulses can be kept out of US trade policy.

7.6   STRUCTURE OF THE REMAINING CHAPTERS

Although the US maintains a substantially open trade regime, most US trade policy falls into the category of import 'management' – that is, import barriers or other practices that reduce imports from abroad. Due to the striking successes of the multilateral trade negotiations (including the Tokyo round), tariff barriers to US imports are relatively small. Consequently Chapters 8 and 9 focus attention upon various aspects of US non-tariff barriers. Chapter 8 considers the trade-affecting aspects of US agricultural policy. Chapter 9 handles US textile and clothing trade policy and rounds off with the remainder of the major non-tariff barriers (NTBs) in US trade policy toward developing countries.

Although free trade has been the overarching principle guiding US policy in the postwar era, barriers nonetheless prevent free-market trade access to the US economy as well as to the economies of its trading partners. The attempts to overcome (or compensate for) these barriers can be called trade promotion, although technically speaking many of these policies only partially offset existing trade restrictions. Two aspects of trade promotion are addressed in Chapters 10 and 11. Chapter 10 focuses upon US efforts to provide preferential access to the US market for goods from selected developing countries. It discusses the Generalised System of Preferences, the Caribbean Basin Initiative, free trade areas, and more recent preferential trade proposals, (most of these programmes provide duty-free trade to beneficiaries, with little change in NTBs). Chapter 11 deals with a hitherto minor aspect of US trade policy – the promotion of US exports. Until the 1980s this policy was handled primarily by the Export-Import Bank of the United States. However in the 1980s substantial agricultural export subsidies were introduced, and numerous bilateral access negotiations were initiated to open markets for US goods.

The nature of trade has been undergoing steady change for decades now, but in the 1980s, as diplomats and businessmen prepared for further multilateral trade negotiations, several 'new' issues came to the forefront. These issues have challenged the multilateral trading system to expand and adapt to the new forms of commerce. In addition the growing interdependence of national economies led to new pushes for more harmonised practices in areas never previously discussed as trade issues. The last two chapters focus on the changing nature of trade and how trade policy is therefore being redefined. Chapter 12 analyses the new issues of services, intellectual property rights, investment, and worker's rights. Chapter 13 concludes this study of US trade policy toward developing countries by commenting on the overall directions of the trading system and the US role within it.

Notes and references

1. Imports on a c.i.f. transactions basis.
2. See Paul R. Krugman, 'The J-Curve Illusion' in *International Economy* (September/October 1989) pp. 75–8, for the arguments of these 'dollar pessimists'.
3. Even with substantial dollar depreciation, other policies will be needed. See Ralph C. Bryant and Gerald Holtham 'The U.S. External Deficit:

Diagnosis, Prognosis, and Cure', in *External Deficits and the Dollar*, Ralph C. Bryant, Gerald Holtham, and Peter Hooper (eds), (Washington, DC: The Brookings Institution, 1988) p. 71.

4. Note that this effect takes place even when a developing country's currency is pegged to the dollar.

5. The 'highly indebted countries' (HICs) are defined by the World Bank to be Argentina, Bolivia, Brazil, Chile, Colombia, Costa Rica, Cote d'Ivoire, Ecuador, Jamaica, Mexico, Morocco, Nigeria, Peru, Philippines, Uruguay, Venezuela and Yugoslavia.

6. The estimate refers to jobs in export industries, intermediate supplier industries, and the service sector, plus community jobs that are indirectly related due to employment multiplier effects. For the methodology see Stuart K. Tucker, 'Update: Costs to the United States of the Recession in Developing Countries' (ODC Working Paper no. 10, January 1986) and Stuart K. Tucker, 'The Costs of Third World Debt: The Loss of U.S. Jobs' (mimeo, 1988).

7. Estimates by the author show that roughly $30 billion of the US trade deficit could be reduced in the early 1990s if developing countries recovered their former rapid growth rates. See John W. Sewell, 'The Dual Challenge: Managing the Economic Crisis and Technological Change', in John W. Sewell and Stuart K. Tucker (eds), *Growth, Exports, & Jobs in a Changing World Economy: Agenda 1988* (US–Third World Policy Perspectives No. 9, Transactions Books in cooperation with the Overseas Development Council, 1988) pp. 10–16.

8 US Agricultural Policies

Stuart K. Tucker

Some US import restraints represent the longstanding influence of significant US business and political interest groups. Hence US imports of agriculture and clothing products have been restrained since before a significant US commitment was made to multilateral free trade. Yet the persistence of these policies can not always be explained by the continuing influence of these groups. In addition, the major trading partners of the US have resisted the rigours of the international marketplace in these sensitive sectors. Thus, despite garnering an ever-increasing world-wide support for freer international trade and more effective multilateral oversight, the US and some of its industrial allies find themselves maintaining policies that are somewhat anachronistic and often expensive, reducing national as well as global welfare. These once 'temporary' mechanisms have become entrenched cancers in the international economy.

At one time 'management' of selected imports was justified as a way to help an industry adjust. The US has been particularly weak in implementing alternative methods of adjustment assistance for industries and individuals hit by competing imports. However today the justifications for protection have widened to include support for 'strategic industries' or protection of the 'social contract' or retaliation for perceived unfair practices abroad. In a climate of increasing competition for stagnant or dwindling world markets, the political impetus for 'managing' trade – that is, restraining it – has strengthened. The proliferation of protectionist pressures has been rapid. The US, though in principle resisting this trend, has been party to a number of the new arrangements for managing imports. The big challenge of the Uruguay round is to overcome this trend and set the international trading system onto a new footing.

8.1 THE AGRICULTURAL DIMENSION

In the mid-1980s farmers around the world faced depressed commodity prices, huge debts and stagnating trade. Although populations and

113

Table 8.1   US agricultural trade with developing countries, 1980–8
(billions of dollars)

	Exports	Imports	Balance
1980	17.5	12.2	5.3
1981	18.4	11.7	6.7
1982	14.9	10.0	4.9
1983	15.7	10.6	5.1
1984	16.1	13.0	3.2
1985	12.7	12.9	−0.1
1986	11.0	13.6	−2.6
1987	12.5	12.5	0.0
1988	16.4	12.7	3.7

Source: US Dept of Commerce, Bureau of Census, *Highlights of U.S. Export and Import Trade*, various issues.

consumption have increased, production has grown faster. Much of the global agricultural overproduction and depressed markets has resulted from government subsidies, especially in industrial countries. Both the US and the Third World have a strong interest in reducing the level of farm subsidies – production subsidies in industrial countries are high. Furthermore in 1986 roughly 48 per cent of Third World agricultural exports to industrial countries were affected by non-tariff barriers (Laird and Yeats, 1988; Nogues, Olechowski, and Winters, 1986). Between 1980 and 1986 world food prices fell by 38.5 per cent, undermining farm production incentives in the many food-short countries of the Third World. Cash crop prices also slumped from 1980, making it difficult for these currency-poor countries to pay for even cheap food imports.

Developing countries have a substantial interest in reforming agricultural policies, and the US stake in better agricultural policies is also large. The value of US agricultural exports fell 40 per cent between its peak in 1981 and its trough in 1986 (Table 8.1). Despite some improvement in recent years, agricultural exports in 1988 were still 15 per cent below the 1981 level. Meanwhile federal government farm programmes were costing $31 billion by the fiscal year 1986 – more than $13 000 for each American farmer (Table 8.2). After 1986 the farm economy picked up and the cost of US federal farm programmes fell to $17 billion in 1989 – although this was still twice the size of the 1980 level. US federal farm programmes still represent

Table 8.2 US agricultural production subsidy equivalents, 1986

	Value of production ($ billions)	Value of US policy to producer ($ billions)	Production subsidy equivalent (% of production)
Wheat	9.2	5.8	63
Corn	20.4	10.1	50
Rice	1.5	1.1	72
Sorghum	2.2	1.1	49
Barley	1.4	1.0	76
Oats	0.5	0.1	16
Soybeans	9.4	1.2	13
Dairy	17.6	10.4	59
Sugar	1.7	1.4	83
Beaf and Veal	20.9	2.4	12
Pork	9.5	0.7	8
Poultry	8.9	1.5	17
Total	103.0	36.9	36

Note: State subsidies included.

Source: USDA, *Estimates of Producer and Consumer Subsidy Equivalents: Government Intervention in Agriculture, 1982–6.*

a substantial portion of net farm income (40 per cent of the 1988 income).

8.2 US PRODUCTION SUPPORT AND GLOBAL SURPLUSES

In the early 1970s world food production was very close to the level of world food consumption, and stored cereal stocks amounted to about one-seventh of a year's consumption. But in 1973–4 a series of bad harvests in many regions of the world, inflationary macroeconomic policies, and speculative hoarding by most industrial countries led to world food shortages. In response to this crisis, global food production, except in Africa, grew rapidly – considerably outstripping consumption and resulting in a dramatic increase in global stocks. World cereal stocks in 1985 were 147 per cent higher than in 1974, amounting to 27 per cent of annual consumption.

With domestic consumption growing at only about 1 per cent annually but US farm productivity growing more rapidly, US farmers relied heavily upon export markets for their earnings (31 per cent of farm sales in 1981). The world food crisis in the early 1970s encouraged US farmers to increase production. However the 1980s found many US farmers deeply indebted, with loans tied to land dropping rapidly in value as worldwide overproduction became apparent. US agricultural exports dropped from a high of $43 billion in 1981 to just over $26 billion in 1986 and more than 200 000 American farms went out of business during this period.

8.3 IMPACT ON THE THIRD WORLD

Up until 1981 the Third World was a net exporter of agricultural goods to the rest of the world. Developing countries, especially lower-income ones, depend heavily upon the agricultural sector for employment and production. In 1980 63 per cent of the Third World's labour force was employed in agriculture. In low-income Asian and African countries the ratios are even higher (71 and 78 per cent respectively). Low-income countries in Africa are especially dependent upon export earnings from agricultural commodities (68 per cent in 1982–4). In low-income Asian countries agriculture contributes to 36 per cent of GDP. Even middle-income developing countries (predominantly in Latin America and Asia) remain dependent upon agriculture for employment (53 per cent in 1980) and exports (45 per cent in 1982–4) when oil-exporters and the few major exporters of manufactures are excluded (World Bank, 1986).

8.3.1 Production and food security

The share of developing countries in world cereal production is substantial – more than double the US share. However most of these countries consume all of their production and many are major importers of additional food commodities. Five of the seven major Third World wheat producers are net wheat importers. Only a few developing countries – such as Argentina with wheat, and Thailand and China with rice – are major cereals exporters and hence compete with the US in global markets. Thus the US share of the cereals trade is double the Third World share (36 per cent compared to 18 per cent in 1985).

At first glance it would appear that a world-wide glut would benefit the Third World through low import prices. In the short-term this is true only when these countries have the necessary purchasing power to buy imports. Recessionary macroeconomic policies in the 1980s, rising trade barriers, Third World debt service problems, industrial countries' export subsidies, and generally low prices for developing countries' export crops have combined to drastically reduce Third World purchasing power.

In the long-term a primary goal of Third World countries is to increase domestic production as a buffer against the volatile world market. However ever-increasing cereals 'mountains' in industrial countries and artificially low prices greatly undermined the efforts of food-short developing countries to increase production and thus increase security against future food disasters. Many countries, from the standpoint of economic efficiency and comparative advantage, should be growing their own food rather than importing temporarily cheap food.

For some developing countries the current glut is also suppressing food exports. Although the Third World provides only 6 per cent of the world's wheat exports, it has been estimated that its share would nearly double if the wheat policies of industrial countries were liberalised (benefitting Argentina, Turkey and India with exchange earnings increases amounting to about $1.5 billion) (Zeitz and Valdes, 1986).

8.3.2 Export crop production and earnings

Although malnutrition remains widespread in much of the Third World, a major obstacle to increasing per capita food consumption is widespread poverty throughout the Third World and, for food-importing countries, the lack of foreign exchange earnings to purchase imported food. It has been estimated that the people of developing countries would increase immediately their daily caloric consumption by 50 per cent if they had the means to afford it.[1]

Increases in national income and foreign exchange earnings, which are needed to boost food consumption in developing countries will be difficult to achieve under prevailing trends. Only a minority of Third World countries have the option or ability to sell manufactures to gain foreign exchange, particularly since the onset of protectionist pressures in the 1980s, and developing countries' cash crops suffered severely in the 1980s due to a commodity price depression. Moreover agricultural products, especially in processed forms, face high trade barriers in industrial countries, including the US. US non-tariff barriers in 1986 covered over 32 per cent of US imports of developing countries' agricultural products (Laird and Yeats, 1988). The Third World's share of US agricultural imports actually decreased during the early 1980s. For example US sugar quotas, imposed in 1982, have reduced US sugar imports by 72 per cent. The EC also maintains high barriers and production subsidies. The World Bank estimates that the Third World's export share would increase nearly 75 per cent following sugar trade liberalisation, adding some $2 billion to the earnings of low-income countries (Zeitz and Valdés, 1986).

By 1986 the world sugar price had dropped 80 per cent from the 1980 level and 84 per cent from the 1974 level. Despite increases since 1986, the world sugar price remains considerably below the level many analysts would consider to be a free market price. Similarly the Third World's export share of beef would double if the trade in beef were to be liberalised (Zeitz and Valdés, 1986). High tariffs and quantitative restrictions are used by the industrial world to protect ranchers from losses. In addition to this and in response to the milk glut caused by decades of dairy production subsidies in industrial countries, the US and the EC implemented a herd slaughtering plan that greatly increased the supply of beef. Also the Multi-Fibre Arrangement, which limits Third World textile and clothing exports to industrial countries, has reduced the world demand for cotton fibre – a substantial portion of which is supplied by a large number of Third World countries (64 per cent of world production; 52 per cent of world exports).

The three major exceptions to these trends, the beverage commodities of coffee, cocoa and tea, have fared well in recent years. However production is concentrated in a few developing countries, and reliance upon the export earnings from these commodities to pay for food imports greatly endangers nations with periods of feast and famine because price and supply volatility is high. Efforts to stabilise these price fluctuations have largely failed due to the lack of consensus between consumers and producers over the primary goals of commodity stabilisation agreements.

8.4   US INTERESTS IN REFORM

US agricultural policy reform is necessary to save the US farm sector, jobs, export markets, budgetary costs and trade relations. The long-term health and viability of the agricultural sector depends upon reform of current US farm programmes. Real net farm income was lower in the 1980s than in any of the previous four decades, and the farm credit system has been strained by debt. Distortions of cropping patterns is also endangering soil quality in the US.

US farmers account for only 3.2 million jobs out of a total labour force of 125 million, but connections between farm output and other parts of the economy are substantial. The National Agricultural Forum estimates that in 1982 farm supply service industries, farming itself, food and agricultural raw material processing, food transportation, and food wholesaling and retailing services combined to account for 25 million jobs and 20 per cent of the US GNP (US GAO, 1985).

In 1981 agricultural exports comprised 18.6 per cent of total US exports. The subsequent decline in US agricultural exports to developing countries ($7.4 billion from 1981 to 1986) resulted in the loss of about 230 000 jobs, whereas an additional 265 000 jobs would have been created if the trends of the 1970s had been maintained in the 1980s. Thus a total of nearly 500 000 jobs in farming and farming-related input and service sectors were lost from 1980 to 1986 due to the reduction in purchasing by the Third World.[2]

Developing countries represent the most important source of future demand for US food exports. US domestic consumption is growing by about 1 per cent annually, while cereal consumption in developing countries is growing by about 3.5 per cent – an annual increase of about 34 million metric tons. Developing countries had increased their cereal imports at a rate of 4.3 per cent annually to make up for their production shortfall – thus the Third World's share of global imports increased from 41.3 per cent in 1974 to 45.6 per cent in 1985. By the year 2000 it is projected that developing countries will be importing 54 per cent of traded world cereals (Avery, 1985).

Recent evidence indicates that those countries that have the highest increases in agricultural production are also the most likely to experience high food import growth due to the income effect of successful agricultural production. One example of this trend is Brazil, which in 1974 was a major cereal exporter. By 1985, despite a production growth rate of 2.9 per cent, Brazil's cereals exports had dwindled to a trickle and were swamped by imports, which grew at 6.4 per cent. This import expansion was largely attributable to a per capita growth in income and consumption; Brazil's per capita production also increased during this period. Robert Paarlberg (1987) summarised the issue: 'food imports went up faster when poor country farmers were doing well and making money than when they were doing poorly and losing money'. Of course this kind of analysis rests on the assumption that the policies of industrial countries, recessions and debt crises do not inhibit Third World exports and imports.

A major factor behind the call for US policy reform is the costly nature of current farm programmes. The $26 billion farm spending in 1986 must be contrasted with net farm sales (domestic and overseas) of about $50 billion for commodities covered by federal programmes. In addition US consumers pay a price which is higher than the world price and some federal spending goes to administrative costs. One estimate places the total loss to the US economy in 1985 at $5 billion (Gardner, 1985). The World Bank estimates that for every dollar transferred to US farmers, $1.38 is lost by consumers and taxpayers (World Bank, 1986). Using this ratio for 1986 farm expenditure, consumers and taxpayers lost $36 billion while farmers gained only $26 billion, meaning that the US economy lost $10 billion. As a result of the US policy the rest of the world incurred losses of the same magnitude as those of the US.

Agricultural subsidies also translate into higher food prices for consumers in industrial countries. For instance the industrial countries spend roughly $150 billion per year subsidising bumper crops. In other words, each American spends $126 per year subsidising farm programmes through higher taxes and grocery prices. Likewise Japanese food prices would fall by 60 per cent and Europe's by 32 per cent if all agricultural support programmes were scrapped.

Reforming the policies of industrial countries may be the only way to avoid damaging trade and subsidy wars among allied countries. The EC subsidised its farmers to the tune of $22 billion in 1986 and still has substantial import barriers. The Japanese continue to boost internal prices for food way above the world market price. In a spat over the entrance of Spain and Portugal into the EC in 1986, the US and the EC traded threats of tariffs and subsidies, largely in the field of agriculture. Current GATT negotiations could be jeopardised by the continuing lack of consensus on moderation of trade subsidies within the GATT system.

8.5 SUGAR POLICY

Sugar policy is one of the most deleterious US trade practices that affect developing countries. US sugar producers have received special treatment since the 1933 Agricultural Adjustment Act authorised a sugar import quota system to cover up to 50 per cent of the domestic market. In 1955 the US received a waiver from the newly-created GATT allowing continued operation of the existing sugar programme, even though the programme violated the newly-adopted principles for international trade. Since then US policy has oscillated between the imposition of quotas and other forms of intervention aimed at supporting the incomes of US sugar producers. The last period without quotas was 1975–81.

Under the Agriculture and Food Act of 1981, US sugar producers are protected from market volatility through an import fee. Particularly after the 1974 collapse of the International Sugar Agreement, the international sugar market was plagued with wildly fluctuating prices. World sugar prices plummeted from 21 cents per pound in 1975, to 8 cents in 1977, and then soared to 30 cents in 1980. However the import fee programme was not entirely satisfactory to either producers or Congress.

Through the EC's Common Agricultural Policy (CAP), Europe was able to rise from a net importer to a major exporter of sugar. During 1971–81, gross sugar exports by the EC grew by 315 per cent, while the world sugar trade grew by only 34 per cent (USDA, May 1987). By the end of the 1970s domestic sugar growers were calling for US price support and a stronger import protection scheme than was provided for by the 1981 Act. Furthermore the US Congress, concerned about the budget deficit and the cost of running the import fee programme, urged that the sugar programme operate at no cost to the government budget.

In response to this budgetary concern and to sugar growers' demands, the US Department of Agriculture devised in 1982 the present system of import quotas to guarantee a minimum net domestic price of 18 cents per pound to domestic producers. The effect of the policy is to indirectly subsidise domestic producers by making consumers pay artificially high prices. In the food Security Act of 1985, the no-net-cost requirement was formally mandated by Congress.

The price floor is maintained through a 'non-recourse' loan programme. Under this system the US Department of Agriculture USDA) provides loans to sugar producers through the Commodity Credit Corporation (CCC) in exchange for sugar as collateral. If the market price is not higher than the value of the loan (21.8 cents per pound), producers may keep the loan money and forfeit the collateral sugar to the CCC without suffering any other penalty. In other words, the government has no recourse but to accept the sugar in lieu of repayment.

The programme's second prong is a system of import quotas, which are adjusted by USDA every year to constrain sugar imports and bolster domestic prices. Historically, during quota-free periods US sugar growers have held about 55 per cent of the home market, leaving almost half of the market for foreign competitors. With quotas, foreign imports have steadily decreased, leaving almost 90 per cent of the market to domestic producers. The effect of the loan programme and the quotas has been to keep the domestic market price both stable and high – averaging 21 cents per pound from 1982.

With the imposition of trade sanctions against Nicaragua in 1983 and South Africa in 1986, the US Congress unevenly reallocated these countries' quota shares to other producing countries. In November 1989 Congress passed a reallocation of Panama's quota to Bolivia and the Caribbean Basin Initiative (CBI) beneficiary countries. The Caribbean Basin Initiative enhancement bill (called CBI2) further calls for an uneven reallocation of unused quota shares and a guaranteed minimum quota level for CBI beneficiaries, regardless of the level of the total import quota necessary to maintain the domestic price.

In September 1989 USDA announced that the sugar import quota would change from 1.125 million metric tons for twelve months through December 1989 to 1.99 million metric tons for twenty-one months through September 1990. The time period extension – from 31 December 1989 to 30 September 1990 – linked to the 860 000 ton quota increase would allow producers additional time in which to fill their 1989–90 quotas. However on an annualised basis this actually represented a *decrease* in the total import quota levels by about 1 per cent.

8.5.1   Third World interests

The US sugar programme effectively protects the American sugar industry not only from world price fluctuations but also from its European and Third World competitors. This policy has had adverse effects on Third World producers in three ways: (1) their share of the US sugar market has continually declined, (2) the downward pressure on world sugar prices has caused a significant reduction in their overall sugar export earnings, and (3) unemployment has risen as sugar production has been curtailed.

Foreign imports to the US amounted to about 4.4 million tons per year during 1975–81. The 1989 quota allowed only 1.2 million tons to

Table 8.3   Top suppliers of US sugar imports, 1975–89
('000 short tons, raw value)

Country	Average annual Imports 1975–81	Quota 1989	Change (%)
Dominican Republic	774	204	−74
Philippines	594	183	−69
Brazil	639	168	−74
Australia	366	96	−74
Guatemala	210	56	−74
Argentina	188	50	−74
Peru	179	47	−74
Panama	125	34	−73
El Salvador	113	33	−71
Colombia	106	28	−74
Costa Rica	67	23	−66
Honduras	45	21	−53
From CBI countries:	1660	442	−73
From developing countries:	3981	1129	−72
Total Sugar imports:	4394	1238	−72

Sources: John Nuttall, 'Evolution of Sugar Import Policies and Programs, 1981–1988', FAS Staff Report no. 8, November 1988; 'Status of 1989 U.S. Sugar Import Quota', FAS Report, 1989; Jasper Womach, 'Sugar Policy Issues', *CRS Issue Brief*, 20 March 1989.

be imported, and this represented a 73 per cent fall in Third World exports to the US market due to the sugar quota programme. In 1989, the sugar quotas restricted imports to about 12 per cent of the US sugar market. Costa Rica, the Dominican Republic and the Philippines respectively witnessed a 66 per cent, 74 per cent, and 69 per cent decline in their exports to the US compared to their average annual exports to the US during 1975–81 (Table 8.3). Caribbean Basin countries as a whole saw their export levels fall 73 per cent, from a 1975–81 average of 1.66 million tons per year to only 442 200 tons in 1989 (Womach, 1989).

Some portion of Third World sugar exports do receive the high prices offered in the US market, but most of their production is forced onto the world market, where prices are artificially low due to the global sugar surplus created by the combined effects of the import policies of the EC, the US and other industrial countries. Since most Third World production is sold at the lower world price, the net effect of the falling share taken by the US market is a deep cut in Third World sugar export revenues.

Most studies suggest that US import quotas provide benefits to Third World producers in the form of guaranteed higher prices, but they also recognise that US and EC imports would be vastly larger without the quotas (Hufbauer, Berliner and Elliott, 1985; Gardner, 1985). A study undertaken on behalf of the World Bank suggests that the world market shares of developing countries would jump from 33 per cent to 57 per cent if industrial countries were to liberalise their sugar trade. The net effect would be a gain of about $4 billion in export revenues for developing countries, with 42 per cent of the gain captured by Latin American producers (Zeitz and Valdes, 1986).

If US imports, in the absence of quotas, had returned to the level prevailing in the 1975–81 period and the price had been 15 cents per pound (considered by some analysts to be the free market price), then foreign suppliers would have suffered about $947 million in lost sales in 1989. The higher price they received for their quota shares provided them with a gain of about $149 million in 1989. Thus the net direct loss attributable to the US quota system in 1989 was roughly $800 million. The Caribbean Basin countries' net direct loss attributable to US sugar quotas has been over $300 million per year since 1986; their total losses during 1982–9 amounted to about $1.8 billion. Moreover the depressed world prices during this period also reduced their earnings on exports to other markets. As a point of comparison, although exports of manufactured goods from the Caribbean Basin have been on the upswing due to the CBI, these gains have been dwarfed by the loss in export revenue from sugar – the region's most important export commodity apart from coffee.

The countries most severely affected are those that rely heavily on sugar as a major export crop. After Fiji and Mauritius, the Caribbean and a few Central American countries are the most 'sugar-dependent' producers in the world. A case in point is the Dominican Republic, which relied on sugar exports for more than 30 per cent of its export earnings in 1984. As the US is the Dominican Republic's largest market for sugar, comprising roughly three-fourths of its sugar exports, sugar export earnings have shrunk dramatically – its exports in 1975–81 averaged 774 000 tons, but its 1989 quota was only about 204 000 tons.

The US sugar programme has also caused a significant loss of jobs among Third World nations, particularly those in the Caribbean. Julio Herrera, a spokesman for the coalition of Caribbean sugar producers, notes that in the Dominican Republic alone, five sugar mills have closed since the US sugar programme began in 1982 (Bureau of National Affairs). The overall decline in US sugar import quotas since 1982 has translated into 400 000 jobs lost among the 22 Caribbean Basin nations.[3] In contrast the growth in Caribbean Basin's manufactured exports created less than 136 000 jobs in the region during 1983–8 (Tucker, LASA Paper, 1989). During that same period the region's labour force grew by about 2.3 million. The sugar programme has had a profound impact on various countries' ability to accommodate their growing populations and simultaneously address the problems of the poor.

8.6 US AGRICULTURAL POLICY OPTIONS

The primary goal of US farm programmes is to protect farm income and support prices. A variety of policy tools are used to raise the domestic prices received by farmers, facilitate production, enhance export and divert acreage away from excess production of commodities.

The 1985 Farm Bill was passed with the need for competitiveness by US farmers in mind. The bill allows for gradual reductions in price supports, continued income support, more vigorous export promotion, and an acreage reserve system to leave fallow land which is suffering from soil erosion. The income support system is however tied to agricultural production levels, thus encouraging production and undermining other aspects of the law. As world prices have fallen, budgetary expenditure has escalated, in part because the target prices were frozen and are only now beginning to decline slightly.

The need to further reform current US policy has stimulated a number of proposals, which vary with regard to specific commodities and mechanisms but fall into the following categories.

8.6.1 Export promotion

A number of proposals call for greater emphasis on recapturing US shares of world markets. These generally rely upon greater levels of export promotion – including in-kind subsidies and export subsidies – in a larger number of overseas markets. In addition marketing loans, which finance low-priced sales at home and abroad and are used for rice and cotton crops (the 1985 Farm Bill), are being proposed for other commodities, such as wheat.

Export-reliant reform proposals tend to call for the least amount of change to the policy and by and large ignore the world market situation. Export enhancement will encourage continued overproduction by US farmers, and if other countries also continue their current practices global prices will continue to fall. The US may capture a greater share of the trade volume, but this will be counterbalanced by falling unit prices. Of course there is no guarantee that the US will capture more market shares – other countries have been willing to protect their shares by 'outspending' US programmes in most commodities. The US may find itself entangled in an agricultural trade war that would destroy all hope of success at the GATT negotiations. This policy would be most damaging to developing countries due to the effect it would have on food production, prices, and market access. Such a strategy would also entail even higher US budgetary costs.

8.6.2   Market-led adjustment

The Organization for Economic Cooperation and Development (OECD), the major leaders at the Tokyo summit, and major international institutions have all called for this approach. Recognising that target prices and loan rates are too high under current global conditions, in its budget requests and US administration proposed drastic cuts in price (and income) supports. This approach falls short of totally dismantling federal programmes, but is aimed at bringing incentives more into line with market conditions. By letting domestic prices fall, the least efficient farmers will leave farming, production will fall, and the more efficient producers will be in a better position to compete on world markets.

This market-led strategy would have a positive impact upon world markets, but it also implies that the higher-cost US farmers – usually the younger, newer producers – will bear the major part of the burden of adjustment. Farm income would drop drastically as price supports fell. Many commercial farms as well as small farms would be forced out of business. The budgetary costs of such a programme would be low. World cereal prices would rebound as production fell, thus hurting food-importing countries' balance of payments, but the greater production incentives would in the long term enhance food security in the Third World. Liberalised US imports of cash crops would more than compensate most developing countries for higher food prices.

8.6.3 Production controls

Several proposals call for government-orchestrated mandatory production controls, using acreage diversion plans to reduce US production and increased price supports to raise domestic prices and incomes. To complement this strategy the domestic market would have to be protected against cheaper foreign products.

The burden of adjustment under production controls would also fall heavily upon US farmers. However administrative costs, in the form of equity questions and budgetary commitments, would be high. Furthermore controls would involve a unilateral abandonment of US export markets so long as other countries continue to encourage overproduction. This policy would not help Third World crop exporters as US imports would have to be restricted in order to maintain high domestic price targets.

8.6.4 Targeted income support

This approach (embodied in proposals by Senators Boschwitz and Boren) would buttress farm income with subsidies regardless of the level of production. Market prices would remain the production incentive. This 'decoupling' of benefits from production would allow US farmers to reduce production in the face of low prices, thus equilibrating supply with demand without losing their shirts.

This income support approach would cost the government more than a market-led approach, by bolstering short-term US farm sector income, but would be cheaper than production controls or export promotion. The likely production reductions and price increases would help world markets to iron out distortions and return to balance. Essentially relying upon market forces, this proposal offers Third World producers a much better situation than exists today.

The optimal solution for the current world agricultural crisis is to greatly increase incomes and purchasing power in the Third World through growth-oriented macroeconomic and debt policies. World farm trade cannot hope to see vigorous growth without widespread global economic growth. However inequitable income distribution patterns, budgetary austerity and debt crises are not going to disappear from the Third World overnight. With the world experiencing a glut of agricultural produce it is inevitable that some US farmers will be forced out of business.

The targeted income support payments approach is a good way to support US farmers in the short term without damaging Third World interests, while longer-term solutions are sought.

8.6.5   The Uruguay round

The US cannot correct world agricultural problems on its own – without coordination and cooperation from other industrial countries. The burden of adjustment will unjustly fall on the shoulders of either US or Third World producers. The Uruguay round of GATT negotiations offers such an opportunity for cooperation. There is some evidence that other industrial countries are willing to consider reducing their production subsidies.

Although part of the solution to the present world agricultural crisis lies in adjustment and openness to competition, binding multi-lateral agreements can help industrial countries to reduce their subsidy bills without risking the loss of markets to foreign subsidies.

In the Uruguay round of GATT negotiations, the issues of agricultural subsidies and their role in world farm commodities trade policy were debated and finally left unresolved. The US offered two proposals in Montreal that not only ran counter to its traditional stance on agricultural subsidies, but also to the historical position of GATT. The US proposals included a plan to eliminate all trade-distorting agricultural subsidies and a decoupling scheme. The Montreal negotiations on agricultural subsidies ended in deadlock in December 1988, but were followed by an 'agreement to disagree' in April 1989.

The first US proposal, dubbed the 'Zero Option', represented a major break from the traditional US (and other GATT member's) stance on agricultural subsidies. Nevertheless, acutely aware of the negative implications of such subsidisation programmes, the US realises that the costs of agricultural subsidies have outweighed the benefits for industrial and developing countries alike. Although seemingly contrary to their historic position on this issue, many US farmers are willing to accept this proposal – if foreign farmers do likewise. The reason, according to Barbara Rudolph (1988), is that American farmers believe that US agricultural productivity 'would give them an edge if competition were fair'.

In order to encourage its trading partners to follow suit, the US adopted a 'beggar-thy-neighbour' policy with respect to agricultural subsidies. For example the US continued to flood the world market with cheap food, which forced other countries to either cut their quotas and subsidies or increase their subsidies to farmers to meet the difference between falling international and domestic prices. The prices for soybeans, corn and wheat by 1990 had already plummeted from 10 per cent to 30 per cent. Congress also ordered the US administration to institute a new marketing-loans programme to bring about a fall in rice and cotton prices as well.

The Zero Option did not receive a warm welcome in Montreal. The EC vehemently opposed it on the ground that the US proposal demanded too much too soon. Wily de Clerq, the chief EC negotiator, implied that the politically powerful nine million EC farmers would certainly oppose the elimination of the subsidy payments upon which their livelihoods depended. As the common agricultural policy is at the heart of the EC and its farming industry, the Zero Option would constitute 'open heart surgery' for the EC.

However the Zero Option became more and more flexible as the talks continued. It ceased to call for the complete elimination of all subsidies to farmers and instead focused on those price supports that distort trade. This would enable the EC to gradually shift its spending from price to income support. The Cairns Group (a group of thirteen major agricultural exporters, including Canada, Australia, New Zealand, Argentina, Brazil, the Philippines and Thailand), on the other hand were more receptive to the US proposal.

The second U.S. proposal – 'decoupling' – constituted a plan to separate government support payments from farmers' planting decisions. Under the system operating at the time, the federal support payments encouraged overproduction, which only served to push prices down even further. In an attempt to decouple the system, Senators Rudy Boschwitz (a Minnesotan republican) and David L. Boren (an Oklahoman democrat) attempted to include a modified decoupling proposal in the 1985 farm bill. The attempt failed because the Congressional Budget Office published a study showing that the plan would costs $51 billion over a three-year period. In retrospect that would have been a bargain. In the first three years of the 1985 bill, farm-bill income stabilisation cost $69.5 billion.

There are concerns however over the domestic implications of decoupling. The first is that decoupling would be no less costly than the existing subsidies programme. The difference would be that the burden of cost would shift from the consumer to the taxpayer. This could be a politically difficult issue. American farmers moreover worry that agricultural support would be more visible in a decoupled system. The more visible agricultural support schemes are, the more vulnerable they become to cuts and changes. This is precisely what would be best for improving those US policies which affect US–Third World interests.

Since progress on agricultural issues in the Uruguay round was slow, in October 1989 the US proposed to GATT members that the first step toward the elimination of world trade-distorting agricultural policies should be the conversion of all quota restrictions and other non-tariff distortions to their tariff equivalent. Then these tariffs should be reduced over a specified time to the level of bound tariffs. In addition existing tariffs should be reduced over 10 years.

Moreover, the US proposed phasing out agricultural export subsidies over five years; classifying internal support measures more systematically and eliminating the most trade-distorting, while disciplining the less-detrimental ones; and setting up an international process for dispute settlement and harmonisation of sanitary and phytosanitary regulations and barriers.

Notes and references

1. Speech by Maurice Williams before the International Dairy Conference, The Hague, The Netherlands, 29 September 1986.
2. Author's calculations based upon methodology used in ODC Working Paper no. 10, 'Update: Costs to the United States of The Recession in Developing Countries', by Stuart K. Tucker (January 1986).
3. According to José Orive, Chairman of the Caribbean Basin Initiative Embassy Group (a Washington-based, intergovernmental coalition of Caribbean nations).

9 US Textile Trade Policy and the Proliferation of Managed Trade

Stuart K. Tucker

Enacted initially in the late 1950s as a temporary protective scheme to stem import surges, US textile policy has been widely adopted elsewhere and has become an intransigent feature of the world trading system. The practices initiated between the US and Japan have spread to virtually every textile product and to every country with a significant textile and clothing trade. The industries involved in textile and clothing production provide good jobs and upward mobility for Third World workers, while in industrial countries they are either being mechanised or are becoming dying industries. Although production in industrial countries has been noncompetitive for decades, the extreme trade restrictions remain in place under the pretence of helping the industries adjust.

No other barrier to world trade does as much economic damage – to workers, to consumers, and to world income – as the current international textile trade policy. The constantly growing nature of this protection over the course of 30 years is the foremost example of how the lightest step into trade intervention can create a political snowball effect that can be nearly impossible to stop. It also shows how bilateral protection between industrial countries is also often only a short step away from dramatic curtailment of Third World trade interests.

9.1 THE 'TEMPORARY' AGREEMENT

The 'arrangement regarding international trade in textiles', commonly known as the Multifiber Arrangement (MFA) is the international agreement designed to provide orderly trade in textiles and clothing. The MFA, which came into force in 1974, has been renewed three times – in 1978, 1982 and 1986 – and the current MFA will be in effect until 31 July 1991.

The first MFA was an extension of the efforts in the mid-1950s to regulate world trade in textiles and clothing as the US faced increasing imports from Japan. Initial negotiations were conducted under the auspices of GATT. As a result of these talks the US and Japan signed a reciprocal trade agreement in 1957, granting tariff concessions to the Japanese on certain products and establishing a market disruption mechanism in the US. Under the Trade Agreements Act, the US Tariff Commission determines whether the concessions lead to Japanese imports that would pose a threat of injury or market disruption to the US market. If a market disruption determination were made, the commission could apply tariff relief for the domestic industries. At the same time the Japanese agreed to voluntarily reduce cotton textile exports for five years (Ghadar, Davidson and Feigenoff, 1987).

In November 1959 talks were initiated once again under GATT to take a multilateral approach toward limiting the influx of textile imports to developed countries. The meetings produced a list of the elements of market disruption, an agreement among the countries that claims of market injury would be resolved between the parties involved, and a permanent GATT body, the Committee on Avoidance of Market Disruptions.

In July 1961 the 'short-term arrangement regarding international trade in cotton textiles' (STA), essentially the first multilateral agreement governing the trade of cotton textiles, was created. The STA covered 64 categories of cotton products and specified both the condition of market disruption and the procedures by which an importing country could react to such conditions. This was transformed into the 'long-term cotton arrangement' (LTA) in February 1962. After several renewals and expansion in scope of the bilateral accords, the LTA was converted into the 'arrangement regarding international trade in textiles', or the Multifiber Arrangement (negotiated in 1973 to stop market disruption by bringing some order into the negotiations for bilateral agreements).[1]

MFA I was renewed as MFA II, which ran from January 1978 to December 1981. MFA II, contained a provision which allowed for 'jointly agreed reasonable departures from particular elements [of the arrangement] in particular cases'. In practice it permitted the EC to discriminate between suppliers to renegotiate downward the 6 per cent growth level through separate bilateral agreements.

Then in January 1982 MFA III (January 1982 to July 1986) was signed. MFA III eliminated the 'reasonable departures' clause and provided greater latitude in negotiating bilateral agreements to set lower growth rates for the largest suppliers. It also contained an anti-surge provision to avoid surges of imports under unfilled quotas. However the most important aspect of MFA III was the implementation of a 'call' system in US policy. The US decided in December 1983 to institute a trigger system, whereby consideration of a possible case of market disruption could be initiated when (1) imports reached at least 20 per cent of production, and (2) imports had risen by 30 per cent in the previous 12 months and imports from an individual supplier (company) reached 1 per cent of US production (Goto, 1988).

MFA (IV) was renewed in August 1986 to remain in effect until the end of July 1991. During the negotiations for renewal of the arrangement, the Reagan administration was intent on getting further restraints on a wide range of products from Hong Kong, South Korea and Taiwan. In particular the administration sought to limit the growth of imports from the usual 6 per cent to between 0.5 per cent and 1.5 per cent per year. The US was able to extract these concessions, which provided for broader product coverage and stricter restrictions. Also the reasonable departures clause was restored and product coverage was extended to cover vegetable fibres and silk blends.

9.2 US IMPLEMENTATION

The MFA serves as an umbrella for bilateral agreements between countries. Importing countries tend to attach further import restrictions in the form of tariffs and non-tariff barriers to work in conjunction with the MFA. The US currently has 43 bilateral textile agreements (each lasting between three and six years) and has in place 1200 quota restraints on individual textile and clothing categories. Approximately 90 per cent of textile and clothing imports from developing countries are subject to some form of import restraint. The three largest suppliers for the US (South Korea, Hong Kong and Taiwan – Table 9.1) are limited by the agreements to an aggregate annual growth rate of 1 per cent.

The average textile and clothing tariff rate is 17.4 per cent, which is six times higher than the average for all non-textile imports. The average tariff rate for clothing alone is even higher – 19 per cent

Table 9.1   US textile and clothing imports from top suppliers covered by the MFA

	1984	1985	1986	1987	1988	1984	1985	1986	1987	1988
	(billions of sq. yd equiv.)					*(billions of dollars)*				
Total	10.16	10.84	13.08	13.74	12.85	14.73	15.99	19.67	23.47	23.38
Of which:										
Hong Kong	1.05	1.05	1.18	1.22	1.07	2.39	2.53	2.93	3.56	3.34
Taiwan	1.58	1.60	1.72	1.60	1.39	2.45	2.44	2.85	3.26	2.96
Korea	1.17	1.14	1.33	1.35	1.21	1.87	1.85	2.21	2.71	2.67
China	0.99	0.98	1.68	1.74	1.61	1.11	1.14	2.05	2.37	2.24
Total – top four	4.79	4.77	5.90	5.91	5.28	7.82	7.96	10.05	11.90	11.21
(%)	47	44	45	43	41	53	50	51	51	48
Italy	0.51	0.53	0.49	0.39	0.29	0.74	0.86	1.04	1.08	1.07
Japan	0.74	0.72	0.80	0.60	0.44	1.02	1.02	1.17	0.96	0.76
Philippines	0.24	0.27	0.29	0.34	0.37	0.38	0.41	0.45	0.62	0.73

Source: US International Trade Commission, *U.S. Imports of Textiles and Apparel Under the Multifiber Arrangement: Statistical Report Through 1988* (Washington, DC, June 1989).

(Table 9.2). The tariff equivalent of US quotas on textiles was 21.8 per cent in 1987 and the rate for quotas on clothing was 28.3 per cent (USITC, October 1989). The tariff equivalent of all US clothing trade barriers was estimated to be about 53 per cent in 1986 and for textiles the tariff equivalent was 28 per cent (Cline, 1987).

Import limits in these agreements can be aggregate or product-specific or flexible. Carryover and carryforward provisions allow the transfer of unused import quotas from year to year and a change from category to category within the same year. Some agreements require an export control system in the supplier country. Even those categories without specific limits are usually covered by 'consultation levels' – whereby the US government asks for negotiations when imports reach a certain level. In the absence of a bilateral agreement, Congress has authorised the executive branch to take unilateral action.

The responsibility for the administration and implementation of the textile and clothing agreements lies with the Committee for the Implementation of Textile Agreements (CITA) and the Office of the US Trade Representative (USTR). CITA determines when and if market disruption has occurred and requests consultation with the government involved. CITA is an interagency body, composed of representatives from the Department of Commerce, the State Department, the Treasury, the Department of Labor, and the US Trade

Table 9.2   Sample of US clothing tariffs on Caribbean goods, 1988
(duties collected divided by dutiable imports)

Import	Average duty (%)
Body-supporting garments	18.0
Girl's man-made fibre knit coverings	22.7
Lace or net body-support garment	32.0
Lace underwear	22.7
Men's cotton knit jackets	21.0
Men's cotton knit suits, shirts	21.0
Men's cotton knit t-shirts	21.0
Men's cotton suits and slacks	16.5
Men's man-made fibre disposable	29.2
Men's other cotton knit shirts	21.0
Men's other cotton shirts	21.0
Men's wool suit coat	22.4
Other underwear, not ornamented	18.2
Womens' man-made fibre trousers	30.0
Women's cotton knit athletic wear	16.5
Women's cotton knit blouses	21.0
Women's woven cotton blouses	16.5
Women's woven cotton jumpsuit	8.0
Women's woven cotton shirts	16.5
Women's woven cotton nightwear	14.0
Women's man-made fibre blouses	30.0
Women's man-made fibre coats	17.0
Women's man-made fibre dresses	22.7
Women's man-made fibre knit blouses	34.6
Women's man-made fibre knit overalls	17.0
Women's other cotton knit blouses	21.0
Women's other cotton knit shirts	21.0
Women's other woven apparel	29.1

Source: US Department of Commerce unpublished data.

Representative's Office. The Department of Commerce chairs the committee. No public interest or private industry groups are formally represented on the committee. However the American Fiber Textile and Apparel Coalition (AFTAC) regularly meets with CITA. The AFTAC includes representatives from the American Textile Manufacturers Association, the Man-Made Fiber Producers Association, the Amalgamated Clothing and Textile Workers Union, and the International Ladies Garment Workers Union.

Actual negotiations are carried out by the Chief Textile Negotiator (an office carrying ambassadorial rank) in the office of the USTR.

The Department of Commerce's Office of Textile and Apparel (OTEXA) monitors the imports affected by bilateral agreements under the MFA under the direction of CITA.

9.3 THIRD WORLD CONCERNS

Exporters of textiles and clothing from developing countries have fared well in their export earnings and market shares in developed countries in spite of the MFA, the tariffs and the NTBs. Sales growth was rapid and the restraint agreements allowed producers to capture rents due to higher prices. Nevertheless these exporting countries could have earned more without the existence of these policies and agreements.

The textile and clothing industries have traditionally been the means by which developing countries begin to industrialise. This is because the raw materials are relatively more available, the industries require less capital than for most other exportable manufactures, and the tasks can be handled by generally unskilled labour. These industries are very attractive to developing countries as a primary source of export earnings.

Over the last thirty years the newly industrialised countries have played an increasingly important role in the textile export industry. Not only are they able to take advantage of low labour costs, but they have favoured export-oriented industries during development and have enacted measures to protect their domestic industries from foreign competition. The combination of inexpensive labour and industry targeting has allowed newly industrialised countries to ably compete with the US and other OECD countries in both the textile and clothing industries and to capture large shares of the import markets of each of these countries. By 1985 the four leading textile and clothing exporters to the US were Taiwan, South Korea, Hong Kong and China, who together accounted for 45 per cent of all textile and clothing imports (Table 9.1).

There is a double-edged sword for these newly industrialised countries in exporting textiles and clothing to industrial countries. The tariff rates on these products increase with each stage of processing – while the average tariff rate of fibres imposed by major importers is around one per cent, that of clothing is often more than 20 per cent. As these countries attempt to modernise their textile and clothing industries through the use of more technologically-advanced equipment and processing methods, they will face higher tariff rates in the US.

Despite the MFA and tariffs on textiles and clothing coming into the US, newly industrialised countries' exports to the US increased 14 per cent annually during 1980–7, and were generally above the formal growth limits of the MFA (USITC, June 1989). In 1980 textile and clothing imports equalled 4.8 billion square yard equivalents (SYE). Imports steadily climbed from 1981 to 1987 (13.1 billion SYE) but growth then slowed in 1988 and declined in 1989 to 12.9 billion SYE (Table 9.1). In 1989 imports amounted to 26 per cent of apparent US consumption (USITC, June 1989). The value of textile imports during 1985–8 increased by $1.5 billion (nearly a one-third increase). Imports from developing countries during that period increased by more than one-third.

Clothing imports rose even more dramatically. For each dollar's worth of clothing exported, roughly $15 worth was imported into the US. Moreover one-third of all garments sold in the US are manufactured overseas. These ratios are higher for sweaters and women's cotton slacks. The majority of these imports are from the Asian newly industrialised countries. The value of US imports from developing countries between 1985 and 1988 increased by nearly 50 per cent.

9.4 IMPACT

Since almost all clothing exports and half of textile exports go to industrial countries, Third World textile and clothing exporters are heavily dependent on these markets. As such the MFA, and the restrictions that often accompany it, causes revenue losses by reducing the size of sales. Although some rents are gained by having higher prices, the lost sales amount to far more than the rents. One study estimates that the removal of the MFA quotas and tariffs would lead to an increase in US imports of 245 per cent and world welfare would increase by more than $17 billion (constant 1986 dollars), while US welfare would increase by $2.6 billion. All textile- and clothing-exporting Third World countries would benefit; some exporting countries would gain as much as an 800 per cent export increase, while a few would only gain a 20 per cent or 30 per cent increase. Most exporting countries would see their exports increase by between 100 per cent and 200 per cent (Trela and Whalley, 1988). According to a separate study by UNCTAD, if all textile and clothing restrictions – both tariffs and NTBs – were removed, Third World textile and clothing exports to the US, the EC and Japan would increase by $15 billion (UNCTAD, 1986).

Even if tariffs were unaltered, the removal of MFA quota restrictions would have a substantially positive effect on world welfare – about $16 billion according to Trela and Whalley – although more of the benefits would accrue to industrial countries, and US imports would increase less (133 per cent). Although aggregate net welfare of developing countries would still increase by $5 billion, the removal of quotas without altering tariffs would actually hurt a handful of countries in Asia (Hong Kong, Macao, Pakistan, Singapore and Thailand).

Trade diversion from more-restricted countries to less-restricted countries has been another result of the MFA. The less-restricted countries are also often afforded 'guaranteed market shares' through the system, even though smaller Latin American producers, for example, are unable to fill their quotas. The unfilled quotas are not reallocated in spite of the ability and desire of other producers to meet the quota.

Foreign direct investment in exporting countries is also distorted by the MFA. Heavily restricted countries like Hong Kong attempt to circumvent tariffs and quotas by investing in other countries, such as Bangladesh, Jamaica and the Dominican Republic. The World Bank gives an account of how many firms in the Asian big three have invested in the Dóminican Republic and Jamaica to set up clothing factories. The inflow of capital from the Asian firms has been a boon to these less restricted and smaller producers and has enabled the Asian exporters to avoid tariffs and stricter quotas. However the recipients of this investment do not gain as much as they might in the absence of barriers. The high US tariff rates have forced Caribbean producers, for example, to upgrade the quality of clothing shipments in order to compete in the narrower, higher cost market. In general Asian investments in clothing production have not integrated well into the local economies and are very likely to leave the country at the first sign of a changing economic wind.

The cost to the US of continued protection of the textile and clothing industries is staggering. One source estimates that retailers lost as much as $40 billion as a result of the MFA. Based on estimates of the Federal Trade Commission, the MFA restrictions cost consumers between $302.773 and $550 916 per job protected (Alexander et al., 1989). Other estimates are lower, putting the consumer cost at about $135 000 per textile job protected and total consumer cost at about $20 billion (Cline, 1987). In any case the costs are extremely high on a national scale.

Moreover, the burden fell disproportionately on the lower-income families who would have bought the cheaper imports – thus reducing the income of the bottom quintile of US families by 4 per cent. In fact the consumer losses of the lower-income families exceeded the job gains of the low-income textile and clothing workers (Cline, 1987).

Furthermore the import quotas represent an 'unwanted and unnecessary burden' on those US clothing producers who import fabrics which are in short supply or not available in the US in the quantities they need.

9.5   OUTLOOK

Many developing countries are insisting upon commitment to a phasing out of the MFA as part of the final Uruguay round package. Formal negotiations on the post-MFA IV era did not begin in earnest in 1990, but general commitments were required in the Uruguay round to avoid the mass desertion of developing countries.

Recognising the need to change the MFA, the EC announced in July 1989 its support for phasing out the MFA and implementation of strengthened GATT rules and disciplines in the textile and clothing trades. The US, on the other hand, avoided public discussion of any governmental proposals, hoping to show significant victories in other Uruguay round negotiations before opening up the domestic debate over the textile trade. However several US import and retail associations banded together to try to force a more open public hearing on the future of textile trade policy. Beginning in December 1989, US negotiators began to sketch publicly the US position – which is that the textile and clothing trades should eventually be integrated into the GATT system of trade rules.

Thus the Uruguay round, if concluded successfully and in a timely fashion, is likely to provide a global consensus on how to renegotiate the MFA. If that consensus is to be for trade liberalisation, then subsequent proposals will have to provide measures to satisfy a variety of interests, mainly those of exporters concerned with reducing arbitrary diplomatic interventions and increasing markets equitably, importers hoping to reduce costs, and import-competing producers demanding safeguards from injurious import surges.

Without doubt the prospect of a phased reduction of textile protection will provoke outcries among import-competing producers. The political task will be to (1) gain a commitment to reduce protection over a reasonable period of time without appearing to be abandoning domestic industry, and (2) gain domestic allies for the reduction by showing progress toward liberalisation in other priority areas such as agriculture and services.

9.6   PROLIFERATION TO OTHER INDUSTRIES

Although textile and clothing trade barriers are the most significant and longstanding barriers to US–Third World trade in manufactured goods, other US manufactured imports have been subjected to an increasing number of trade restraints, particularly non-tariff measures. According to one estimate, the major US nontariff barriers (NTBs) affected – both covered directly by and affected indirectly by the NTBs – 36 per cent of US import value in 1966 and 45 per cent of US import value in 1986 (Laird and Yeats, 1988). Table 9.3 gives an idea on how widely the NTBs were used in 1986. Some of this increase can be attributed to the faster growth rate of imports subjected to restraints (after all, faster-growing imports draw political attention to the restraints). However even the number of import categories covered by NTBs has increased in recent decades.

The US use of NTBs increased particularly sharply in the 1980s. In 1981 4.8 per cent of US non-petroleum import categories were covered by NTBs, while in 1986 the frequency of NTBs in US imports had increased to 6.5 per cent. US NTBs in the 1980s continued to focus upon the fastest growing sectors, yielding faster-growing ratios for import value covered than for categories covered (Laird and Yeats, 1989). Furthermore US NTBs in 1986 covered more US imports from developing countries (19.1 per cent) than imports from industrial countries (16.6 per cent).

Most of the new voluntary export restraints (VERs) created in the 1980s were responses to the pursuit or threatened pursuit of anti-dumping or countervailing duty investigations. With the passage of the Omnibus Trade and Competitiveness act of 1988, the executive branch has been under increased pressure to launch bilateral negotiations to eliminate priority trade barriers in other countries. The new law contains stricter. timetables for showing progress to avert US retaliation. These negotiations (governed by Section 301 of US trade

Table 9.3   Incidence of selected US nontariff measures on imports, 1986 (percentage coverage of import value)

Import category	NTM coverage ratio
Agriculture:	
Sugar and honey	91.9
Dairy products	87.8
Oil seeds and nuts	87.0
Crude animal and vegetable matter	11.0
Manufactures:	
Clothing	76.4
Iron and steel	76.3
Transport equipment	41.1
Textiles	34.5
Travel goods	18.9
Other metal manufactures	11.0

Source: Sam Laird and Alexander Yeats, *Quantitative Methods for Trade Barrier Analysis* (World Bank, 1989) p. 138.

law) lend themselves well to the establishment of VERs.

Towards the end of the 1980s the incidence of initiations of anti-dumping cases increased substantially. During 1981–5 an average of less than 50 cases per year were started. After 1985 roughly 100 cases per year were initiated (IMF, September 1989).

9.6.1   Steel

In 1984, after 15 years of various forms of VERs and price floor mechanisms to protect steel, the current US steel policy was initiated. A successful industry-initiated escape clause petition in 1984 led President Reagan to direct US Trade Representative to negotiate VERs with all significant suppliers in order to reduce imports to 18.5 per cent of domestic consumption. Agreements were reached with the EC and 19 other countries, including a number of developing countries (Brazil, Korea, Mexico, South Africa, Trinidad and Tobago, Venezuela and Yugoslavia). These VERs mainly limited carbon steel – but also some stainless steel – imports. The VERs require exporters to obtain export certificates from their governments. In cases of short supply, the US Commerce Department may grant licenses for additional imports. In 1989 President Bush authorised two-year and six month extensions to these VERs (with an increase in the import ratio target to 19.1 per cent), during which time the US sought to eliminate trade-distorting practices in the steel sector.

In the early years of the programme the VERs had a wide effect on US steel imports, but as the international demand for steel subsequently picked up the restrictiveness of the VERs declined. In 1986–7 VERs reduced US steel imports by about 16 per cent – in 1988 they only caused a 2 per cent reduction. The restraints had an equivalent effect as an *ad valorem* tariff of about 4.3 per cent during 1986–8. VER limits on specialty steel products were equivalent to 8 per cent tariffs in 1986–8 (USITC, October 1989).

The net effect of US VERs on steel has been a domestic price increase of about 25 per cent, on average, above Japanese prices during 1969–85 (The Stern Group, 1989). By 1988 US steel imports (excluding semifinished steel) were down to 18 per cent of consumption (USGAO, 1989).

9.6.2 Automobiles

NTBs on transport equipment (automobiles) cover a significant portion of US trade in this sector. However automobile VERs are not comprehensive among major suppliers as are those for steel. Instead the restraints are maintained simply on Japanese exports to the US. Each year since the expiry in 1985 of the formal VER, Japan has unilaterally announced that it would keep to a 2.3 million unit ceiling (about 25 per cent above the formal limit in the negotiated agreement prior to 1985). While these restraints do not directly impinge upon the few existing suppliers from developing countries, the indirect effect is to make more leeway for Third World automobile exports to the US without threatening damage to US producers. However the very existence of Japanese restraints means that suppliers in developing countries must worry about future market access should Japan choose to eliminate the practice.

9.6.3 Machine tools

In 1986 the Reagan administration completed a review of the national security implications of imports of certain machine tools and proceeded to negotiate VERs with Japan, Taiwan, West Germany and Switzerland. Only Japan and Taiwan agreed to restraints, effective from 1987 to 1991, and attempted to keep imports at either 1981 or 1985 market share levels depending upon the product. The VERs required the exporting countries to issue export licenses. The administration also warned other suppliers not to increase their market shares from 1987 to 1991.

Imports from the two signatories, Japan and Taiwan, represented substantial portions of US consumption of numerically controlled lathes and machine centres. In 1987 Taiwan supplied 25 per cent of US consumption of non-numerically controlled lathes and 19 per cent of milling machines. The agreements however were not entirely binding, as Taiwanese exports to the US in 1987 and 1988 exceeded the export ceilings. Japanese products however remained below the established export ceilings. Overall the VERs reduced machine tool imports by about 14 per cent in 1987 and 3 per cent in 1988, having an effect equivalent to a 4 per cent tariff (USITC, October 1989).

9.6.4 Footwear

This product area stands out as the one major case in which the Reagan administration resisted and rolled back NTB protectionism. In 1981 President Reagan chose not to extend the orderly market arrangements (OMAs) that had been signed with Korea and Taiwan on the non-rubber footwear trade. In 1985 Reagan went against an ITC injury determination and cabinet advice by rejecting proposed auction import quotas. Instead he ordered the Department of Labor to establish a trade adjustment assistance and retraining package for footwear workers.

However, despite these efforts to resist protectionism, the Reagan and Bush administrations have repeatedly been unable to overcome opposition by the US footwear industry to duty-free entry of imports from Caribbean basin countries through the CBI (see Chapter 10). Footwear also remains excluded from the Generalised System of Preferences (GSP) programme of duty-free entry for manufactured products from developing countries. US footwear tariffs, ranging from 6 per cent to 20 per cent, are generally higher than average US MFN tariffs (Pearson, 1989).

9.6.5 Semiconductors

The market-sharing agreement concluded in 1986 with Japan on trade in semiconductors essentially aimed to monitor the prices of Japanese semiconductor exports not only to the US but to the world. Though the effectiveness of the agreement has been called into question in recent years, the theoretical effect of complete compliance would be to keep global semiconductor prices above the free market level, thereby damaging the competitiveness of computer manufacturers without access to lower-priced chips inside Japan and the US. The EC and a handful of the newly industrialised countries are the likely losers should this sort of NTB (essentially, a cartelisation agreement) ever become fully effective.

9.6.6 Government procurement

The 1988 omnibus trade law contained strengthened 'Buy America' provisions in order to encourage greater fairness in government procurement of non-sensitive goods and services. This law will likely focus greater attention on compliance by signatories of the GATT Code on Government Procurement. However the discriminatory practices of developing countries (none of which are signatories to the GATT Code) are exempted from coverage by the 1988 act.

Note

1. For a description of the mechanisms of the MFA, see Goto, 1988.

10 Import Promotion: Preferential Arrangements

Stuart K. Tucker

For the most part US tariffs are low. However in selected and sensitive labour-intensive product areas the tariffs are very high, paralleling the non-tariff barriers restraining trade in the same categories. The US Generalized System of Preferences (GSP) was instituted in the early 1970s as a way of improving relations with developing countries. The lowered protection was seen as affordable since many developing countries were deemed unable to supply significant quantities of the manufactured products that benefited most from the preferential treatment.

By the mid-1980s the striking successes of the newly industrialised economies of East Asia revealed weaknesses in the GSP programme. Most of the GSP duty-free imports were from four newly industrialised countries and Brazil. US concerns that the GSP programme has wide benefits for many lower-income developing countries, allied with more protectionist concerns about the success of the newly industrialised countries, produced demands for 'graduation'. Though most analyses say that such graduation will not necessarily aid the poorer countries in capturing a larger market share, the policy has been followed with the hope that it will send the message that successful developing countries must take on more responsibilities in the multilateral trading system.

At the same time the economic crisis of the early 1980s led many observers to note that relations with key developing countries were suffering due to limited trade opportunities. The CBI and talk of a US–Mexico free trade pact both reflect US concern for the economic wellbeing of 'strategic' neighbours. Unfortunately these efforts have born little fruit and in fact have drawn the criticism that they represent the leading edge of regionalism/bilateralism and the disintegration of multilateral trade.

At first free trade agreements (FTAs – such as exist with Israel and

Canada) were waved to back US threats that if its trading partners did not fully participate in the Uruguay round, the US was prepared to develop regional blocs for its own benefit. Those FTAs that were established, however, were clearly defined as issues of national interest that should not trouble world trading partners. Prominent US officials fear a drift toward regionalism, but US businessmen seem more concerned that the US should get its foot in the door to any promising initiatives (such as a Pacific Rim agreement) so as not to be left out. Though policy has wavered on FTAs, the commitment to making the Uruguay round work is receiving the primary efforts of the trade bureaucracy and political leaders.

10.1 US TARIFF STRUCTURE

US MFN tariffs are low and generally near the averages of industrial countries. Applied US tariffs on food items are lower than the averages of industrial countries, but applied US tariffs on manufactured goods are slightly higher. The overall average applied US tariff is 3.4 per cent (Table 10.1).

However, this average disguises large variations among trade categories. Low-wage industries, such as textiles, clothing, footwear and handbags, are protected by considerably higher average tariffs (and even higher peak tariffs in particular categories facing large import competition). Tariffs in such categories often run above 10 per cent, with 20 per cent tariffs, or even 40 per cent tariffs on narrowly-defined items. About 17 per cent of US trade line items are covered by tariffs higher than 10 per cent (2.3 per cent of the line items have tariffs above 20 per cent) (Erzan and Karsenty, 1989). This tariff structure is particularly important for developing countries, which are often the major source of US imports of such labour-intensive items.

In fact the US tariff structure discriminates against developing countries by protecting such low-wage industries. The average (trade-weighted) tariff applied to industrial countries is 3.4 per cent, but the tariff applied to developing countries is 4.5 per cent (Laird and Yeats, 1989). Even those countries receiving duty-free access for certain manufactured items under the GSP programme (see below) continue to face stiffer trade-weighted average tariffs (3.6 per cent) than industrial countries. Of course these averages reflect the actual structure of trade flows, not discriminatory US treatment, which is prohibited by the most-favoured-nation (MFN) treatment principle of GATT.

Table 10.1 Post-Tokyo round tariffs of the US and all industrial countries (average *ad valorem* percentages)

	United States			All industrial countries		
	(1)	*(2)*	*(3)*	*(1)*	*(2)*	*(3)*
All food items	4.1	3.5	3.6	6.4	5.3	5.5
Food and live animals	3.8	3.2	3.4	6.5	5.3	5.6
Oilseeds and nuts	1.4	1.0	0.3	5.3	4.0	4.5
Animal and vegetable oils	0.9	1.0	0.1	0.1	0.2	0.4
Agricultural raw materials	0.3	0.3	0.1	0.8	0.5	0.5
Ores and metals	1.9	2.2	1.1	2.3	1.5	0.9
Iron and steel	4.3	5.0	3.5	5.1	3.4	3.0
Non-ferrous metals	0.7	0.7	0.3	2.3	1.3	1.1
Fuels	0.4	0.4	0.3	1.1	0.6	0.6
Chemicals	3.7	3.9	1.0	5.8	3.1	3.7
Other manufactures	5.6	4.9	6.6	7.0	4.7	6.7
Leather	4.2	2.7	1.4	5.1	3.1	3.2
Textile yarn & fabric	10.6	12.1	9.0	11.7	7.9	8.4
Clothing	20.3	18.1	17.8	17.5	11.9	14.6
Footwear	11.7	9.5	9.4	13.4	9.0	10.1
Other items	4.2	3.6	4.0	3.8	3.3	3.8
All products	NA	3.4	3.6	NA	3.0	2.7

1. Average most-favoured nation tariff rates
2. Average applied tariff rates
3. Average tariff for GSP beneficiaries

Source: Sam Laird and Alexander Yeats, *Quantitative Methods for Trade Barrier Analysis* (Macmillan, 1989) p. 326.

Countries without MFN status face the very high tariffs that were established by the Smoot–Hawley law (Tariff Act of 1930). Only a few tariffs of selected minor categories have been altered for non-MFN trade. MFN treatment was denied to all communist countries except Poland and Yugoslavia.[1] Such countries were only to be allowed MFN status if they fulfill the free emigration requirement of the Jackson–Vanik amendment and if they sign a bilateral commercial treaty with the US providing reciprocal nondiscriminatory treatment.[2]

10.2 THE MAQUILADORA PROGRAMME

The 'maquiladora' programme was established to allow US companies to base certain assembly and processing operations outside the

US (both to take advantage of low wages and to spur development in host countries) and not be penalised by tariffs on the portion of the imports originating in the US. The maquiladora programme thus allows for duty-free treatment of the US component of an import assembled from US materials.

Now classified as Section 9802 of the harmonised system of tariffs, this programme was originally covered by sections 806.30 and 807 of the US tariff code.[3] Section 806.30 allows for non-precious metal products processed overseas from raw materials originating in the US to enter the US partially free from duty. The portion of the product that originated in the US is subtracted from the value of the import before duties are applied. Section 807 has similar provisions, but is applied to manufactured goods (such as clothing, transport equipment or electronics) which are assembled from intermediate goods (such as textiles, transport equipment parts or electronics parts) originating in the US.

A company invoking section 9802 can own an offshore facility, use contractors or engage in joint offshore ventures as long as the following conditions are met: (1) the exported parts and material must be ready for assembly without further fabrication; (2) the items must not lose physical identity in the process; and, (3) the items must not increase in value or be improved in condition except by being assembled.

Section 9802 is predominantly used for machinery and equipment assembly operations, but has been used for clothing in Mexico and the Caribbean basin. Section 9802 clothing operations require that the fabric be spread, cut and assembled in correct parts for sewing. The garments often need to be finished and packaged after they are reimported. Mexico is the most important source of products imported under the 9802 programme. Other users of section 9802 for the textile and clothing trades are Barbados, Costa Rica, Colombia, the Dominican Republic, Guyana, Haiti, Honduras, Jamaica and Panama.

Imports under the 9802 programme increased rapidly in the mid-1980s. They accounted for 17 per cent of total US imports in 1987, but only 9 per cent in 1984. The foreign value-added portion of these imports increased by 160 per cent from 1984–7, while total US imports grew by 24 per cent. These products accounted for 19 per cent of US electrical machinery imports in 1987 and 59 per cent of transportation equipment imports. Nearly 7 per cent of US clothing imports entered under the maquiladora programme (USITC, December 1988).

However the share originating in developing countries has declined as section 9802 trade with Canada and Japan increased more rapidly. About 42 per cent of the former section 807 imports (about 99 per cent of section 9802 imports are from the former section 807 category) originated in developing countries in 1984, but by 1987 this figure was down to 26 per cent. In 1987 Canada supplied 31 per cent of section 807 imports; Japan accounted for 22 per cent; Mexico for 13 per cent; and Korea, Singapore and Malaysia provided a combined total of 8 per cent.

Although the dutiable portion of 9802 imports is still substantial (81 per cent), most analysts find the programme benefits both the US and the host countries of the maquiladora plants. In Mexico between 1977 and 1986, maquiladora production grew by $4.5 billion and created 172 000 new Mexican jobs. According to one estimate, elimination of the programme would increase Mexican production costs by 50 per cent (Godshaw, et al., 1988; Schoepfle and Perez-Lopez, 1988).

10.3 THE US GSP PROGRAMME

In 1964, at the urging of the secretary-general of the UN Conference on Trade and Development, developing countries called upon industrial countries to preferentially provide non-reciprocal tariff reductions for Third World products. In 1965 the GATT articles were modified to accommodate such programmes, and by 1970 many industrial countries had pledged to enact GSP programmes.

In 1974 the US enacted its Generalized System of Preferences (GSP) programme, thereby granting nonreciprocal duty-free access for about 3000, mainly manufactured, products from 140 developing countries. The programme has been amended and extended and will now operate through to early July 1993. As of mid-1989 the programme covered 4100 tariff lines under the harmonised tariffs system for 136 developing-country beneficiaries. About 47 per cent of US tariff categories are eligible for the GSP programme.

The US GSP provides reduction of duties to zero on all eligible items. However agricultural items are not included and certain import-sensitive manufactures are also ineligible: textiles and clothing, watches, selected electronics, selected steel products, footwear, handbags, luggage, flat goods, work gloves, leather clothing and selected glass products. Furthermore items subject to import relief under the GATT escape clause are excluded. Finally, a product-specific graduation mechanism is used to reapply duties to items from specific countries when they are deemed to be competitive (determined to be any country-specific import category exceeding $82.5 million in 1988 or 50 per cent of total US imports of the item). The US president has discretionary graduation authority as well as the ability to waive competitive product graduations. Each year the executive branch reviews the trade data and private sector petitions to determine further graduation action. However, as of 1985 32 beneficiaries have been designated as least-developed beneficiary developing countries and are thereby guaranteed duty-free treatment – the usually mandatory competitive graduation criteria are ignored.[4]

Most developing countries (except for Arab oil producers – OPEC members) were eligible to benefit from the programme in 1974. All industrial countries and communist countries were ineligible. To take effect in January 1989, President Reagan used his discretionary graduation authority to remove from eligibility Hong Kong, Korea, Singapore and Taiwan, saying that these countries had 'achieved an impressive level of economic development and competitiveness, which can be sustained without the preferences provided by the programme'. Furthermore, due to amendments regarding the observance of worker's rights in GSP beneficiary countries, the beneficiary status of Romania, Nicaragua, Paraguay, Chile, Burma and the Central African Republic was suspended. Reviews of Haiti, Liberia and Syria were underway. Also, due to an allegation of expropriation, Venezuela's status is under review.

In 1988 duty-free US imports under the GSP programme amounted to $18.4 billion (just over 10 per cent of total US imports from developing countries and 13.3 per cent of imports from beneficiary countries). About $6.1 billion of beneficiary imports were not allowed due to competitiveness graduations. Over 90 per cent of these product graduations applied to imports from seven newly industrialised countries, including the four Asian tigers. Product and administrative exclusions combined to remove $31.6 billion of imports from GSP duty-free status in 1988.[5] With the removal of the four Asian newly industrialised countries from the US GSP programme, Mexico and Brazil became the top beneficiaries (accounting for over 40 per cent of 1989 imports under the programme). However most analyses say that the country and product graduations will not have the effect of stimulating poorer countries to greatly increase trade to fill the gap left by these graduations.[6]

Due to the limited manufacturing diversification in many developing countries and the extensive product graduations, the US GSP programme has had a limited, although positive impact on the trade of developing countries.[7] Nonetheless it is one of the few large-scale efforts by the US government to promote trade with developing countries specifically. Most other US trade policies toward developing countries restrict trade in a discriminatory fashion or only positively affect a small handful of countries. Therefore the GSP has come to represent the pillar of the US policy of offering 'trade rather than aid' to stimulate development. The GSP has failings similar to those of the CBI which are analysed below, and therefore is only of little help to the development process.

10.4 THE CARIBBEAN BASIN INITIATIVE[8]

The hallmark of the Reagan administration was its emphasis on private sector development. Just as the administration pushed for deregulation in the US economy, it attempted to spread the faith about laissez-faire economics at the international level. With the Caribbean Basin Initiative (CBI), it was hoped that, by breaking the chains that restrain commerce, the full economic potential of the region would be realised. Unfortunately the 'unshackling' of trade, not surprisingly, has produced minimal results. Past trade restraints on much of the region's exports have been minor; the most deleterious 'chains' remain in place; and the former 'slave' has few resources for dealing with centuries of commodity-dependence, just like American Blacks had little money or education to make effective utilisation of their emancipation in 1863. Certainly the 'unshackling' was a correct action – but one of limited value in the absence of appropriate steps to alleviate the economic distortions created by centuries of dependence.

10.4.1 The trade provisions

The central policy instrument of the CBI is the non-reciprocal preferential treatment of goods from the region – a policy aimed at augmenting the region's growth and diversification through enhanced export access to the US market. Although the US government expressed hope that the programme would be complemented by similar programmes in other industrial countries, the CBI is markedly bilateral.

The Caribbean Basin Economic Recovery Act (CBERA) reflected the desires of the Reagan administration. The trade provisions written into the CBERA allow the US president to grant duty-free treatment for twelve years to all imports from designated Caribbean basin countries, except for those textiles and articles of clothing that are subject to textile agreements under the Multi-Fiber Arrangement: footwear, handbags, luggage, flat goods, work gloves, and leather clothing excluded from GSP eligibility; canned tuna; petroleum and petroleum products; and watches and parts if they contain any materials produced by communist countries. In addition sugar and beef products lose duty-free treatment if the beneficiary country fails to submit a 'stable food production' plan (to deter beneficiaries from shifting production away from food crops to take advantage of duty-free access for sugar and beef).[9] In any case sugar and beef products remain limited by quotas. All countries in Central America as well as those adjoining the Caribbean Sea, except Colombia, Cuba, Mexico, Venezuela and French territories, are eligible for designation, although some countries have not applied for such status.[10] For a product to be eligible, at least 35 per cent of direct cost must be attributable to processing in a beneficiary country (US-made components may comprise fifteen of these percentage points). Finally, products comprised of foreign materials must be 'substantially transformed' in a beneficiary country.

10.4.2 Evolution since passage

Without question, promotional efforts have been highly visible. While some of these efforts can be criticised for reckless use of dubious figures,[11] the US government has seen these activities as crucial to the effort to overcome business sector inertia in investment and import sourcing decisions. Several officials admit that the promotional efforts elevate expectations far above what the CBI can expect to produce, but this effort, they say, has beneficial effects by attracting the attention of businessmen to the inherent advantages of conducting business in the basin. In addition to these efforts, a variety of complementary programmes are of value to the countries of the Caribbean basin.[12] In March 1986, in an effort to extend access to the US market in the area of clothing, the Section 807 programme was modified to provide guaranteed access to Caribbean basin countries. However these products are often subject to tariffs and guaranteed access is still subject to 'surge' provisions to avert unexpected increases. Finally, changes in the tax code have allowed Puerto Rico to use its Section 936 funds for twin-plant investments in Puerto Rico and the Caribbean basin. Only a limited number of projects have been funded to date.

10.4.3 Assessment of the CBI

The record of the CBI has been disappointing. While the programme is not a failure, its slow start and the probable future direction of US trade and foreign aid policy make it unlikely that the high expectations created since the announcement of the programme will be fulfilled. In short, the CBI is largely irrelevant to the economic dilemmas of Central America and the Caribbean, as shown in the lack of real export growth to the US (Table 10.2).

A major reason for the poor economic performance of these areas is that they are extremely dependent upon a narrow range of primary commodity exports. Except for coffee, the world prices of these commodities had dropped dramatically by 1990. As also happened after past commodity busts, Central America and the Caribbean are suffering terribly for their general lack of economic diversification.

The 1980s witnessed an increase in the US share of exports from Central America: 32.3 per cent in 1980, 35.2 per cent in 1983 and 37.9 per cent in 1986. On the surface this would seem to indicate that the CBI has been rather successful, at least in diverting Central American exports to the US market, if not in creating new exports. However the CBI had little if anything to do with this shift. In fact if coffee is taken out of the balance, the export gain is virtually erased. The rest of the gain can be explained by products not eligible for duty-free access under CBI.

Duty-free imports under CBERA amounted to $578 million in 1984, and then grew at a moderate rate of $791 million in 1988. Imports under the Generalized System of Preferences (GSP) programme declined 40 per cent between 1984 and 1988 and the GSP utilisation ratio also declined, indicating that some of the import gains from CBERA imports were due not to trade creation, but to the simple accounting procedure of shifting the mode of access. In fact Caribbean basin utilisation of GSP on GSP-eligible items dropped from 61 per cent in 1984 to 32 per cent in 1988 (USITC, September 1989). Of the top twenty products entering under CBERA in 1986 (accounting for 72 per cent of CBERA imports), only 44 per cent were provided new preferences (USITC, September 1987). The

Table 10.2   Increase in US imports from Central America and the
Caribbean basin, 1983–8 (millions of constant 1985 dollars)

	Caribbean basin	Central America
Total US imports	−4068	80
Of which:		
Food	−538	−231
Beverages and tobacco	−22	−18
Crude material	−104	−8
Mineral fuels	−4532	−34
Oils and fats	2	0
Chemicals	190	10
Manufactured goods, by material	130	53
Machine and transport equipment	−157	−40
Miscellaneous manufactures	1081	340
Not elsewhere classified	−119	8
Agricultural commodities	−533	−275
Non-agricultural commodities	−3536	356
Petroleum	−4520	−33
Textiles	55	27
Clothing, except footwear	932	300
Total mfg. (SITC 5–9)	1124	372

Source: Calculations based on US Department of Commerce, *Highlights of
U.S. Export and Import Trade* (various December issues).

other 56 per cent would have been duty free under GSP or most-
favoured-nation treatment. According to a more recent estimate,
only $297 million of CBERA imports in 1988 received new duty-free
treatment. Thus the new duty free imports represent less than 5 per
cent of imports from CBI countries. For comparison, each year new
trade due to the CBI was more than offset by the estimated revenue
losses due to US sugar import quotas (Tucker and Chambers, 1989).

If one looks in isolation upon non-primary-product trade, growth
has been respectable, though not outstanding. However the growth
of manufactured exports is coming from a small base and is not
apparently attributable to the CBI. A comparison of the manufacturing sector's performance in 1983–6 with the two previous years (prior
to the enactment of the CBERA and a period of recession in the US)
shows very little impact by the CBI (or tariffs in general).

Another telling sign of the limited impact of the CBERA trade provisions is the relative standing of basin producers in relation to other suppliers to the US market. Between 1984 and 1988 overall US imports from CBI countries fell from constituting 2.8 per cent of total US imports to only 1.4 per cent (USITC, September 1989).

Investment is a central determinant of economic growth and trade performance by Central American and Caribbean countries. The Department of Commerce conducted a survey of US investment in the region to ascertain the trends. For the survey 642 companies (of all nationalities) reported new investments of $1.6 billion (about half of which related to CBI trade), and the creation of more than 116 000 full- and part-time jobs between 1984 and 1987 (USDOC, 1988). While the data indicates a shift of interest on the part of investors toward non-traditional exports, the data does not take into account major planned disinvestments – such as Reynolds Aluminum in Jamaica, United Brands in Costa Rica, and Exxon in the Netherlands Antilles. However other estimates show that the indirect and direct employment generated by US imports of manufactured goods from seven major CBI countries amounts to as much as 136 000, suggesting that the Commerce Department survey may be underestimating the job creation (Tucker, December 1989). However a large part of the investment that is taking place in the Caribbean basin is not related to the CBI.

10.5 OTHER PREFERENTIAL INITIATIVES

The US is currently implementing or considering two enhancements of the GSP preferences, one initiative for Andean countries and one initiative for 39 least-developed countries.

10.5.1 The Andean initiative

On 1 November 1989 President Bush, as part of US efforts to decrease the flow of illegal drugs, announced a package of trade initiatives intended to expand legal trade opportunities for countries in the Andean region: Bolivia, Colombia, Ecuador, Peru and Venezuela. The bilateral part of the Andean initiative involved: (1) an expedited review of GSP product eligibility for Andean countries, leading to a July 1990 announcement about GSP changes for these countries; (2) technical assistance to help Andean exporters with GSP procedures; (3) an assessment of what technical assistance the US may be able to provide Andean countries to improve their legal trade; and (4) GSP access for six categories of handicraft textiles and further investigation into the possible expansion of the textile trade, consistent with the current MFA. On the multilateral side the US government would: (1) negotiate to re-establish the International Coffee Agreement; (2) undertake accelerated negotiations on tariffs and NTBs with Andean participants in the Uruguay round of GATT trade talks; (3) consult with other industrial countries (at the quadrilateral talks) to determine areas of cooperation to assist Andean countries to improve trade performance; and (4) encourage multilateral development banks to provide technical assistance to promote Andean exports.

With coffee negotiations stalled, the major visible element of the Andean initiative was the change in GSP access (initially for textiles, but potentially for a much wider list of products). However this initiative will only have an impact if new tariff lines are affected. Andean countries already have very high GSP utilisation ratios (around 95 per cent, compared to 75 per cent for all beneficiaries). The main limiting factor for their imports is not their lack of understanding of how to get the most out of the current GSP programme, but rather the exclusion of products from the GSP which matter most to their economies. The US trade representative received 139 petitions for review in this process, Decisions will be announced in mid-July and implemented on 1 August.

10.5.2 Enhanced access for the least developed developing countries

As one of the last acts of the outgoing Reagan administration in January 1989, the US trade representative requested an ITC study of the probable economic effects of complete tariff elimination for over 3100 tariff line items in the US Harmonized Tariff Schedule for each of 39 developing countries (termed by USTR as the 'least developed developing countries'), including 31 low- and middle-income African countries, six low- and middle-income Asian countries, one low-income Latin American country, and one middle-income Pacific country. The outgoing USTR was thereby initiating a six-month review that would allow the US president to eliminate duties on these products as an early Uruguay round tariff concession in 1989.

By 1990 the Bush administration had not publicly endorsed this unilateral tariff initiative, although this kind of concession to the poorest countries would be consistent with US negotiating positions at the Uruguay round. However the original idea of publicly endorsing such an initiative at the Montreal mid-term meeting of the round had failed to capture the imagination of the outgoing administration in late 1988 and was buried by the last-minute agriculture policy negotiating tangle that eventually required a delay until April 1989 before adoption of the Montreal mid-term package.

10.6 FREE TRADE AREAS

The economic crisis of the early 1980s led many observers to note that relations with key developing countries were suffering due to limited trade opportunities. Both the Caribbean Basin Initiative and talk of a US–Mexico free trade pact reflected US concern for the economic well-being of strategic neighbours. These efforts have drawn the criticism that they represented the leading edge of regionalism/bilateralism and the disintegration of multilateral trade.

At first US bilateral 'free trade areas' (FTAs) were used to back US threats that, if its trading partners did not fully participate in the Uruguay round, the US was prepared to develop regional blocs for its own benefit. Those FTAs that had already been established (with Israel in 1985 and Canada in 1988), however, were clearly defined as issues of national interest that should not trouble world trading partners.

US business is concerned that the US should get its foot in the door to any promising initiatives (such as a Pacific Rim agreement) – especially if the Uruguay round results are disappointing. Though US policy has wavered on FTAs, the US commitment to making the Uruguay round work is receiving the primary efforts of the trade bureaucracy and political leaders. As the Uruguay round comes to a close, the US government would begin acting upon western hemisphere FTAs in case this alternative policy is the wave of the future.

The appeal of FTAs stems from a number of different concerns. Many people are worried about the functioning of the GATT system, which seems too slow and negotiations too complex, whereas bilateral accords might be more quickly accomplished. A second concern is the management of the political fallout of extreme bilateral trade imbalances. FTAs might afford a mechanism to achieve trade liberalisation and more balanced trade flows.

The US International Trade Commission surveyed a number of

leading experts on Pacific Basin trade on the various issues surrounding FTAs (USITC, March 1989). The majority of these people resoundingly supported the improvement of the GATT multilateral system as the priority objective of US trade policy, considering this the best means to achieve trade liberalisation. Most argued that FTAs should only be pursued after the results of the Uruguay round had been evaluated. Some even suggested that simultaneous talk of FTAs would indicate that the US was abandoning the multilateral trading system and this would undermine the GATT talks. Only a few people suggested that studies of FTAs during the GATT talks would actually provide a positive stimulus to the multilateral negotiations. A distinct minority said that FTAs should be vigorously pursued regardless of ongoing GATT talks.

In 1990 attention shifted to Mexico and a North American FTA. The US and Mexico conducted formal sectoral talks from Spring 1990 through to November 1990, which laid the groundwork for the FTA talks. However Mexico expressed its desire to more fully integrate itself into GATT, which it had only recently joined. Thus, for Mexico as well as the US, the Uruguay round remained the primary focus.

Academic work on FTAs warns against an overly ambitious policy. Potential FTAs hold little promise of substantial trade reform beyond minimal tariff reductions (since US NTBs will not be brought bilaterally to the bargaining table). Most trade barriers can only be reduced multilaterally or unilaterally – bilateral solutions run counter to existing global commitments. Bilateral liberalisation creates discriminatory practices which undermine multilateral bargaining leverage. FTAs among countries not at comparable levels of development involve messy bargains and complicated rules which are best left to multilateral fora. FTA negotiations undermine multilateral bargaining credibility. Widespread FTAs would tend to create disruptive trading blocs rather than positive trade liberalisation. Finally, little change in bilateral trade imbalances will result from FTAs. In sum, FTAs are clearly suboptimal. While the multilateral track is functioning, a parallel bilateral track is a waste of effort, at best (Schott, 1989).

Notes and references

1. Afghanistan, Albania, Bulgaria, Cuba, Czechoslovakia, Estonia, German Democratic Republic, Kampuchea, Laos, Latvia, Lithuania, Mon-

golia, North Korea, Romania, USSR and Vietnam.
2. The US president has limited authority to waive the emigration requirement.
3. The Harmonized Tariff Schedule of the US was adopted in the Omnibus Trade and Competitiveness Act of 1988, and became effective in January 1989.
4. The least-developed beneficiary developing countries are Bangladesh, Benin, Bhutan, Botswana, Burkina Faso, Burundi, Cape Verde, Central African Republic, Chad, Comoros, Djibouti, Equatorial Guinea, The Gambia, Guinea, Guinea-Bissau, Haiti, Lesotho, Malawi, Maldives, Mali, Nepal, Niger, Rwanda, Sao Tome and Principe, Sierra Leone, Somalia, Sudan, Tanzania, Togo, Uganda, Western Samoa and Yemen Arab Republic.
5. 1988 GSP trade data from *The President's Report to Congress on the Generalized System of Preferences As Required By Section 505(B) of the Trade Act of 1974, As Amended* (1989).
6. For analysis of the reasons that lower-income countries will be unable to take advantage of graduation of competitors, see Joseph Pelzman, *The U.S. Generalized System of Preferences: An Evaluation and an Examination of Alternative Graduation Programs* (Report prepared for the US Department of Labor, October 1983).
7. See Stuart K. Tucker, 'The U.S. GSP Program: Trade Preferences and Development', ODC *Policy Focus*, no. 6 (September 1984) for analysis of the benefits of the GSP programme.
8. This section draws heavily upon Stuart K. Tucker, 'Trade Unshackled: Assessing the Value of the Caribbean Basin Initiative', in William Ascher and Ann Hubbard (eds), *Central American Recovery and Development: Task Force Report to the International Commission for Central American Recovery and Development* (Durham, 1989: Duke University Press pp. 357–92).
9. Countries that have had duty-free treatment suspended for sugar and beef products include Antigua, Aruba, the Bahamas, Barbuda, Montserrat, the Netherlands Antilles, St. Lucia, and St. Vincent and the Grenadines.
10. Designated beneficiary countries include: Antigua and Barbuda, Aruba, the Bahamas, Barbados, Belize, the British Virgin Islands, Costa Rica, Dominica, the Dominican Republic, El Salvador, Grenada, Guatemala, Guyana Haiti, Honduras, Jamaica, Montserrat, the Netherlands Antilles, Panama, Saint Christopher-Nevis, Saint Lucia, Saint Vincent and the Grenadines, and Trinidad and Tobago. Non-designated countries eligible to apply for designated status include: Anguilla, the Cayman Islands, Nicaragua, Suriname and the Turks and Caicos Islands.
11. See US General Accounting Office, *Caribbean Basin Initiative: Need for More Reliable Data on Business Activity Resulting From the Initiative* (August 1986) and various testimonies given at hearings before the Subcommittee on Oversight of the House Committee on Ways and Means, 25 and 27 February 1986.
12. For an explanation of these complementary programmes as well as Section 807 and Section 939, see Stuart K. Tucker, 'The Caribbean Basin

Initiative: Elevated Expectations and Limited Means', (November 1986), a paper presented at the symposium on 'Selective Preferential Arrangements Between Developed and Developing Countries (Mini-NIEO)' held by the Institute of Development Studies of Helsinki University, 28–30 November 1986, Helsinki, Finland.

11 Export Promotion: Market Access, Credits and Aid

Stuart K. Tucker

Traditionally the US has resisted large budgetary commitments to export promotion. Instead it has relied on multilateral negotiations, bilateral negotiations, technical assistance to exporters and the generic benefits of growth and development to increase markets for US goods. However the economic turbulence of the 1980s created perceptions of imbalanced commitments and unfair practices. The US Congress responded with pressure on the executive branch to act unilaterally if necessary to defend critical trading interests. Section 301 negotiation procedures were modified. Export credit 'warchests' were authorised. Subsidies for agricultural exports were established in the 1985 farm act to bolster both US trade and US negotiators. Concern grew substantially regarding the possible negative impact of multilateral aid on US trade. Although each of these efforts is portrayed as standing up for US rights and potentially assisting the liberalisation of the trading system, each is more likely to hurt the trading interests of developing countries than to help.

11.1 BILATERAL NEGOTIATIONS AND SECTION 301

In the late 1980s the US government started taking a new approach to export promotion. Bilateral and multilateral negotiations to liberalise foreign markets (especially for US exports) are being supported by threats of trade sanctions (section 301 legislation). The 1988 trade act regularised this process, putting more pressure on the executive branch to vigorously pursue bilateral negotiations under section 301 (with a stricter timetable). The 'Super 301' provisions require annual identification of unfair trade practices and priority countries for negotiations.

In May 1989 the Bush administration chose to initiate a minimal

161

number of such negotiations – enough to fulfill the law without creating havoc for the multilateral talks in Geneva. Korea and Taiwan escaped identification as priority countries due to the 'last minute', unilateral trade concessions offered by them. In addition to the well-publicised complaints against Japan, the Bush administration identified Brazil's import licensing system and India's barriers on foreign investment and insurance as unfair barriers and tried to initiate negotiations.

Brazil was already in the process of revising its licensing procedures to a manner more consistent with US trading interests. Furthermore Brazil saw the prospect of trade retaliation (required under the 1988 trade act if no progress is made in negotiations) as a minor annoyance. The Brazilian government inaugurated in mid-March 1989 may show more interest in harmonious trade relations with the US.

India, having exported only $3.2 billion to the US in 1988, saw little to lose if sanctions were imposed and showed a willingness to discuss these issues only in a multilateral context. Nonetheless the unilateral Indian trend toward liberalisation of investment restrictions may undercut the basis for sanctions.

By April 1990 the Bush administration was facing another deadline for initiating section 301 actions against priority countries. The lack of significant progress with Japan and the unwillingness of Brazil and India to engage in serious bilateral negotiations led to significant Congressional pressure for stronger action in 1990. However the Bush administration's minimalist interpretation in 1989 and 1990 and its desire not to undermine the Uruguay round indicate that future 'super 301' actions are likely to be minor.

Parallel to this process was the 'special 301' provisions for monitoring the protection of intellectual property rights (see Chapter 12 for more details). In 1990 the administration attempted to avoid bilateral confrontation with developing countries and did not seek negotiations with any countries.

However in 1992 the Uruguay round trade package would be presented to the US Congress for enactment of implementing legislation. If a majority in Congress perceive that the problem of unfair trade practices remains unaddressed by the Uruguay round, then they may look to the results of the section 301 negotiations for guidance in future action. The Bush administration is trying to make Super 301 look effective without disrupting multilateral interests. If the 301 actions are perceived as ineffective by Congress, then more restrictive, unilateral, and potentially protectionist amendments to the section 301 process may be offered. Legislative history shows that Congress will have significant leverage for passing such legislation while the Uruguay round package is being considered.

In effect, through section 301 the US is pursuing a policy of *ultimata* to promote fairer international trade – although its actions are aimed primarily at giving *US industries* market access (with the multilateral implications still unclear). These actions may have a positive effect on world trade, including the trading interests of developing countries, if the negotiations are handled diplomatically and the results are multilateral. On the other hand this unusual export promotion mechanism is also very likely to fail and lead to import protection. In any case the negotiations can be no substitute for widespread liberalisation through GATT. Unilateral *ultimata* have no place in GATT negotiations. The US government must walk a tightrope to keep section 301 negotiations from backfiring.

11.2 THE ROLE OF US GOVERNMENT EXPORT CREDITS

Subsidies have not been used very widely in the post-war period; often they have been restricted to the defence industry and to technological research and development. However the US has attempted to provide assistance to exporters in the form of information services. More concretely – through Eximbank – the government has attempted to provide a mechanism to compensate exporters for some of the failings of private markets. Yet in the 1980s US official export credits shrank and more often than not acted as a procyclical force (see Table 11.1). As a negotiating tool, a mixed credit war chest was established in the late 1980s to assist with capital goods sales. This small fund serves to match what are perceived as unfair credit offers by competing export credit agencies of industrial countries. Thus the emphasis at Eximbank has shifted away from providing substantial credit for export sales to developing countries which desire to buy US goods, and focuses instead on subsidised credit to combat the selected sales of other industrial countries.

A significant addition to US trade policy in the late 1980s was the use of the Export Enhancement Program (EEP) to boost US agricultural exports. This programme has been riddled with problems, both for the US taxpayer and the farmers receiving the benefits. Yet current US policy is to maintain these export subsidies as a way of

Table 11.1   US Eximbank's financial highlights (billions of dollars)

	Loan authorised	(Direct credits)	Guarantees	Insurance authorised	Exports supported
1978	3.4	2.9	0.6	3.4	10.6
1979	4.5	3.7	0.9	4.1	13.6
1980	4.6	4.0	2.5	5.5	18.1
1981	5.4	5.0	1.5	5.9	18.6
1982	3.5	3.1	0.7	5.1	12.1
1983	0.8	0.7	1.7	6.8	10.4
1984	1.5	1.1	1.3	5.8	10.4
1985	0.7	0.3	1.3	6.5	9.3
1986	0.6	0.4	1.1	4.4	6.4
1987	0.6	0.3	1.5	6.4	9.3
1988	0.7	0.5	0.6	5.1	6.5

Sources: *Annual Reports of the Export-Import Bank of the United States*, Fiscal years 1979, 1980, 1982, 1984, 1986 and 1988.

improving US negotiating leverage at the Uruguay round. Thus, in an effort to fight EC agricultural policies, the EEP is boosting US grain exports to developing countries, much to the detriment of Third World producers.

11.2.1   Export credits in the 1980s

During the 1980s, amid the traumas of debt and trade imbalance, the drying up of private export credits was overlooked. While debt rescheduling captured the media headlines, a parallel retrenchment by commercial banks was underway. The commercial, short- and medium-term credits offered by industrial countries to facilitate trade transactions with the Third World dropped from $29.4 billion in 1981 to $13.8 billion in 1986. *Net* disbursements of such credits went from $10.5 billion in 1981 to *minus* $1.6 billion in 1986 (OECD, 1985, 1988). That is to say, in 1986 commercial banks in industrial countries received more in repayments of past credits than they lent. In short, private export credits were not available to facilitate the expansion of imports by developing countries in the late 1980s.

When the private sector fails to perform a set of activities necessary for the proper functioning of free markets, the government has a legitimate responsibility to correct these market failures by intervening with an appropriate government-run response. Indeed this was the philosophy that led to the creation of the Export-Import Bank of the United States (Eximbank) in the 1930s.[1] The current activities of Eximbank are geared to fulfil three roles: promoting US trade, facilitating Third World development, and enhancing the US position in bilateral and multilateral trade negotiations.[2]

The fundamental purpose of US official export credits is to finance activities that the private sector considers too risky or insufficiently profitable. Over the years, as industrial countries' buyers gained strength and creditworthiness, Eximbank's role has shifted toward finance for US exports to developing countries. Eximbank, as a public-sector institution, is most useful when it steps up in market activity during economic slumps. Thus Eximbank should play a counter-cyclical role by promoting US exports at precisely the time when business activity is slow.

Third World buyers who have difficulty finding private capital receive an economic boost from the provision of official export credits and guarantees. In addition to the benefits of access to such credit, lower-income developing countries receive the added assistance of credit at lower interest rates than are commercially available even to more creditworthy buyers. The OECD arrangement on export credits has established separate interest rate categories to allow agencies in industrial countries to provide this low-cost finance according to the level of development of the recipient. Finally, the tied aid pro-gramme throws grant money into the deal to make the financed project even more affordable for the lower-income developing countries.

In recent years Eximbank has been called upon to serve as a weapon for trade negotiators. Eximbank has always had the implicit role of 'levelling the playing field' so that purchasing decisions could be made on the basis of product competitiveness rather than on the basis of unequal financing terms. In the 1980s Eximbank activities followed two new paths. First, the increasing use of tied aid by other countries raised worries that this 'aid' was not being spent for de-velopment purposes but for commercial gain. Hence the current mixed credit war chest is meant to counterbalance subsidised financ-ing. Second, Eximbank was called upon to provide subsidised financ-ing for the sale of US goods in US markets in cases where foreign competition for the sale was itself subsidised. Aimed primarily at Japanese and Brazilian goods, this policy was intended to bolster US bilateral trade negotiations in the hope that subsidies and trade barriers would be reduced in these countries.

11.2.2   The mixed credit war chest

By creating a war chest of funds to finance mixed credits, it was hoped that the US would be able to match the subsidies offered by other countries and thus cause them either to stop using the aid subsidies for commercial gain or to spend even more aid, making it overly costly to use the aid subsidies for commercial gain (hence it might be safe to assume that the money was being spent on a legitimate development aid project).

In an ideal world Eximbank would be able to use these funds to win the 'competition' for providing the best credit terms. This, combined with a competitive product, would yield an American sale. Other countries would then have to decide whether to up the ante by giving larger subsidies in their financing bids or to cease offering such large subsidies. If the other countries were to back away from larger subsidies, then the war chest would be serving its purpose of deterring unfair credit deals for commercial gain. On the other hand, if the other countries were to raise the ante then the US would have to raise its subsidies or risk losing the sales. The gamble in all this is that other countries may not raise the ante because of the high costs which would be incurred. The incentive therefore for the other countries to back down resides solely in the size of the US war chest – the smaller the war chest, the less incentive there would be to back down.

11.2.3   The developmental impact

Unfortunately mixed credit sales have effects other than those upon trade negotiations. The use of a subsidy to make a commercial sale attractive is, in effect, an offer to a country to make a decision it might not otherwise make. In short, the aid can be trade-distorting. By paying the buyers to buy a different product than they would have, the credit agency has twisted the preference of the buyers. If those buyers, without the attraction of the mixed credit, were making economically rational choices, then the mixed credit could be luring the buyers into a bad decision. In the end an altered choice may be the wrong choice with regard to the development of the buying country.

On the other hand, if the buyers would have bought the product anyway, then the mixed credit would not result in trade distortion and would be a simple transfer of money to the buyers. In short, under this circumstance the mixed credit would play a positive developmental role. Of course if this were the case, then the trade negotiation aspect of the credit would be defeated, because the credit agency would not have to counterbalance the foreign competitor's offer in order to win the sale.

Thus mixed credit only aids development if it is not trade-distorting and is consequently not playing a trade negotiating role. Similarly, mixed credit only serves as a bargaining tool in trade when it distorts trade and is therefore playing a negative role in the process of development. The central determinant is whether buyers will change their decisions following an offer of mixed credit. Since this is likely to happen more often when the subsidy element is high, a fairly straight-forward conclusion is the following. The higher the level of the subsidy in a *commercially-oriented* mixed credit, the less positive (or more negative) the role the credit plays in the process of development. Yet a low level of subsidy is not as likely to succeed in accomplishing the trade negotiation objective. In sum, mixed credit is a unidimensional policy tool which can only achieve one of these two objectives.

11.2.4 Eximbank finances

During the period 1981–8, total Eximbank authorisations fell from $12.9 billion to $6.4 billion. During this time Eximbank direct lending fell dramatically – from $5 billion to $465 million (a 91 per cent drop). Insurance and guarantees also declined, although less dramatically. The net result of this drop in direct lending was not only a drop in the value of US export sales supported by Eximbank but also a decline in the effectiveness of US authorisations. Whereas overall authorisations fell more than 50 per cent, the decline in Eximbank-supported US exports was 65 per cent – from $18.6 billion in 1981 to $6.5 billion in 1988. Thus in 1981 one dollar of Eximbank authorisations supported nearly $1.50 in US exports; the ratio in 1986 was barely above one-for-one.

The decline in direct lending has been particularly damaging for US trade with low-income and lower middle-income developing countries. These countries are typically less creditworthy. Private lenders are unwilling to lend to them, even with insurance and guarantees. In effect the direct lending programme is the only sure way Eximbank can provide aid to trade with these poorer countries. Thus the virtual disappearance of the direct lending programme has reduced the developmental role of Eximbank.

Relative to the demise of US direct lending, US mixed credit funds have been extremely small. During 1987 and 1988 less than $86 million was spent in war chest actions.[3] Thus while the US Eximbank was reducing its direct credits by roughly $4.6 billion (1981 compared to 1988), it was wielding a minuscule mixed credit fund as a stick in trade negotiations. This drop in direct lending led to a decline in Eximbank's worldwide exposure from $38.4 billion in 1981 to $27.4 billion in 1988. However the reliability of Eximbank's outstanding portfolio was severely damaged over the same period. Delinquent loans rose from $888 million to $2.7 billion. The ratio of delinquent loans compared to loans receivable has changed from 5.6 per cent to 27.4 per cent.

The rising cost of borrowing in the 1982–5 period outpaced Eximbank revenue increases and Eximbank's net income has been negative since the beginning of 1982. Eximbank lost an average of $445 million annually during 1987–8, and as a result of this lengthy period of losses, in 1988 it used up the last of its reserves (which were $2.2 billion in 1981) and began to eat into its capital. Eximbank staff do not expect net income to be positive until well into the 1990s.[4]

This brief review of Eximbank lending shows that the institution is playing a smaller role in US trade during a period in which it should be more active. Eximbank is facing a serious capital crunch that will only serve to impair its ability to play a positive role in the future. Though not a major holder of delinquent debt claims, the official nature of Eximbank makes its actions on delinquent loans highly political. Thus the US Congress must consider seriously its actions with regard to Eximbank's future in the world trade and financial system. Eximbank is in danger of falling into obscurity and irrelevance.

11.2.5 Export credit recommendations

In essence the war chest is bad for development, is too small to have any effect on trade negotiations, and is an inefficient (and overly costly) tool for promoting US exports. If it is politically impossible to do away with the war chest, the US Treasury Department should retain the primary role, since it is in the best position to use the war chest to support US negotiating objectives (which is the only reason to have such a policy tool). The US Congress should recapitalise Eximbank to allow it more freedom to manoeuvre when handling bad debts and encouraging continued operation at low interest rates to borrowers. The US should increase the authorisation ceiling for the

Eximbank *direct lending* programme in order to better promote US exports and to provide much needed financing to lower-income countries. Finally, *new* funds should be provided for US Agency for International Development (AID) to use for development purposes; most of this aid would be spent on US goods anyway and the growth impact would help to further US trade.

11.3 AGRICULTURAL EXPORT SUBSIDIES

The US offers agricultural subsidies through the Export Enhancement Subsidy Program (EEP). Created in the mid-1980s, the EEP was designed to combat heavily-subsidised EC exports. However it has exceeded that role and it now also affords the federal government more control over the market and supply of agricultural commodities.

Under the EEP system the US Department of Agriculture compensates agricultural commodity exporters at a discount overseas by giving them government-owned products to meet the difference between world prices and the (generally) higher US prices. Practically speaking the USDA announces a certain amount of sales of a particular commodity to a certain country (an 'initiative'), and then agricultural commodity companies bid for the sale (Cloud, 1989). EEP sales had reached $8.9 billion by November 1989. The market value of EEP bonus awards was $2.6 billion, of which $1.8 billion went for wheat sales (77 per cent of which went to five countries: the former USSR, China, Algeria, Egypt and Morocco).[5]

Recent administrative changes (such as loosening the 'cost-effectiveness' requirement, and the 'additionality' of sales requirement) allowed for greater use of EEP subsidies. Farm groups and many congressmen supported avidly the extension and even the expansion of the EEP in sweeping farm legislation under consideration. However the effectiveness of the EEP has been called into question. First, it is not a cost-free programme, as was initially maintained. Furthermore it has had significant negative effects on Third World economies. In the process of underselling European competitors, the EEP has simultaneously undersold producers in developing countries as well. This has had the effect of squeezing out the rural farmer, worsening the agricultural trade balances of developing countries and cutting off a vital source of foreign exchange (Strange, 1989).

At the same time the EEP has tended to widen the gap between large and small farmers in the US, which undoubtedly has contributed to the rash of small-farm bankruptcies. Since multinational companies and producers of large commercial agricultural commodities reap the lion's share of the subsidies, smaller farmers gain proportionately less from the EEP. In 1986 the small farmers comprising nearly three-fourths of all US agricultural land received less than 10 per cent of federal payments. This is quite ironic because the programme was designed with the small family farmer in mind. The President's Council of Economic Advisers similarly concluded in a report evaluating the overall effects of the EEP that, 'the benefits do not reach those most in need' (Shapiro, 1988). Moreover the US EEP may incite retaliation from those countries that are not eligible for the programme. The full economic and diplomatic effects are still unclear.

Evidence abounds of weaknesses in the EEP. A USDA report concluded that the EEP only increased agricultural exports by between 10 and 30 per cent, and only about 20 per cent of the increase in wheat exports since 1987 has been related to EEP (USDA, 1989). Moreover only 10 per cent of those wheat sales covered by the EEP were 'additional' sales (that is, had not been anticipated) (Bailey, 1989). Furthermore some grain exporters believe that the EEP has actually cost them exports by making buyers hesitate until the EEP bonuses had been announced, and then by foreign purchasers reducing their US imports in order to remain eligible (Paarlberg, 1989).

Although the economic costs of the EEP are quite small in comparison with other such arrangements, many trade experts do not seem convinced of the need for such a subsidy. Nevertheless, in spite of its effectiveness having been called into question, the EEP remains relatively popular with Congress and many farmers. Its supporters still maintain that EEP has allowed the US to gain a larger share of the world market. Despite the analytical arguments against the EEP, pro-farm groups were determined to extend and expand the programme in the 1990 farm bill.

Although the Bush administration showed little desire to expand the use of the EEP it did propose, in its 1990 farm proposals, that the programme should be extended, arguing that unilateral abandonment of the EEP would undermine the US negotiating position at the Uruguay round. Of course this argument ignored the fact that the EEP was costing the US budget more than it was damaging EC agricultural interests. The EC simply increased subsidies to compensate its farmers for the US EEP. The added subsidy costs incurred by the EC were only about half the US budgetary cost of the EEP

(Paarlberg, 1989). Furthermore the actual size of these subsidies were still small compared to the overall EC farm budget (less than 2 per cent).

The US EEP will not be eliminated prior to the end of the Uruguay round. However the costs do not justify its being extended, particularly once the multilateral negotiations have been concluded.

11.4 WORLD BANK LENDING AND US COMPETITIVENESS

The debate over the use of mixed credits in the promotion of sales by industrial countries to the Third World is now being accompanied by a debate over the trade neutrality of World Bank projects. Although soybean producers have been the most vocal opponents of World Bank aid to Third World producers (Brazil in particular), other groups have also come together to fight foreign assistance that is perceived as detrimental to US trade interests.

One of the protectionist aspects of the draft of the 1988 trade bill was a provision to deny bilateral aid to competitors for US export markets – these legislative efforts were diluted before enactment of the 1988 act. Therefore efforts to constrain multilateral and bilateral aid on the basis of US trade concerns have been effectively resisted thusfar, but the erosion of the consensus behind US foreign aid in recent years may give new openings for additional trade-linked aid provisions.

Notes and references

1. See Richard E. Feinberg, *Subsidizing Success: The Export-Import Bank in the U.S. Economy* (Cambridge University Press, 1982) for more information on the economic logic behind the creation of Eximbank.
2. See Rita M. Rodriguez (ed.), *The Export-Import Bank at Fifty* (Lexington Books, 1987) for evaluations of Eximbank's activities from the mid-1980s, including a number of analyses on the issue of mixed credits. In that volume, 'Export Credits in U.S. Trade, Development, and Industrial Policy' by Richard E. Feinberg and Stuart K. Tucker discusses an additional role – that of promoting US industrial policy.
3. Statement by John A. Bohn Jr. before the House Banking Committee, 25 February 1988.
4. Ibid.
5. Statement by Allan I. Mendelowitz before the House Agriculture Committee, 16 November 1989.

12 New Trade Issues
Stuart K. Tucker

Perhaps out of a sense of US impotence in the macroeconomic sphere, a number of new initiaves have been thrust forward to assist US international commerce. Free trade area initiatives arose from a sense of frustration with the enforcement mechanisms of the GATT system. Proposals for services and intellectual property rights reflect the emerging strength of US high-technology and service-oriented companies in US politics as well as within the international economy, while also showing the unwillingness of manufacturing industries to take the lead in opening up trade. Workers' rights legislation reflects the concern for human rights which is prevalent in American foreign policy combined with new fears for the low-skilled US manufacturing workers who were affected by stiff import competition during the 1980s. Congressional efforts to place conditions on financial flows to multilateral agencies (to the effect that the foreign aid should not damage US industries) increased dramatically as companies and farmers faced stiffer international competition in the 1980s. The investment plans of developing countries are being scrutinised for their potential to increase US capital goods exports.

More traditional trade issues still command the top priority in multilateral negotiations. However if the US concerns embodied in these initiatives are not met with responsible efforts by trading partners, US leadership in the GATT system will not be sustained. The concerns of specific US industries will drive US policy toward isolation as multilateralist advocates become discredited. The Uruguay round will not solve all the problems of the world economy overnight. But the trading system rests at a critical juncture both in terms of economic prosperity and in terms of the US leadership role.

12.1 SERVICES

Services can be defined loosely as 'activities that produce an intangible and/or non-storable output' (Sapir, 1985). The primary service activities include accounting, banking, advertising, business and professional and technical services, construction, engineering, communications, health, insurance, information, legal services, motion pictures, tourism and transportation. About 76 per cent of US employment is in the services sector, which also accounts for over 90 per cent of new jobs created. In 1988 services exports amounted to about $90 billion, leaving the US with a $20 billion surplus. During the 1980ᶜ US services exports grew by approximately 150 per cent.

Broadly speaking, both developed and developing countries would benefit from a liberalisation of trade in services in terms of efficiency and competitiveness. The industrial countries would accrue large trade benefits from more liberal trade in services, since services constitute a large portion of their total exports. Many industrial countries maintain services trade surpluses, which would increase with greater liberalisation. Another benefit exists for the US: that of gaining political support from powerful lobbies whose interests lie in liberalising international trade in services.

Many developing countries fear that the liberalisation of international trade in services will put them at an even greater disadvantage in terms of their government's sovereignty and of developing their domestic service industries. However just as there are vastly different levels of development among Third World countries, there are also differing views on the costs, and the magnitude of these costs, of freeing-up the trade in services. For instance Brazil and India have led a number of developing countries in opposing the inclusion of discussions on the trade in services in the Uruguay round. Yet Hong Kong and Singapore are less adamant on this issue, and to some extent welcome the talks (Malmgren, 1986).

Some developing countries fear that only the interests of industrial countries will be represented in the final Uruguay round package. Third World countries are concerned that the US position on the trade in services has focused mainly on those service industries in which the US has a strong comparative advantage and not on those in which developing countries are most competitive, such as construction and other labour-intensive services. The implication is that policy guidelines may also ignore these service industries, which would serve to both harm and hinder Third World economic development.

The protection of infant industries in developing countries is likely to be the most significant argument in opposition to opening up the trade in services. The potential of these industries may not be realised if an immediate liberalisation takes place, because it would not allow them time to develop and become competitive in world markets.

Also a liberal trade in services may have serious balance of payments ramifications for developing countries. Most developing countries are already net importers of services, so freeing this trade would tend to worsen their large and still growing negative balance on services and increase the burden on their balance of payments.

On the other hand many developing countries could benefit, in the long-term, from a liberalisation of the trade in services. Third World countries that insist on developing indigenous service industries could deprive their goods-producing industries of lower-cost services and state-of-the-art technology imported from developed countries. It may be less expensive for them to import the services in which they do not have a comparative advantage and to concentrate on those service industries in which they are most competitive. For example, less costly banking and insurance services would aid production in and export from these countries, and an increase in construction service abroad would help alleviate the pressure on their balance of payments.

Without services economic development would become an even more difficult and slow process. Access to the least expensive and most advanced services can greatly improve the growth prospects of developing countries.

12.1.1 Integrating services into GATT

The existing framework for the GATT negotiations may be inadequate to deal effectively with the complexities associated with trade in services. This is true primarily because technology is revolutionising the structure of the service economy at such a rapid pace that the existing talks are unable to keep up with the changing needs of the sector. At this juncture it is vital to establish a viable framework that would provide not only stability to this rapidly changing and growing industry, but also set up guidelines for market behaviour and the settlement of disputes.

Two approaches to the trade in services have emerged in the Uruguay round of trade talks. The sectoral approach attempts to deal with services on a sector-by-sector approach using the existing organisations to establish guidelines. The general approach on the other hand seeks to set up broad, overarching international regulations that would provide direction when solving particular problems.

The developing countries, led by India and Brazil, were opposed to the setting up of a multilateral framework for negotiations on the trade in services. Nevertheless agreement was reached in the 1984 GATT session that a working group would be established by the chairman of the contracting parties 'with a view to compiling and distributing information on service industries with the support of the GATT Secretariat'. Subsequently the ministerial declaration which launched the Uruguay round of the GATT talks called for a framework for the trade in services that would promote the 'economic growth of all trading partners and the development of developing countries'. The Uruguay round did establish a separate negotiating group for services, although this runs parallel to the goods negotiations and the two negotiations will be integrated at the final stage of the Uruguay round.

The goal of these multilateral negotiations, then, must be to establish a framework of principles and rules for services transactions, including the elaboration of possible disciplines for individual sectors, the expansion of such trade under conditions of transparency and progressive liberalisation, and provisions for the development of developing countries.

12.1.2 The US position

Although Uruguay round negotiations will only produce some general guidelines for future services trade negotiations, it is vitally important for the US to show some substantive progress in these discussions. US political support for GATT would be likely to wane in the absence of progress on services (and agriculture) by the end of 1990.

The impetus for placing intellectual property rights and trade in services under the aegis of GATT appears to have come largely from the private sector. The US private sector has been working diligently with the US government to refine its proposals and positions in the Uruguay round and to garner support among their counterparts in other industrial countries. 'The extent and nature of private sector participation in these negotiations are unprecedented, and the success of the initiative is virtually dependent upon the resourcefulness and effectiveness of these efforts' (Baldwin and Richardson, 1988).

In October 1989 the US presented a draft proposal for a general agreement of trade in services (GATS). This outlined broad rules for the trade in services and allowed for annexes for specific sectors. It included legal language on the obligations of the signatories as well as provisions for the settlement of disputes and other procedural issues. The following principles were included: national treatment, the right of establishment, the right to provide cross-border services, temporary entry of service providers, transparency, non-discrimination, prohibition of injuries subsidies, the right to national regulations, limits to restrictions on payments and transfers across borders, and non-discriminatory treatment by government-designated monopolies.

The proposal also called for automatic application to all existing and future measures covered by the agreement. However the signatories would have the right to take limited, temporary reservations for existing measures that do not conform. Additionally the US suggested that the signatories may decide against extending the benefits of market liberalisation to any signatory taking excessive numbers of reservations. Additional protocols may be negotiated among subsets of signatories.

12.2 INTELLECTUAL PROPERTY RIGHTS

After the Second World War the role and significance of intellectual property increased dramatically in virtually all areas of economic activity. As a result the protection of intellectual property rights (IPR) has emerged as an issue in international trade that has caused significant conflict between industrial and developing countries. Industrial countries seek to establish a uniform IPR protection system that would not only ensure legal protection but also allow a mechanism for recourse against counterfeiting. As much as $25 billion per year, or 20 per cent of the US trade deficit, is lost as a result of piracy and counterfeit trade (Gadbaw and Richards, 1988). In sharp contrast developing countries envision a world where information and the transfer of technology flow freely.

There are essentially three underlying reasons for the growth in importance of protection of intellectual property and its role in development and trade negotiations. First, since the Second World War the role of intellectual property-based products in international trade has increased substantially. Second, advanced communications systems have created a more united global marketplace. Third, the level of research and development required to develop new technologies and products has steadily increased, especially in high technology industries.

These developments, combined with the growing US trade deficit, have roused US policymakers to consider seriously the effects of intellectual property protection on international trade flows. Accordingly the US has tried increasingly to incorporate the protection of intellectual property into the world trade regime, especially with respect to Third World countries. In 1984 the US government began holding bilateral discussions with more than thirty countries concerning trade and the protection of intellectual property rights. In these talks the US tied full protection of intellectual property to benefits from the GSP programme. The Reagan Administration released the *Administration Intellectual Property Rights Policy Statement* in April 1986, which argued: '1) the provision of intellectual property protection will enhance the competitiveness of all nations, developing as well as developed and 2) the failure of all nations to protect intellectual property rights distorts and creates inefficiencies in international trade flows'. The 1988 Omnibus Trade Act amended section 301 to include special provision for identifying priority countries for IPR negotiations (this provision is called 'special 301'). The US maintains a 'watch' list of (mostly developing) countries that are under review regarding their IPR practices, but as yet no negotiations have been initiated. The administration is under periodic pressure to announce its intentions, and consequently several of these countries could be subjected to section 301 bilateral negotiations if the political atmosphere changes. As there is likely to be little progress on IPR in the Uruguay round, the US is poised to launch further unilateral initiatives.

12.2.1 Pivot of the conflict

Industrial countries relay reports of 'losses, difficulties, distortions, impediments, and obstacles' by companies, exporters and associations. Instances of piracy were greatest in India, followed by Brazil, Taiwan, the Republic of Korea, Mexico, Argentina and Singapore. The industries most affected by these pirate sales were those producing pharmaceuticals, computers, audio recordings, video recordings, software, agricultural chemicals, semiconductors, and books. The principal complaints against the pirating countries are identified as: their total lack of any laws aimed at protecting patents, trademarks and copyrights; the narrow range covered by what protection they do afford, under which several categories of products or processes are not protected; the brief duration of any such protection; their misuse of compulsory licensing provisions, particularly for patents; and the absence in these countries of adequate and effective enforcement of laws pertaining to copyright and so on.

However industrial countries essentially have a monopoly on

patents and advanced technology. For instance, during the 1970s, of
the 3.5 million patents in existence, only 6 per cent were granted by
developing countries. 'An overwhelming majority of these patents –
as high as 84 per cent – were owned by foreigners, mainly by the
transnational corporations of the five major developed market economy countries'.[1] According to developing countries, any provision
for extending the duration of patents would prolong the monopolistic
profits enjoyed by companies in industrial countries. Strong patent
protection would therefore increase the already high costs of acquir-
ing technology and would thus slow the rate of development.

From the point of view of the transfer and development of technology, developing countries see the issue as one of regularising the
profits of exploitative foreigners. However industrial countries argue
that protection is vital if companies are to engage in the research and
development activities that are necessary to help improve living
standards in the Third World.

12.2.2 GATT initiatives

Intense negotiations and activity in the UN, UNCTAD and WIPO
have taken place in past decades to revise the conventions and
national patent systems applicable to IPR. Frustration with progress
in these efforts has led the US to suggest that IPR be incorporated
directly into GATT. Industrial countries are attracted by GATT's
enforcement and dispute settlement features – these are areas in
which they feel the UN World Intellectual Property Organization
(WIPO) has been largely ineffective.

At the Punta del Este meeting the Group of Ten (Argentina,
Brazil, Cuba, Egypt, India, Nicaragua, Nigeria, Peru, Tanzania and
Yugoslavia) submitted a draft resolution which contained no refer-
ence to intellectual property and was confined to traditional areas of
GATT. Nevertheless, at the urging of industrial countries, the Uru-
guay round negotiations did include trade-related aspects of IPR.

At the Montreal mid-term meeting, IPR remained one of the
unresolved issues. By April 1989 a framework agreement was
adopted which encompassed US objectives, including application of
GATT principles, standards and principles of protection, means of
enforcement, and dispute settlement procedures. However significantly different negotiating positions have remained. India and
Brazil have continued to lead the opposition to comprehensive rules
for IPR.

12.2.3 US bilateral initiatives

In the late 1980s the US charged India, Brazil and South Korea with abuse of intellectual property rights, and in May 1989 it initiated section 301 actions against India and Brazil in areas touching upon these rights. Korea escaped action being taken against it because of its 1987 adoption of the International Copyright Convention and additional last minute efforts in early 1989 to avoid being named a priority country. May 1989 saw the establishment of a priority watch list of eight countries[2] and a watch list of seventeen other countries, all of which were to be monitored for IPR issues during 1989–90.

12.2.4 Recommendations

Knowledgeable observers of IPR issues note that US bilateral initiatives in the area are undermining multilateral objectives. Furthermore US policy is seen to be overly moralistic and to be ignoring the very real economic issues of developing countries. Clearly the US negotiators do have a strong mandate to pursue wider IPR protection, but the issue is one of tactics. Some leeway may exist for selective accords with developing countries in multilateral fora. However the fully-fledged comprehensive GATT approach will gain few adherents (Wells, 1989).

12.3 TRADE-RELATED INVESTMENT MEASURES

At Punta del Este the US tried to interject all the foreign investment measures into GATT. However this was opposed by most countries on ground of national sovereignty. Instead of dealing with the issue of national treatment, the Uruguay round is only addressing measures which restrict or distort trade flows. Negotiations are dealing with definitions of which investment measures should be considered as trade-related and which should be prohibited, and are centred on trade in goods. If trade in services is significantly integrated into GATT, then the issue of all investment measures will be reopened by the US.

12.4   THIRD WORLD WORKER RIGHTS

An issue which has received even less international support is the
linkage of preferential trade benefits to the observance of workers'
rights in the Third World. The US stands alone in its attempts to
place this issue on the GATT agenda. Meanwhile Congress has
imposed a requirement of positive reviews of worker's rights as a
condition for continued receipt of preferential trade access to the US
market (applicable to GSP, CBI and OPIC insurance coverage). A
number of developing countries have had their GSP benefits suspended or revoked because of abuses of workers' rights.

While US actions have been unilateral, a significant economic as
well as a moral case exists for the establishment of internationally-
recognised labour standards in GATT. The deliberate suppression of
improved working conditions can be used to gain competitive advantage. Furthermore, by concentrating profits outside the hands of
domestic workers, aggregate demand is needlessly reduced, thereby
inhibiting national growth.[3]

Of course developing countries are naturally hesitant to invite
actions that might artificially raise their wage levels and take away the
basis of their natural comparative advantage in international trade.
However the workers' rights provisions in US trade law do not
establish unrealistic standards for developing countries. Instead the
law calls for recognition of the principle. The actual application of the
principle in the context of a developing country will vary depending
on the level of development of the country. In no way does the US
workers' rights law require an unsuitable replication of the standards
of industrial countries in poorer nations.

12.5   PROSPECTS

The inclusion of these new issues in the GATT system is by no means
guaranteed. In fact even in services, where some progress is evident,
the disciplines of GATT will not be applied very quickly. Nonetheless
US negotiators are actively engaged in promoting US interests in
these new areas. Because of the decline in basic manufacturing in the
US economy, the *quid pro quo* for US concessions on issues of crucial
importance to developing countries (such as trade in textiles or
agriculture) will be progress in these new issues.

Notes and references

1. *Political and Economic Weekly*, p. 980.
2. Brazil, China, India, Mexico, Saudi Arabia, Korea, Taiwan and Thailand.
3. For a description of the economic rationales surrounding this issue, see Stuart K. Tucker, 'Rapporteur's Report', in *Beyond Subsistence: Labor Standards and Third World Development* (Report of the Symposium co-convened by the Bureau of Labor Affairs of the US Department of Labor and the Overseas Development Council).

13 Trade Policy for the New World Economy

Stuart K. Tucker

The most striking aspect of the evolution of US trade policy is the persistence of old concerns whilst new opportunities and challenges arise. The potential role of developing countries in global prosperity in the 1990s is vastly underestimated even as US conflicts with other industrial countries spill over and taint relations with the Third World. By responding to perceived competitive threats in a piecemeal, reactive fashion, the US government has tended to opt for approaches which restrain selected imports rather than approaches which manage the trade conflicts and set a viable international course.

With regard to trade relations with developing countries, experience has shown that although trade flows far overshadow assistance flows, trade is not a perfect substitute for aid. Indeed even if it were, the reality is that the 'trade instead of aid' slogans were more a justification for reducing grant aid than an indication of willingness to enhance trade relations. The US has been woefully unprepared to adjust to competition from developing countries. Furthermore in governing structure has not allowed strong directive action to mesh US industrial developments with those of the Third World. US businesses have also been slow to respond to Third World opportunities in accordance with growing US interdependency with the world economy. As a result the US commitment to assisting Third World development has staggered in the face of global change.

Ironically the US leadership in world trade is faltering just as the appeal of its free market ideology has reached new heights – with most countries clamouring to join GATT, unilateral liberalisation abounds and internal price reforms and anti-statism are the order of the day. It seems clear that most developing countries recognise that they have more to lose than the US if the liberal international economic order dissolves into groupings of conflictual regional blocs. With US trade leadership ebbing, but still predominant, many recognise that the benefits of more stringent multilateral rules outweigh the costs. Yet, now as before, the US government is quite divided over how much sovereignty it is willing to cede to multilateral mechanisms. Congress has tended to ignore GATT as much as possible. This must change if the current multilateral system is to be maintained and strengthened. If some other approach should come to prevail, it is likely that it will have emanated from chaos as the US government lacks the unity necessary to generate a viable alternative to the system it has created over the last four decades.

13.1 REGIONALISM

The threat of regional accords and other forms of 'plurilateralism' served US negotiators well in getting the Uruguay round started. However, the use of this tool would be far more dangerous than the simple threat. The multilateral system is on soft footing now and the Uruguay round could well end in effective deadlock. US negotiators rightfully argue that without progress on some of these new issues in the talks, then the old issues will remain irresolvable. The constituents of multilateral liberalisation need to be reinforced through a broadening of the benefits. Agricultural and service exporters are needed as counterweights to the more inward-looking manufacturing interests with important stakes on the table. Not one of these issues seems to have much potential for resolution on its own in bilateral or regional discussions.

Some analysts have applauded the US move to form a formal regional agreement. However the regional approach fails to achieve the large multi-state coalitions necessary to pressure the barrier-ridden countries into significant policy change. It may not even facilitate a preservation of the current *status quo* in market access if fears of other regional blocs lead to regional market-sharing arrangements. The talks on forming a Pacific Rim bloc in late 1989 ran directly into the blunt reality that too many nations are necessary to make it work and the key nations have more interest in making the multilateral system work than in forming regional free trade areas. In fact some analyses show that the gains to be had from regional free trade areas are relatively small and the effort may even detract from worldwide trade.

Thus the major issue for the trade negotiators in Geneva is how to extend and enhance the GATT trade negotiating process to fulfill the objectives of the Punta del Este declaration without disappointing political forces expecting a completion of the round in 1990. The solution may be found in revising the role of the GATT secretariat and the dispute resolution system to elevate GATT into something more akin to the originally proposed International Trade Organization (ITO). The Uruguay round should establish a long-term framework for a continuing review of trade policy and for negotiation within this new GATT. Without some such effort to solidify the legitimacy of the multilateral trading system the drift toward regionalism may turn into a headlong change, much to the detriment of world trade.

13.2　MANAGING TRADE CONFLICTS

The large US trade deficit, perceptions of unfairness in global trade practices, and concern that the Uruguay round is faltering have combined to produce a significant willingness within US public and private circles to use more forceful negotiating techniques to gain movement toward more overseas access for US goods. US tactics both in the Uruguay round and in bilateral discussions have become more brinkmanlike. For the most part these efforts are directed at the EC and Japan. Hence, although the current GATT round is more of a North–South round than ever, it is getting hung up on the fundamental issue of the agricultural practices of industrial countries. Other interindustrial-country conflicts, such as in specific sectors of manufacturing, are no longer really bilateral as steel VRAs affect major developing countries, and semiconductor market-sharing agreements and other high-technology issues will affect Third World access to the affordable technologies needed to compete in the new global economic climate. With the high price of clothing in industrial countries, production has been stimulated into luxury items. Some of the expansion in clothing imports to the US has been from the EC, leading to even greater US resistance to open markets.

In short, a wide variety of interindustrial-country conflicts are having large spillover effects on North–South trade relations. Failure to deal with these issues in a multilateral context can only lead, as has happened in the past, to partial agreements among the major industrial powers which leave out the vital interests of developing countries (as well as consumers in industrial countries).

In the pursuit of free trade during the early Reagan years, the US government chose to ignore many of these conflicts, or to respond only on the verbal/ideological level. In the meantime world economic events have pushed the US trade balance deeper into the red. Congress has begun to suggest various forms of trade management to resolve the problem. US executive branch efforts in the late 1980s were directed at mechanisms to quieten Congress. Some of these mechanisms controverted free trade principles, but in general the efforts managed to reduce the pressure from Congress. Failure to get to the roots of the international trade conflicts has left the current administration with a Congress more willing to directly manage trade.

13.3 TRADE AND DEVELOPMENT

The legacy of US trade politics in the late 1980s is that developing countries are now viewed as more of a threat to competition, and trade benefits are now tools to open Third World markets. The developmental aspect of trade with the Third World has been pushed to the back burner. In fact some US trade policies discriminate more against developing countries than against industrial countries. Those which are beneficial to the Third World are seen as 'gifts' which the US is unwilling to call permanent (since these 'concessions' are seen as harmful to the US, although they generally are beneficial).

As the US is unlikely to change its attitude and reorient its trade policy to promote unilaterally Third World development, changes to US policy will most likely come about when the US perceives similar action taking place in other industrial countries. Such action may be formally harmonised or simply coordinated, but domestic political pressures dictate that some international commitments be visible as a driving force. Without such commitments, protectionist forces will obstruct progress.

13.4 POLICY PRIORITIES

Areas for immediate action fall into two categories: the difficult and crucial, and the easy and less useful. The most important actions, such as liberalising both the trade in clothing and trade-distorting agricultural policies, or resolving the debt crisis, are also the most difficult. Although attempts to harmonise GSP systems, export credit policies and trade-related aid may be more easily accomplished, they are also less significant for Third World development.

The main cause for hope with regard to progress is the changing nature of world trade, which has made a number of unregulated issues (in an international sense) grow in importance. These issues, such as services, trade-related intellectual property rights, and trade-related investment, are gathering political weight in industrial countries. Those with interests in US–Third World trade should be able to find grounds for compromise and concession involving opening up US manufacturing and agricultural trade in return for access to global service and investment markets. Unfortunately progress on the new issues will be delayed by lack of definition and data. Meanwhile the Third World's need for employment expansion in light manufacturing and agriculture is immediate and pressing.

Updating the systemic rules is another area in need of attention. As US economic influence declines, US desire for meaningful international rules may increase as it sees its own vulnerability, or it may decrease as it looks inward for nationalistic economic solutions. The internationalist impulse is likely to be stronger and this will make the US a more willing ally of the Third World in seeking dependable multilateral trade rules. In this regard a Japan that can say 'no' may be useful, by pointing to the fact that the US should not expect unilateralism to work.

13.5   EMERGENCE OF JAPAN IN US–THIRD WORLD TRADE

Japan can be a useful ally to the Third World in opening up US markets for clothing, having been in the suppliers' camp on the MFA. Similarly the US should find numerous Third World allies in bringing about changes to Japanese agricultural policy. US and Japanese technical assistance to the Third World will be important for those middle-range developing countries with little technological capacity, while both countries can do more to promote trade with the least developed countries through coordination of credit policies. Finally, and perhaps most importantly, debt relief for the major debtors can dramatically improve trade prospects worldwide. On this, US–Japanese coordination is a must.

Although the debt crisis has weakened the pro-trade coalition in the US, the forces for liberal trade are still substantial. Conflict management and positive multilateral cooperation will be more possible if the trade imbalances incurred in the 1980s can be quickly remedied through macroeconomic and debt policy coordination in the early 1990s.

Part III

European Trade Policies towards Developing Countries

14 Structural Change and Foreign Trade in the EC

Jamuna P. Agarwal

14.1 STRUCTURAL CHANGE

Notwithstanding some important differences in detail, the general pattern of structural change appears to be largely the same in the EC as in the US or Japan. This is not very surprising in view of the interdependence of these economies resulting from international trade and mobility of resources, especially capital, across their geographic boundaries. A marked decline in the share of agriculture during the last three decades and a rise in that of services is clearly noticeable in all three regions. The portion of GDP produced by manufacturing and other industrial activities has also been declining in all three regions. This process – often called deindustrialisation – has made the greatest headway in the US.

More important particularities of EC developments emerge with respect to structural change within manufacturing. In their study commissioned by the EC Commission, Buigues and Goybet (1985) concluded that European policy focused more on preserving old declining industries than on providing an adequate environment for expanding industries. This conclusion is supported by the development of foreign trade. The EC has been able to reduce imports of goods which compete with contracting industries. This is contrary to an efficient policy which should allow liberal imports of goods produced by contracting industries so that they can be phased out (Hiemenz and Langhammer, 1988, p. 22). A similar conclusion is reached by another study (Donges and Glismann, 1987, p. 15) emphasising that the notorious deterioration in the performance of the West European countries since the early 1970s is associated with protective measures and subsidies which favour declining activities and delay the necessary process of restructuring.

Detailed data on structural change within manufacturing are presented in Table 14.1 at the three digit level of the international standard industrial classification (ISIC). The shares in value added

Table 14.1 Industrial structures in the EC, the US and Japan, 1973–4[a] and 1985–6[a] (percentages)

ISIC	EC Share in manufacturing, value added 1973–4	1985–6	EC Share in manufacturing, employment 1973–4	1985–6	US Share in manufacturing, value added 1973–4	1985–6	US Share in manufacturing, employment 1973–4	1985–6	Japan Share in manufacturing, value added 1973–4	1985–6	Japan Share in manufacturing, employment 1973–4	1985–6
Expanding industries:												
384 Transport equip.	9.27	11.01	10.52	11.63	11.59	12.85	10.54	11.07	9.33	10.47	8.53	8.65
383 Electrical mach.	8.90	9.78	10.27	10.88	8.67	11.05	9.73	11.58	10.23	15.22	12.00	16.34
352 Other chem. prod.	3.73	4.05	3.08	3.64	4.54	5.54	2.49	2.72	4.00	5.00	1.96	1.96
342 Printing, publ.	3.21	3.77	3.62	4.01	5.32	7.45	5.77	7.95	4.19	5.22	4.19	5.03
311 Food products	8.36	9.90	7.38	8.64	8.47	9.00	7.28	7.25	6.62	7.98	8.31	9.85
356 Plastic products	1.90	2.31	2.00	2.64	1.78	2.51	2.04	3.16	2.70	3.38	2.73	3.77
385 Professional goods	1.56	1.48	1.73	1.62	3.02	3.96	2.70	3.46	1.42	1.67	1.95	2.11
Total	36.94	42.31	38.60	43.05	43.40	52.36	40.56	47.18	38.51	48.95	39.68	47.70
Contracting industries:												
371 Iron and steel	7.38	5.09	5.94	4.49	5.29	2.35	4.65	2.50	8.12	5.65	4.75	3.55
351 Industrial chem.	6.45	5.99	3.57	3.73	5.13	4.33	2.43	2.26	5.12	4.22	2.35	1.75
321 Textiles	4.93	3.65	7.55	5.89	3.68	2.74	6.11	4.85	6.07	3.67	9.07	6.21
353 Petroleum refineries	3.80	4.03	0.42	0.45	1.74	1.37	0.54	0.49	1.39	1.02	0.26	0.22
322 Clothing	2.45	2.15	4.95	4.09	2.90	2.21	6.33	5.02	1.49	1.41	3.61	4.23
369 Non-metal prod.	3.19	2.98	2.79	2.73	2.22	2.02	2.20	2.02	3.75	3.07	3.53	2.94
323 Leather and prod.	0.49	0.42	0.68	0.58	0.24	0.14	0.44	0.28	0.25	0.24	0.34	0.39
324 Footwear	0.75	0.70	1.38	1.28	0.45	0.23	0.93	0.50	0.19	0.17	0.28	0.29
331 Wood products	1.71	1.29	1.98	1.88	2.11	1.62	2.82	2.63	3.27	1.70	4.70	2.83
355 Rubber products	1.44	1.30	1.69	1.52	1.52	1.08	1.53	1.15	1.25	1.24	1.31	1.34
361 Pottery, china etc.	0.65	0.61	1.04	0.82	0.17	0.13	0.26	0.19	0.45	0.39	0.72	0.68
362 Glass and products	1.07	0.92	1.18	1.03	0.93	0.79	0.96	0.80	0.93	0.96	0.67	0.61
372 Non-ferrous metals	1.53	1.34	1.53	1.40	2.00	1.16	1.61	1.38	2.32	1.25	1.49	1.10
Total	35.84	30.47	34.69	29.88	28.40	20.17	30.79	24.06	34.59	24.99	33.08	26.13

Stable or stagnating industries:												
382 Machinery, n.e.c.	10.97	11.94	11.02	11.90	11.80	11.32	11.48	11.77	11.71	12.90	11.35	12.06
381 Metal products	5.88	5.55	7.36	7.16	6.95	6.09	7.63	7.75	7.03	6.46	7.83	7.57
313 Beverages	2.87	2.68	1.58	1.54	1.43	1.67	1.03	0.96	1.57	1.31	1.08	0.69
341 Paper and prod.	2.63	2.47	2.59	2.44	3.99	4.16	3.45	3.50	3.34	2.47	2.73	2.31
332 Furniture, fixtures	1.79	1.64	2.29	2.21	1.34	1.36	2.22	2.44	1.06	0.94	1.64	1.47
314 Tobacco	1.72	1.64	0.47	0.46	0.71	1.21	0.36	0.28	0.40	0.20	0.37	0.16
390 Other industries	0.95	0.94	1.20	1.18	1.64	1.31	2.25	1.81	1.47	1.58	2.09	2.01
354 Petroleum, coal prod.	0.27	0.28	0.11	0.12	0.33	0.35	0.22	0.24	0.31	0.19	0.16	0.13
Total	27.09	27.15	26.63	27.00	28.20	27.47	28.64	28.75	26.90	26.06	27.25	26.39

Note: a. Averages of two years.

Sources: UNIDO, 1989; The World Bank, 1988; own calculations.

and employment are averages of 1973–4 and 1985–6 in order to avoid disturbances of yearly figures. Further, the 28 industries included in the table are divided into three groups. The first includes those industries which have increased their shares in manufacturing value added either in all three regions or by over 10 per cent of the initial share in at least two of the regions (expanding industries). The second group consists of industries whose shares in manufacturing value added have declined either in all three regions or by over 10 per cent of the initial share in at least two of the regions (contracting industries). The third group encompasses the rest of the industries which show no clear sign of expansion or contraction (stable or stagnating industries).

The following conclusions can be drawn from a comparison of the three regions on the basis of these data:

– Expanding industries have expanded less in the EC than in the US and Japan. Similarly – or, more precisely, consequently – contracting industries have contracted much less in the EC than in the other countries. In terms of percentage points, structural change observed in expanding and contracting industries of the EC was only one-half to two-thirds of that observed in Japan and the US.
– Labour/output ratios (the share in value added divided by the share in employment) of expanding industries as a group have increased and those of contracting industries have declined in all the regions. But the decline in the EC was much smaller than in the US and Japan. Thus the conclusion reached in other studies (for example Hiemenz and Langhammer, 1988; Donges and Glismann, 1987), namely that the EC countries have arrested the decline in productivity by protecting structurally weaker industries, also appears to hold (given the continuation of such policies) on the basis of this more up-to-date and broader set of data.
– Whereas the shares of stable or stagnating industries in manufacturing value added and employment were nearly equal in all the regions (between 26 per cent and 29 per cent), they differed remarkably with regard to expanding and contracting industries. In 1985–6 only a little more than two-fifths of manufacturing value added and employment could be attributed to expanding industries in the EC. In the US and Japan the corresponding shares were about 50 per cent. Thus the scope for structural adjustment within the manufacturing sector of the EC appears to be considerable.
– Structural changes of the past appear to be employment-neutral in

Table 14.2   Growth of manufacturing value added and employment in the
EC, the US and Japan, 1973–4 and 1985–6 (per cent per annum)

	Value added[a]			Employment		
	EC	US	Japan	EC	US	Japan
ISIC 3 Manufacturing total	6.48	8.18	10.94	–2.10	–0.75	–0.27
Expanding industries[b]	7.81	10.04	13.39	–1.13	0.62	1.41
Contracting industries[b]	4.93	4.87	7.68	–3.42	–2.95	–2.39
Stable or stagnating industries[b]	6.51	7.92	10.66	–1.98	–0.72	–0.56

Notes: a. In current $US.
         b. For definition see Table 14.1.

Source: UNIDO, 1989; The World Bank, 1988.

the sense that an increase (decrease) of the shares in value added
had been accompanied by an increase (decrease) of the shares in
manufacturing employment. Employment neutrality of structural
change within the industrial sector is not to be confused with the
effect of technological progress on employment. Total manufacturing value added has increased in all the regions, although manufacturing employment declined in the period under observation. A
comparison of growth rates at a disaggregated level shows that in
expanding industries the US and Japan were more than able to
compensate for jobs lost as a result of technological progress
through higher production while the EC had a negative rate of
growth in employment in these industries (Table 14.2).

14.2   FOREIGN TRADE

The EC has experienced almost no trade disequilibrium over the last
three decades. Its import/export ratio has oscillated around 100 per
cent. The more noticeable point about the EC is that its trade regime
has so far resulted in trade diversion. Its member countries now
export more to each other than they did a decade earlier. The share
of trade within the EC has increased in total world exports as well as
in their exports to the rest of the world (UNCTAD, 1989). In view of
this development it is not surprising that EC trading partners are
looking to the planned complete liberalisation of internal trade with
some anxiety, in spite of the EC's repeated assurances that it will

keep open its doors to foreign goods and services (see Chapter 19).

Another noticeable feature is that the share of food items in EC imports – as opposed to its exports – dropped (UNCTAD, 1989, Tables 4.1 and 4.2). This is a direct result of the EC's agricultural policy, which on the one hand has been protecting the farmers of its member countries against external competition, whilst on the other hand it has been promoting the export of the EC's surplus production of food through substantial subsidies. Such export policies have tended to depress the world price level to the disadvantage of exports of developing countries (see Chapter 16).

Within the manufacturing sector, the findings of recent studies (Buigues and Goybet, 1985; Donges, Schmidt et al., 1988; Hiemenz and Langhammer, 1988) that EC trade policies were oriented more towards preserving sunset industries than towards the promotion of structural change are supported by Table 14.3. Import (export) specialisation indices show that imports to the EC have fallen in industries facing weak to moderate demand (sunset industries) in relation to imports of these goods to all the OECD countries, as well as in relation to total manufacturing imports to the EC and OECD. This is contrary to the expectation that the EC, as a highly developed region, would increase import and decrease export of these items in conformity with its comparative advantages. In contrast to this, the EC has lost relative market shares in both domestic and foreign markets in the case of high-demand and technology-intensive (sunrise) industries. This shows that these industries have been neglected by EC policymakers, and pressure for more support (that is, subsidies) is bound to increase in the future.

With regard to imports from developing countries and their impact on structural adjustment, an analysis of trade data shows that the Third World as a group has in fact succeeded in penetrating the markets of the EC and other industrialised countries in quite a number of agricultural and manufactured products, as measured by increasing import shares (Table 14.4). In the case of manufactured products, developing countries supplied about one-third of total imports to North America and Japan while their share in manufactured imports only amounted to a little over one-fifth in the EC. Regarding the EC more specifically, developing countries have made progress with respect to their shares in extra-EC imports, but many of the shares for traditional and for more advanced products – such as machinery and other manufactures – were still considerably lower than in North America. This relatively poor performance in EC

Table 14.3 Trade specialisation of manufacturing industries of the EC, 1972–83

	Import[a] specialisation	Change[b] 1972–83	Export[a] specialisation	Change[b] 1972–83	Technology content
Industries facing weak demand:	12.7	1.13	−0.04	1.11	+0.17
Miscellaneous products	1.38	−0.30	1.23	+0.18	n.a.
Textiles, leather, clothing	1.10	+0.16	1.06	+0.13	low
Steel, metal ores	1.12	−0.13	0.95	+0.10	low
Metal goods	0.82	+0.17	1.32	+0.19	low
Construction materials, non-metallic minerals	0.93	+0.05	1.21	+0.24	low
Industries facing moderate demand:	0.88	−0.04	0.97	−0.03	.
Rubber and plastics	0.68	+0.08	0.97	−0.11	medium
Transport equipment	0.61	+0.20	0.84	−0.08	medium/high
Paper, pulp, packing, printing	1.49	−0.13	0.50	+0.04	low
Food, beverages and tobacco	1.03	−0.42	1.00	+0.10	low
Industrial machinery	0.92	+0.16	1.25	−0.05	medium
Industries facing high demand:	1.01	+0.13	0.96	−0.11	.
Electrical equipment, electronics	1.10	+0.24	0.89	−0.08	high
Information technology, automated office equipment, precision instruments	1.34	+0.23	0.64	−0.19	high
Chemicals	0.83	−0.02	1.16	−0.02	high

Notes: a. Import (export) specialisation is defined as $(T_{i,e}: T_{i,o}): \left(\sum_i T_{i,e} : \sum_i T_{i,o}\right)$, whereby T = imports (exports) of industry i, e = EC of 10 member countries and o = OECD.
b. Difference in import (export) specialisation between 1972 and 1983.

Source: Hiemenz and Langhammer, 1988, Tables 1 and 3.

Table 14.4 Share of developing countries in imports of the EC, the US and Japan, 1974–75[a] and 1985–86[a] (percentages)

	EC[b]		US/Canada		Japan	
	1974–5	1985–6	1974–5	1985–6	1974–5	1985–6
Primary products	72.09	57.14	89.87	75.76	63.65	64.99
Agriculture	44.86	54.90	79.95	78.86	32.71	38.59
Coal, petroleum, natural gas	92.18	62.92	97.78	81.89	82.97	81.40
Other mining and quarrying	32.39	35.08	54.31	39.78	46.61	45.94
Manufacturing	19.79	22.65	32.95	33.11	31.49	31.09
Food, beverages and tobacco	42.03	48.33	45.79	35.09	46.97	28.81
Textiles	36.60	37.30	39.64	41.41	41.61	39.66
Clothing	47.73	61.23	62.77	74.31	63.47	57.80
Wood products, paper & printing	6.29	11.58	42.74	43.93	18.06	21.67
Rubber	4.31	18.14	5.42	29.80	21.71	13.66
Chemicals	18.20	15.87	23.27	19.05	11.50	16.21
Petroleum and coal products	34.15	43.25	87.01	74.27	82.68	75.46
Non-metallic mineral products	5.20	14.78	12.81	25.76	22.78	40.85
Ferrous & non-ferrous metals	29.29	24.47	18.12	26.04	34.09	42.75
Transport equipment	3.08	7.46	2.74	6.13	2.17	3.77
Machinery and other manufactured goods	7.16	13.65	24.05	31.83	12.90	19.17

Notes: a. Average of two years.
           b. Shares in extra-EC imports.

Source: UNCTAD, 1981 Supplement and 1989, Table 7.1.; own calculations.

import markets seems to reflect retarded structural adjustment and protection for the EC's sunset industries.

What matters with respect to the competitive position of developing countries in EC markets, however, are not import market shares but shares in apparent consumption. Table 14.5 shows that manufactured imports from developing countries grew faster than domestic consumption in the EC and North America in the 1974–5 to 1985–6 period. The developing countries' market shares increased particularly in industries facing low demand growth, such as the EC's sunset industries. The most remarkable change in market penetration in all three regions occurred in clothing, and by 1985–6 the developing countries had captured a sizable share of the domestic markets for clothing in both the EC and North America. On average however, the developing countries' share in the consumption of manufactures had remained fairly low, at around 3 per cent in the EC and North America and less than 1.5 per cent in Japan. Apart from the MFA products – textiles and clothing – the EC market shares held by developing countries significantly exceeded the 2 per cent mark only in machinery and other manufactured goods. From this observation it seems safe to conclude that imports from developing countries may have enhanced structural change in the EC, but certainly could not be considered as having had a disruptive effect on domestic suppliers.

A similar result was presented in a study by Schumacher (1981) for the German Government. He estimated the effect on employment of imports by the EC-6 (West Germany, France, Italy, the UK, the Netherlands and Belgium) on the basis of data for 1970 and 1977 and found the following:

- The decrease in employment in the manufacturing sector resulting from imports from developing countries ranged between 0.9 per cent (Italy) and 3.7 per cent (the Netherlands). This was only a small portion of the total loss of employment associated with imports from all sources.
- The loss of jobs attributable to technological changes was considerably higher than that related to imports from the Third World.
- The jobs created through exports to developing countries outnumbered the jobs lost through imports from them by a factor of 1.5 (the Netherlands) to 6.44 (Italy). For West Germany it was 2.3.
- In the textile, clothing and leather industries, for which calculations were done separately, unemployment resulting from imports from developing countries was relatively higher than for the manu-

Table 14.5 · Share of DCs in apparent consumption of the EC, US/Canada and Japan, 1974–5 and 1985–6[a] (percentages)

	EC		US/Canada		Japan	
	1974–5	1985–6	1974–5	1985–6	1974–5	1985–6
Food, beverages and tobacco	2.40	2.02	1.36	1.13	2.71	1.04
Textiles	2.84	4.98	1.74	3.23	1.71	2.13
Clothing	7.67	17.88	7.40	24.56	7.02	8.86
Wood products, paper and printing	0.79	1.58	0.53	1.23	0.69	0.78
Rubber	0.16	1.48	0.23	2.64	0.33	0.28
Chemicals	1.50	1.63	0.91	1.12	0.65	1.06
Petroleum and coal products	2.10	4.84	7.30	5.63	5.73	7.75
Non-metallic mineral products	0.13	0.56	0.36	1.70	0.18	0.58
Ferrous and non-ferrous metals	3.24	1.86	1.48	1.56	1.94	1.65
Transport equipment	0.17	0.88	0.16	0.80	0.05	0.09
Machinery and other manufactured goods	0.74	3.29	1.58	6.21	0.56	0.88
Total manufactures	1.71	2.84	1.72	3.42	1.48	1.43

Note: a. Two-year averages.

Source: UNCTAD, 1981 Supplement and 1988.

facturing sector as a whole. The net balance of employment attributable to imports and exports was negative except in Belgium and Italy. But even in these industries, technological unemployment turned out to be much higher than that accounted for by imports from developing countries.

Apprehension about the negative impact of imports from developing countries during the 1970s has to be viewed in the light of rising unemployment, oil crises, adverse trade balances, and the slowing down of growth at that time in most developed economies. Since the early 1980s some of these problems have disappeared. But the measures introduced against the imports from developing countries not only still prevail (due to institutional inflexibility), but – as will be shown – seem even to have increased (for example due to pressure from interest groups. Subsidies and trade protectionism give rise to vested interests which focus on safeguarding their rent-seeking activities. Once they have been created it is difficult to remove them, even though more liberal trade policies would be welfare-increasing both for the EC and suppliers in developing countries. The low share in apparent consumption in the EC compared to the US indicates considerable scope for growth in imports from developing countries if import barriers were to be removed.

15 EC Protectionism against Developing Countries – General Tariff and Non-tariff Trade Barriers

Ulrich Hiemenz

15.1 THE COMPOSITION OF EC TRADE POLICIES

At present the EC is a customs union with a common external tariff, a common agricultural policy (CAP) and some jointly administered non-tariff trade barriers. Other non-tariff trade barriers have remained the responsibility of member governments, but these are – at least according to the rules – only implemented with the consent of the Brussels administration. Successive rounds of multilateral trade negotiations have resulted in substantial reductions in the level of the common external tariff. The remaining, on average rather low, tariff rates either do not apply to exports from developing countries or apply only beyond a certain volume of imports (tariff quota) according to the preferences granted to developing countries under the Generalised System of Preferences (GSP). This picture changes however when the CAP is taken into consideration. Variable levies on certain agricultural products may amount to rates beyond 100 per cent depending on the nature of EC interventions, the chosen CAP price level, and world market prices (see Chapter 16).

The brunt of protectionist measures against imports from developing countries applied by the EC has shifted from tariff to non-tariff barriers. The catalogue of non-tariff devices employed to discourage imports into the EC is rather long, and it is virtually impossible to capture all the details due to the complexity of many of the measures and a lack of sufficient transparency. Broadly speaking, important non-tariff barriers consist of voluntary export restraints (VERs), licensing and quotas, EC surveillance, and antidumping procedures. Other measures, such as technical regulations and standards, public procurement or minimum prices, either barely apply to developing countries or cannot be assessed in terms of their protectionist impact. Likewise public and private distortions of competition such as subsidies, cartels and private VERs had to be excluded from this study. They are likely to constitute substitutes for border protection in agriculture, shipbuilding and the steel industry as well as in textiles and clothing, but a comprehensive analysis of these distortions would require a separate study since their importance differs greatly from country to country.

The following sections provide a general overview of the measures applied, an assessment of their quantitative effects and an evaluation of their relevance for exporters in developing countries. Some of the more complex policy instruments, such as the GSP, the CAP and the Multi-Fibre Arrangement (MFA) will be analysed in detail in separate chapters.

15.2 THE COMMON EXTERNAL TARIFF

The harmonisation of the national tariffs of EC member countries to a common external tariff and the removal of internal tariff barriers were accomplished during 1968, roughly a year ahead of the original schedule. However differences still remain in the legal provisions concerning customs administration and tariff implementation (Dicke et al., 1987, p. 24). Such differences among EC member countries can be and have actually been used as unilateral protective devices by individual countries. A famous case in point was the French decision of October 1982 to restrict the customs handling of Japanese video recorders solely to the customs office of the city of Poitiers, which is located far away from harbours and airports.

Reduction of the common external tariff had already started prior to 1968. The EC participated in the 1961–3 Dillon round which resulted in average tariff cuts of 7–8 per cent, and in the 1964–7 Kennedy round which lowered tariffs by 35–40 per cent on average. Following the completion of the customs union in 1968 the EC participated in the Tokyo round (1973–9), during which it was agreed that tariffs would be reduced by one-third in all contracting countries by 1988. The EC actually beat this time-schedule by implementing the new common tariff in 1985 (AB1, no. L320, 10.12.1984). This meant, among other things, lower tariffs for about 250 tariff categories of particular importance to exports from developing countries. On average nominal post-Tokyo MFN tariffs are fairly low and do not differ very much between the EC and other major industrialised countries (Laird and Yeats, 1987, Table 13.3). Using imports as weights, the nominal average EC MFN tariff amounts to less than 5 per cent, which has to be compared to an average rate of 17–20 per cent when the EEC was founded in 1957 (Pelkmans, 1987, p. 19). For developing countries receiving preferences under the GSP, the nominal average tariffs are negligible not only in the EC, but also in Japan and the US. However post-Tokyo tariff rates still differ considerably between product categories. More specifically, nominal tariff rates – even those including GSP treatment – have remained relatively high in product categories in which developing countries have become major exporters. Textiles, clothing and other labour-intensive products belong to the higher tariff brackets in all the major industrialised countries.

It is unlikely, though, that these nominal tariff rates present a decisive impediment to developing countries. First, nominal tariffs are relatively high in product categories which are heavily regulated by non-tariff trade barriers such as the MFA. For these products market access is determined by quotas rather than by tariffs. And secondly, nominal tariffs are an unreliable measure of protection since they merely indicate the margin for domestic price increases. The actual discrimination against foreign suppliers is measured by effective rates of tariff protection, that is the tax on the value added by exporters in third countries inherent in the tariff schedule. Effective rates are higher than nominal rates when tariffs on final products exceed those on intermediate goods (so-called tariff escalation). Estimates of effective tariff protection for selected product categories undertaken by the World Bank confirm the detrimental effects of tariff escalation in the EC as well as in Japan and the US (Table 15.1). Effective rates are considerably higher than nominal rates for many products. They range up to eight times the nominal rate of protection for low value added products such as vegetable oils, and effective tariffs of 30 per cent or more are frequent. In particular processed food is highly protected both in the EC and Japan.

Summarising the effect of the Tokyo round, the estimates presented in Table 15.1 clearly demonstrate that effective tariff protection was reduced but by no means eliminated. Tariff cuts have been low or non-existent for many final goods of which developing countries are major suppliers. Higher tariff cuts for intermediate inputs than for final goods have in some cases even increased the effective

Table 15.1 Post-Tokyo nominal and effective rates of protection for selected manufactured products the EC, Japan and the US (percentages)

Product	EC		Japan		US	
	Nominal	*Effective*	*Nominal*	*Effective*	*Nominal*	*Effective*
Processed meat products	17.9	51.7	22.5	59.6	2.3	4.4
Preserved sea food	12.4	26.5	10.7	23.2	1.1	2.5
Preserved fruits	16.6	40.8	21.8	21.6	20.3	72.5
Processed vegetables	15.1	37.9	17.5	40.2	11.0	20.2
Coffee extracts	13.8	45.5	17.4	76.6	0.0	0.0
Vegetable oils	6.1	50.6	6.2	49.6	0.7	-1.5
Chocolate	0.1	n.a.	24.3	82.6	0.1	0.1
Wood manufactures	4.2	9.2	1.2	1.3	4.7	10.3
Paper and cardboard	2.3	5.5	5.7	13.7	0.3	0.7
Articles of paper	6.0	12.6	3.6	0.7	3.8	8.7
Rubber manufactures	3.0	4.5	3.8	1.1	3.9	-0.4
Cotton yarn	2.3	7.6	3.8	13.7	8.7	18.3
Wool yarn	1.4	1.1	3.9	14.0	12.9	18.1
Jute yarn	2.0	7.2	5.5	19.8	1.3	4.7
Cotton fibres	5.6	11.8	5.9	10.0	10.4	13.5
Wool fabrics	2.7	5.1	11.0	25.3	37.3	85.8
Jute fabrics	4.8	10.0	5.4	5.3	0.0	n.a.
Leather	2.4	6.0	8.5	21.2	3.7	8.1
Leather manufactures	5.5	9.9	12.4	18.6	9.2	17.5

Source: Yeats, 1987, Tables 15.2 and 15.4.

protection of final products in the EC and the US (Göbel et al., 1988, pp. 111 ff). These findings suggest that the EC and other developed countries did not fully honour their Tokyo round commitment to make provisions for a different and more favourable treatment of developing countries.

As far as the EC is concerned the Tokyo round revealed two important shortcomings in the common trade policy (Dicke et al., 1987, pp. 25f). First, tariff concessions in multilateral trade negotiations are the result of tedious bargaining processes among EC member countries. They reflect the smallest common denominator and are therefore much less liberal than relatively open economies such as Germany would be prepared to offer on its own. Secondly, agreement among EC member countries cannot always be reached, and then the EC as a whole is in no position to negotiate at all. In the Tokyo round, the EC was able to support a reduction in tariffs for manufactures, but could not agree to a dismantling of NTBs because of internal dissent over the issue. France in particular demanded the continued application of selective measures. This has resulted in considerable disadvantages for many developing countries because the problems associated with NTBs are often so closely linked with tariffs that they could not be dealt with independently in negotiations. In some sectors (such as agriculture and textiles) many tariff-line items are covered jointly by import duties and hard-core non-tariff restraints such as variable levies, quotas or VERs. In these cases the expected trade expansion resulting from tariff liberalisation will probably not be realised unless some complementary agreement were to be negotiated to relax non-tariff measures.

15.3   NON-TARIFF TRADE BARRIERS

15.3.1   An overview

Empirically assessing non-tariff trade barriers is always fraught with difficulties. From an analytical point of view it would be necessary to estimate the price and quantity effects of NTBs and to compare them to tariff barriers. Such an approach is hardly feasible in the case of the EC. The multitude of NTBs applied, which lack transparency concerning their actual implementation ('grey area measures'), and the selectivity by country and product do not allow meaningful estimates to be arrived at (Deardorff and Stern, 1985). The only avenue open to research to date is an assessment of the frequency distributions of NTBs which measure the share of affected imports in total imports. This 'inventory' method is hardly even the second-best solution though. The share of imports affected by NTBs does not reveal anything about the protective impact of these measures and may even be misleading when prohibitive NTBs reduce imports to almost zero.

Nonetheless the following analysis has to be based on a cautious interpretation of frequency distributions. NTBs applied by the EC against imports from developing countries may be summarised under five major categories: VERs, quotas, minimum or threshold prices, surveillance, and excessive anti-dumping measures. The last of these is utilised purely at the EC level while all other NTBs can be found both at the EC and at the national level. Furthermore it is important to note that there are several ways different instruments (including tariffs) can cumulate in specific product markets. For these reasons an isolated evaluation of just one instrument or to focus on just one level of government, may seriously distort the conclusions.

Table 15.2 provides a comparison of the impact of NTBs (excluding anti-dumping measures) applied in the US, the EC and Germany in 1983. This overview understates current non-tariff protection since NTBs have been used increasingly in recent years. With the above caveats in mind, import shares suggest a higher degree of non-tariff protection against imports from developing countries in the EC than in the US. Close to 30 per cent of manufactured imports and almost 27 per cent of agricultural imports from developing countries were affected by NTBs in the EC while the respective shares for the US amounted to 19 per cent and 25 per cent.

Concerning individual measures, the EC applied more quantitative restrictions on manufactured imports from developing countries than did the US. A similar pattern emerges for surveillance measures and – with respect to agricultural products – minimum prices. The US seems to have utilised more quantitative restrictions in the case of agricultural imports from developing countries than did the EC, but this result is questionable given the almost prohibitive barriers to entry erected within the framework of the CAP. Chapter 16 will provide a more detailed insight into the protectionist impact of this very complex system of regulations. Finally, Germany's manufactured imports from developing countries are hampered by far fewer quantitative restrictions and less surveillance than occurs in Belgium, France and the UK, as the respective shares for the EC and Germany indicate.

Table 15.2   Imports affected by NTBs in the US, the EC and Germany, 1983 (percentage of total)

	US		EC		Germany	
	ICs	DCs	ICs	DCs	ICs	DCs
Quantitative restrictions:						
Agricult. prod.	8.7	18.1	21.3	14.1	12.2	7.4
manufactures	0.4	0.1	1.9	10.7	0.1	2.1
VERs:						
Agricult. prod.	0.0	0.0	0.0	0.0	0.0	0.0
manufactures	11.1	13.0	0.1	17.0	0.0	25.8
Minimum prices:						
Agricult. prod.	4.1	15.2	27.2	13.4	18.7	9.9
manufactures	0.0	0.5	2.1	0.9	2.9	1.0
Surveillance:						
Agricult. prod.	13.0	3.3	2.2	2.7	0.1	1.0
manufactures	5.6	5.6	12.9	14.7	11.0	1.8
NTBs, total:[a]						
Agricult. prod.	23.5	25.1	47.7	26.9	28.5	16.6
manufactures	16.5	18.6	15.2	29.9	13.3	30.2

Note: a. Shares do not add up to total because of cumulation of NTBs in certain markets.

Source: Nogués et al., 1985, Tables 3c, 5c, 6c.

Within the manufacturing sector there is a clear-cut concentration of NTBs on a few import items: textiles and clothing, iron and steel, and automobiles (Nogués et al., 1985). NTBs in the first product category reflect the protectionist impact of the MFA which restricts developing countries' exports of textiles and clothing in a very selective way. Protectionism in the automobile sector consists largely of quantitative restrictions against Japanese imports. To assess the importance of NTBs for specific developing countries, the individual measures and their implementation have to be scrutinised separately.

15.3.2   Voluntary export restraints

VERs have become a popular and convenient method of extending protection to special interest groups without formally violating GATT rules. For the EC, by far the most important single VER consists of the MFA negotiated with 23 countries (as well as close substitutes of the MFA with Mediterranean countries and Taiwan).

In principal the MFA restricts the importation of textiles and clothing into the EC and provides quota rents to both importers in the EC and exporters in developing countries. The successive arrangements have been negotiated at the EC level by the commission for the EC as a whole, but in fact EC quotas have been subdivided in an *ex ante* manner into national quotas for so-called very sensitive and, sometimes, sensitive products. National quotas have then been safeguarded by restricting intra-EC trade by exploiting the provisions of Article 115 of the EEC Treaty. Thus the MFA resembles a quota system rather than a VER. It is extremely selective and discriminatory, and essentially restricts the market access of potent suppliers – especially those from Asia – while providing liberal quotas for least developed countries, which have only a limited capacity to export. Because of the complexity of this arrangement its protectionist content will be evaluated separately in Chapter 18.

The MFA is however only the most visible of a large number of VERs applying to different products, different time periods and different countries of origin. There is no transparency as to the number of national or EC VERs or the products and countries affected as many are privately arranged between importers and producers. The literature has occasionally cited specific cases, but a solid survey of these measures is not available and would be rather difficult and very time-consuming to collect. The only piece of evidence that can be readily referred to is an illustrative list of VERs for non-MFA products, mostly applied at the level of EC member countries, which was presented by Pelkmans (1987) and is reproduced in Table 15.3. The countries affected are mostly Asian developing countries and newly industrialised countries, and the products concerned typically belong to the labour-intensive category in which developing countries and not EC member countries should possess comparative advantage. The last column shows the VERs became popular in the late 1970s and multiplied during the economic recession in the early 1980s. Besides the EC-wide VERs, those negotiated by France, Italy and the UK were most frequent. However it is not clear whether all VERs have actually been enforced, and therefore Table 15.3 should be interpreted with caution.

15.3.3 Quotas

In addition to MFA-based quotas EC member countries maintain a number of so-called unilateral quotas which have been only partly incorporated into EC procedures. Transparency with respect to these

Table 15.3   Illustrative list of VERs applied to EC imports from developing countries

Export country	Import country	Product	First year
Brazil	EC	Footwear	1981
	EC	Steel	1978
S. Korea	Benelux	Simple cutlery	n.a.
	Denmark	Simple cutlery	n.a.
	West Germany	Simple cutlery	n.a.
	France	Non-rubber footwear	1981
	UK	Radio, TV sets (black and white), communications equipment	1980
		Simple cutlery	n.a.
		Footwear (rubber)	1980
		Non-rubber footwear	1978
	EC	Steel	1978
India	EC	Shirts and blouses, dresses	n.a.
Pakistan	Italy	Jute sacks and bags	n.a.
	Italy	Sunblinds and camping goods	n.a.
Thailand	EC	Tapioca	1981
Chile	EC	Sheep and goatmeat	n.a.
Taiwan	UK	Footwear (rubber)	1980
	France	Non-rubber footwear	1981
	UK	Non-rubber footwear	1978
	UK	Radio, black/white TV sets, communications equipment	1980

Source: Pelkmans, 1987, Table 2.2.

quotas leaves much to be desired. In 1986 a long list of quotas at a six-digit NIMEXE level of product disaggregation was published for the EC-12. It is not however clear whether these quotas are actually enforced nor which imports are restricted since quotas often apply to a higher than six-digit NIMEXE-level of disaggregation. To relate these regulations to actual trade flows would be a Herculean task. For these and some other more technical reasons (for details, see Pelkmans, 1987, pp. 25–6) an assessment of the protective impact of quotas and the damage done to developing countries' exports is not feasible.

The available information is summarised in Table 15.4, which presents the number of quotas contained in the 1986 list by four-digit tariff heading of the Brussels Tariff Nomenclature (BTN). Judged by these numbers, France and Italy again emerge as more protectionist

Table 15.4   EEC member states' quotas on third country imports
(non-MFA),[a] 1986

EC Member State	Number of 4-digit tariff headings[a]
Benelux	6
Denmark	7
France	35
Greece	6
Germany	1
Ireland	5
Italy	30
Spain	113
Portugal	44
UK	–

Note: a. Including quotas applied at a more disaggregated NIMEXE-level.

Source: AB1, no. C213, 25.8.1986.

than other older EC member countries. The new entrants to the EC,
Spain and Portugal, still maintain many more quotas than the older
members, but this picture may change when they become integrated
fully into the EC. There is a general tendency towards dismantling
unilateral quotas in preparation for the EC single market. The first
set of six-digit product categories to be freed from quota was recently
agreed upon (AB1, No. L230/6, 8.8.1989).

15.3.4   Surveillance

Surveillance of the imports coming into the EC or into individual EC
member countries is a very sophisticated and difficult to understand
protectionist device. At first glance the statistical monitoring of
selected imports from selected countries should not in anyway restrict
the flow of trade. Surveillance does however create uncertainty
among exporters in that increased imports may trigger protectionist
actions by the EC or by its individual member countries. Under the
MFA such fears are well founded since surveillance is a precondition
for resorting to certain safeguard options, such as the establishment
of national quotas within the EC according to Article 115 of the EEC
Treaty. For non-MFA products surveillance may be a first step towards negotiating a bilateral VER or the introduction of national
quotas.

Table 15.5   EC member state surveillance of non-MFA trade flows, 1985
(number of six-digit NIMEXE products)

EC country	Number of products affected	Eastern Europe	East Asian NICs	China	Other DCs
Benelux	88	62	–	25	5
France	102	22	54	17	3
Ireland	39	39	20	–	–
Italy	117	31	–	14	–
UK	48	6	–	48	–

Source: Pelkmans, 1987, Table 2.5.

Permission for surveillance has to be granted by the Commission. Growing concern about its own competence in trade policies led the Commission to be slightly more restrictive in the 1980s than it was in the 1970s (Pelkmans, 1987, p. 27). Nonetheless surveillance is almost total for the sensitive and most sensitive products of the MFA in the Benelux countries, France, Italy and the UK. The notable exceptions are Denmark, which does not apply any surveillance, and Germany and Greece, who apply relatively little surveillance. This uneven behaviour by individual EC member countries has fuelled the implementation of national quotas within the EC under Article 115 (for details, see Chapter 18.3). Among the exporting countries affected, East Asian newly industrialised countries, China and ASEAN countries figure most prominently (together with Eastern European countries; see Pelkmans, 1987, Table 2.4).

In the 1980s surveillance was also applied to an increasing number of non-MFA products, which in turn resulted in additional Article 115 quotas for those products (Chapter 18.3). Table 15.5 provides an idea of the scope of this practice in 1985. As with the MFA products, surveillance was not carried out in Denmark, Germany and Greece. The countries most affected again include the Asian newly industrialised countries, China and Eastern Europe (and Japan, which is not shown in the table). There is a wide range of products covered by national surveillance – traditional labour-intensive goods such as footwear are included alongside more sophisticated electronic products. Since 1985 the number of products under surveillance has increased, as a more recent list of products under surveillance indicates (AB1, no. C213/45, 25.8.1986). Some countries, such as France and the UK, seem to have replaced unilateral quotas with surveillance in order to continue to control the flow of imports from non-member countries.

15.3.5 Anti-dumping

Anti dumping procedures – one of the older NTB measures – have again come into fashion. Originally dumping simply referred to cases of price discrimination between countries and markets, but had nothing to do with imports being priced lower than their domestic substitutes. This distinction may disappear and anti-dumping measures may turn into protectionist devices depending on how the 'normal value' of a product is determined. If the domestic price in developing countries is chosen as the reference price for the valuation of exports, developing countries appear to be 'dumping' their products on those world markets which grant export subsidies in order to offset the negative effects of import protection on export supply. Such countries could clearly be seem to be discriminated against if their exports were subjected to countervailing duties or other defensive measures.

The EC is a contracting party to the GATT anti-dumping code, whose procedures focus on the 'normal value' of a product and a test of the 'injury' caused by dumping margins (that is the difference between import price and 'normal value'). On both counts the EC is frequently accused of hidden protectionism, although the relevance of this accusation can hardly be substantiated empirically. Anti-dumping cases are usually initiated by companies – through their representative bodies and via the EC authorities – against individual private firms and are usually settled by applying pressure on these firms to raise their prices (the so-called 'price undertakings'), rather than by imposing anti-dumping duties (Göbel et al., 1988, pp. 115–18; Messerlin, 1989, pp. 568–70). To detect protectionist activity would require very detailed case studies of which only one is so far available. Messerlin (1989) has shown for 1980–5 that the EC regulations had a strong protectionist bent. Anti-dumping measures reduced imported quantities by as much as 40 per cent, and anti-dumping duties were rather severe when they were imposed.

The uneven distribution of bargaining power between the EC authorities and individual firms from developing countries, as well as the increasing number of cases initiated against suppliers from developing countries since 1982 (Davenport and Page, 1989, Table 16),

Table 15.6   Anti-dumping investigations,[a] 1980–6

Stage of procedure	Countries affected[b]				DCs in percentage of total
	ICs	DCs	NMEs	Total	
EC:					
Initiated	83	63	134	280	22.5
Confirmed	71	34	108	213	16.7
Negated	26	19	29	74	25.6
Pending	11	15	21	47	31.9
US:					
Initiated	180	137	33	350	39.1
Confirmed	98	78	19	195	40.0
Negated	85	45	7	137	32.8
Pending	17	16	6	39	41.0
Total:[a]					
Initiated	693	385	210	1 288	29.9
Confirmed	397	220	158	775	28.4
Negated	308	125	44	477	26.2
Pending	56	50	36	142	35.2

a. All cases reported to GATT.
b. Includes action taken against exporters from industrialised countries
   (ICs), developing countries (DCs) and non-market economies (NMEs).

Source: Finger and Olechowski, 1987, Table A8.3.

provide further indication that anti-dumping procedures have at least partly become a protectionist device. Table 15.6 provides an overview of these procedures during the 1980–6 period. A comparison of the US and the EC shows considerable differences in the major targets of anti-dumping cases. The EC has focused much more on socialist countries than on developing ones, which were much more frequently accused of dumping by the US. This difference is most striking with respect to the developing countries' share in confirmed cases. The evidence leads to the conclusion that the EC has relied much less on anti-dumping procedures to protect domestic markets than not only the US, but also such countries as Australia and Canada, which are included in the total. Japan has not used this device at all. It might be added however, that in the years 1987 and 1988 the thrust of EC action on cases of dumping shifted dramatically to Japan and developing countries in Asia (Davenport and Page, 1989, Table 16).

15.4 TRENDS AND PERSPECTIVES

Before specific measures with particular relevance to developing countries (CAP, GSP and related treaties, and the MFA) are analysed in greater detail in subsequent chapters, it may be useful to draw a few conclusions from the evaluation presented so far. In the 1980s EC trade policies clearly shifted away from tariff barriers towards non-tariff barriers and from common policymaking towards policy-making at a more national level. Both changes have contributed to an increase in the complexity of trade policies and to reduced transparency with respect to the impact of these policies. Despite some concessions in the GSP, and vis-à-vis Mediterranean and ACP countries, there seems to have been an increase in the overall level of protectionism applied by the EC against developing countries. This new wave of protectionism however does not hurt all developing countries alike. Protectionist measures have become more selective and discriminatory regarding individual products and their countries of origin (for a similar conclusion, see Wolf, 1987). Import barriers have focused on newly industrialised countries in general and on Asian newly industrialised countries in particular, but also on some second-generation exporters following their emergence as competitive suppliers of certain products on EC markets. Even more disturbing is the recent tendency to aim trade restriction at individual firms rather than at countries, as was observed in the case of anti-dumping measures. This threat against firms may be particularly discouraging for new entrants into the international division of labour and may hamper export-oriented economic development in middle-income developing countries.

The changing composition of trade restrictions has rendered trade liberalisation more difficult. The manifold 'grey area' measures (surveillance, unenforced quotas, anti-dumping procedures) have reduced the visibility of protectionism and contributed to greater uncertainty among exporters from developing countries with respect to their future access to EC markets. The observation that special interest groups demanding trade protection are well entrenched in EC member countries (Hiemenz and Langhammer, 1988) does not leave much room for optimism concerning the outcome of ongoing or future trade negotiations. Prospects are further clouded by the question of how the common internal market of the EC envisaged for 1992 may affect trade policies vis-à-vis non-member countries. All these problems will be addressed in some detail in subsequent chapters.

16 EC Common Agricultural Policies and their Impact on the Exports of Developing Countries

Jörg-Volker Schrader

16.1 SYSTEMS AND EXCEPTIONS

As well as by supply and demand, current EC trade in agricultural products is determined by classical trade policy instruments such as tariffs and quotas, and by numerous internal instruments which influence consumption, production and storage. First there is the Common Agricultural Policy (CAP) covering the vast majority of products grown within the EC. The CAP encompasses different market intervention systems depending on the product, and in addition there are numerous exceptions to trade regulations – often for single products and countries. Secondly, a broad group of commodities not included in the CAP are tropical fruits and beverages, spices, and agricultural raw materials for industrial use. For these products GATT regulations and the different preference systems for developing countries are applicable. Thirdly, a group of commodities in between these two basic categories are grain substitutes such as oilseeds, oilcakes, grain by-products (such as bran, corn gluten feed, maize germ, oilcake), citrus pulp, and other protein feed stuff for which trade follows GATT rules and is relatively liberal while EC production of close substitutes or even the same products (some oilseeds) is highly protected.

It is not possible to discuss all the relevant regulations in this chapter. These which are considered important will be defined in a pragmatic way, because even standard statistical criteria such as export shares for certain commodities and/or countries may be misleading since a low share could be the result of the regulation in question and vice versa. Furthermore a clear-cut definition of 'trade policy' and 'towards developing countries' is not possible, if trade and transfer effects for developing countries are to be analysed. Again a pragmatic definition that includes all these policy measures that have major trade or transfer effects will be adequate, since measures directed towards developed countries will also have – via production substitution and trade diversion – significant effects on developing countries.

16.1.1 The Common Agricultural Policy

With two minor exceptions – potatoes and alcohol – the markets of all the commodities produced within the EC are in one way or another regulated by common market organisations. Since all these organisations are ruled by the basic principles of market unity, community preference and common financial responsibility, the basic role of the CAP is one of protection. However the resulting internal allocation of resources, and therefore the trade effects of different commodities, depend to a large extent on which instrument is applied and which policy is pursued. Of major relevance are the yearly decisions on prices taken by the council of ministers. The highly complex and differentiated market instruments for agricultural products can be separated into four broad categories:[1]

1. Internal price support combined with external protection by levies and/or customs duties for most cereals, sugar, milk, beef and veal, pork, certain fruits and vegetables, table wine and seafood, covering more than 70 per cent of total agricultural production.
2. Internal price support for producers and liberal trade,[2] that is, deficiency payment systems, which make up the difference between producers' and consumers' prices, with low prices for consumers or the processing industry for olive oil (with certain specifications), some oilseeds, tobacco, mutton and raisins, covering about 3 per cent of agricultural production.
3. External protection alone for flowers, wine other than table wine, other fruit and vegetables, eggs and poultry, covering about 25 per cent of agricultural production.
4. Flat-rate aid based on acreage or output for durum wheat, cottonseed, flaxseed and hempseed, hops, silkworms, seeds and dehydrated fodder, covering about 1 per cent of production.

This classification is not unequivocal in the sense that the instruments used for each category are the only ones applied to the commodities included in the category. Since the prime objective of the CAP is to protect EC producers, the common aim of all four 'systems' is to increase producer's incomes to above free market levels. Since this is brought about by price support or production-tied aid, internal production is increased, imports are reduced and/or (subsidised) exports are raised above free trade levels. Nevertheless the broad variety of instruments applied leads to different effects on the quantities traded and on world market prices – these will be discussed in some detail.

The main instruments of the levy system are threshold prices at borders and an intervention price. Both prices are derived from a target price, fixed annually by the council of ministers. The intervention price, at which any quantity can be sold to the market authorities, functions as a guaranteed minimum price. The levy on imports to the EC, which is fixed at regular intervals, amounts to the difference between the lowest offer price and the threshold price (for grain, but not for fruit and vegetables, pork, poultry and eggs). For exports the price difference between the (usually higher) EC price and the world market price is compensated for by export subsidies (restitutions) which are differentiated by country of destination. Export subsidies and their regional differentiation in particular have been the cause of heated debates in GATT meeting and were a major topic in the agricultural section of the Uruguay round.

Increasing degrees of selfsufficiency as a logical consequence of the support system have shifted the EC from a net importer to a net exporter of most basic food commodities. This system has also led to continuous sharp increases in the budgetary costs of the agricultural policy. To curb this spending additional instruments to control supply have been implemented. In addition to sugar, where a slightly flexible quota system has been applied since the beginning of the common market, production quotas were introduced for milk producers in 1984. Moreover guarantee thresholds for total EC production were applied for cereals (1982–3), milk (1977–8, combined with a coresponsibility levy) and oilseeds (rape, 1982–3). Should production exceed this quantity, automatic cuts in the guarantee prices should be made, but this measure was rarely taken before 1988.

For several commodities such as beef and veal, live cattle, fruit and vegetables, variable levies on imports were combined with a customs duty. The levy amounts to the difference between the offer price plus customs duty and the guide price (cattle and veal) or the reference price[3] (fruit and vegetables). Of particular relevance to imports is the fact that price competition between foreign suppliers is eliminated in the case of fruit and vegetables, because price differentials in individual offers at the border are levelled by the variable levies. In principal the same effect is achieved for pork, eggs and poultry, when the undercutting of the 'sluice-gate' price, an administratively fixed minimum offer price, is offset by an extra countervailing surcharge. In addition to these principal instruments of internal and trade intervention, there are numerous other regulations and exceptions, but these will not be discussed further.

The second category – internal support prices and liberal trade – encompasses a wide variety of products and a multitude of instruments including variable slaughter subsidies, subsidies for ewes[4] (includes both sheep and goat meat) and processing aid paid to the first buyer of oilseeds. The general consequence of having a deficiency payment system for certain products while markets for close substitutes are highly protected are severe distortions in consumption and the trade structure. This is of particular importance for the markets of grain and grain substitutes, that is oilcakes and other protein feedstuff in combination with manioc. In compound feed, expensive grain is substituted to a large extent by cheaper components. From 1978 (EC-9) to 1987 (EC-12) the import quantity of grain substitutes increased from 12 million tonnes to 18 million tonnes (grain by-products, manioc, citrus pulp) and that of soybean and soybean cake from 18 million tonnes to 22 million tonnes. At the same time the EC's trade balance for grain shifted from a net import of 12 million tonnes to a net export of 17 million tonnes (1987–8) and it was estimated that it would show a surplus of 26.6 million tonnes in 1989–90 (USDA, Grains). In addition to the US (the major exporter of soybean and other protein feedstuff), Brazil and Argentina (soybeans) and Thailand (as the dominating exporter of manioc) have a particular interest in the EC trade arrangements that are on the agenda of the ongoing GATT negotiations. However, with respect to the relatively liberal EC import regime for grain substitutes, it is worthwhile noting that the EC still seeks to limit the import of grain substitutes. The agricultural lobby demands tariffs on imports of oilseeds, and there is an import substitution policy consisting of above-average protection for EC-produced protein feedstuff (oilseeds, peas, beans and so forth) and high premiums for using EC-produced commodities (oilcakes, milk powder) in compound feed.

The third category – external protection as the only protective instrument – is relevant in the case of certain fruits and vegetables for which no internal intervention system exists. The customs duty on these varies between 4 per cent and 21 per cent, depending on the season and on the processing stage of the commodity in question (OECD, 1987, p. 186). Another group of commodities belonging to this category includes poultry and eggs. Protection is brought about by a levy comprising two components: the first is the difference between the cost per unit at world market and EC prices, and the second is a 7 per cent duty on the sluice gate price (calculated minimum production costs under world market conditions). A supplementary amount is charged on offers below the sluice gate price.

Flat rate aid based on acreage or output – the fourth category – is the main or only instrument for a number of commodities (listed earlier). In general flat rate aid has virtually the same effects on trade as deficiency payment systems. The quantitative impact depends on which policy is pursued, but is directed towards import substitution. The number of commodities covered by this policy has expanded since the founding of the EEC – mostly as a consequence of the entry of Mediterranean countries which grow products that are of minor importance to the old member countries.

In summarising this brief outline of the basic systems of the CAP, some preliminary conclusions could be drawn on potential trade and price effects with respect to non-member countries. Given the general policy objective to protect producers (by raising producers' income) the principal effects are an increase in production[5] and exports, shrinking imports and depressed prices on world markets. However the various systems applied to different commodities have an impact on the outcome. The levy system is the most effective system in shielding the internal market against developments on international markets. Since the EC has high shares in most markets, prices on world markets have not only been depressed, but instability has been increased as a consequence of the variable level which stabilises internal prices. Beyond that, competition between foreign suppliers is reduced when the levy is not based on the minimum offer price, but is defined as the difference between a given offer and regulated EC prices. Compared to this system, markets regulated by flat rate aid or external customs duties are to a far lesser degree removed from world markets since consumers and producers within the EC have to react to fluctuations in world market prices. To a limited extent this is also true for a deficiency payment system since at least consumers and industries processing raw products are confronted with changing market conditions. Given the same level of effective protection for producers of different commodities, trade effects are smaller in a deficiency payment system or under flat rate aid than in the case of levies or customs duties. Nominal rates of protection are lower in the first case, and internal consumption is higher than in the latter cases. Similar nominal and effective rates of protection for close substitutes in production and consumption limit the allocative distortions. In reality, the diverging effective rates and extremely different nominal rates for close substitutes which have been brought about by the CAP lead to an aggravation of trade distortions for a given average protection, as discussed above for grain and grain substitutes.

16.1.2 EC trade in agricultural commodities under GATT rules

Whereas the greater part of EC agricultural production was covered exclusively by a levy system,[6] such a system applied to only about 15 per cent of agricultural imports. 43 per cent of imports were subject to customs duties and 42 per cent were totally exempt (OECD, 1987, p. 85). Imports not regulated by a variable levy system fall under the 'common customs tariff' (CCT). CCT includes MFN tariffs, some quantitative concessions for beef imports (Schnoor, 1989, p. 16) and several more general arrangements for trade in meat and dairy products (OECD, 1987, p. 28). The MFN rates vary by product and season for certain fruits and vegetables. With respect to their impact on EC imports, this is either negligible (beef) or at most of minor importance for commodities for which additional levies are charged. For other products covered by the CAP, their impact depends on EC measures that affect the internal supply and demand of the same products or close substitutes in production or consumption. The main agricultural raw commodities covered by the CCT and respective MFN rates are given in Table 16.1.

The main characteristics of the CCT tariff structure are:

- Low or zero rates for tropical beverages and industrial raw materials.
- Low or zero rates for grain substitutes such as oilseeds and oil cakes, manioc and protein feedstuff.
- Medium rates for fruit, vegetables, vegetable oils and spices.
- High rates for certain animals or animal products, but which have a minor or no impact on trade.

Table 16.1   EC MFN tariff rates for agricultural commodities
(percentages)

Product	MFN Tariff Rate
Beef, cattle	20 (quotas applied)
Mutton	20
Vegetables, fresh or frozen	4–21
Fruit partially preserved, but unsuitable in that state for immediate consumption	5.5–16
Bananas	20 (but applied only for Benelux countries)
Vegetable oils	5–15
Spices	5–25
Coffee, unroasted	5
Tea	0
Cocoa beans	3
Oilseeds, oilcake	0
Grain substitutes:	
Corn gluten	0
Citrus pulp	0
Bran	(subject to a levy)
Manioc	6 (VER's with main exporters)
Raw cotton	0
Sisal fibres	0
Natural rubber	0

Sources: Amelung and Langhammer, 1989, p. 45; Menzler-Hokkanen, 1988, p. 90.

The low rates for the first three product categories give rise to a tariff escalation at each stage of processing[7] – this is not shown in Table 16.1 since only raw materials are listed. For tropical beverages, internal consumption taxes are more important than trade measures for EC consumption and imports. These taxes differ widely between member countries – for example there is a 40 per cent tax on coffee in Germany (Cable, 1989, p. 14) and a 110 per cent tax on cocoa in Denmark, but tax on these items is limited to the regular VAT in other EC countries.

A special regulation has been implemented for manioc, which was originally covered by the levy system for the grain market. This levy was restricted to a maximum of 6 per cent of the c.i.f value at the Kennedy round. With imports from Thailand growing rapidly, the

EC negotiated a cooperation agreement with Thailand in 1982, the core of which was a VER for manioc exports valid until 1990[8]. Finally, it should be noted that in all agricultural regulations a safeguard clause is included which enables the EC to adopt promptly any measures needed to defend the EC market against 'serious' disturbance (OECD, 1987, p. 84).

Some special concessions were given for beef and cattle imports, including imports of 211 000 live cattle from Austria, Switzerland and Yugoslavia at reduced customs duties and zero or reduced levies (1988), 65 000 tonnes of beef as a GATT import quota for frozen beef, 504 000 tonnes of veal from Yugoslavia, and 34 000 tonnes of 'Hilton' beef (Schnoor, 1989, p. 16). The potential impact of the CCT tariff structure and of CAP regulations on developing countries or on certain groups of countries is further modified by preferences and concessions. The most important ones will be analysed in the next section.

16.1.3 Preferences by country groups, countries and commodities

16.1.3.1 The generalized system of preferences

The stated objective of the GSP was to promote industrialisation in and exports from developing countries, but a limited number of processed and semi-processed agricultural goods were also made eligible for the GSP from the beginning. In 1983, 385 agricultural products were covered by the GSP (OECD, 1987, p. 26). The GSP provides for duty-free manufactured imports (see Chapter 17), but duties were only partially removed in the case of agricultural products (Table 16.2). Only imports from the least developed countries have been completely free of duties since 1977. However there are no tariff quotas for agricultural imports (as is the case for manufactures) except for two types of unprocessed tobacco, canned pineapple, cocoa butter and instant coffee. All concessions are subject to a safeguard clause to prevent damage to EC internal markets (Weinmüller, 1984, p. 85).

A comparison of MFN and GSP rates yields the same pattern observed for MFN (CCT) rates: the greater the extent of processing, the smaller the preferential margin. With respect to agricultural raw materials, preferential margins on average are necessarily small since MFN rates for major commodity groups are often zero. What remains are slight reductions in the range of 1–2 percentage points for vegetable oils and fats and about 9 percentage points for spices (1982,

Table 16.2   Average weighted[a] and unweighted rates of MFN tariff and GSP preference margins for all agricultural and industrial GSP products, 1982

	MFN-tariff (per cent)	Preference margin (percentage points)
Unweighted rates for all GSP products	8.5	7.0
Weighted rates:		
all GSP products	8.0	6.7
agricultural products	11.8	5.3
industrial products	7.2	7.2

a. Weighted by trade in GSP-covered products.

Source: Borrmann et al., 1985, p. 93.

unweighted; Menzler–Hokkanen, 1988, p. 76). For raw coffee the margin is in general 0.5 percentage points (Amelung and Langhammer, 1989, p. 45) while 5 percentage points apply to the least developed countries. For cocoa beans the GSP rate is zero. The reductions for fruit and vegetables (fresh or frozen) are of particular relevance for the Mediterranean countries and will be discussed below.

The trade effects to be expected from the GSP are very limited for two reasons. First, the GSP does not eliminate tariff escalation and this continues to impede imports of vegetable oils and other processed or semi-processed agricultural products. Secondly, developing countries are the sole suppliers of a large part of the commodities covered by the GSP, and the price elasticity of demand for these commodities is quite low in the EC.

16.1.3.2   The Lomé Convention

Of the different parts of the Lomé Convention only the trade regulations regarding agricultural commodities will be discussed. The basic principle (Article 2) of the Lomé Convention, that 'products originating in the ACP states shall be imported into the Community free of customs duties and charges having equivalent effects', is modified by Section 2 of the same article to the effect that ACP countries are granted only restricted access to EC markets regulated by the CAP. ACP preferences can be described by a classification of products into three categories (Koester and Herrmann, 1987, p. 11):

1. Products originating from ACP countries which can be imported duty-free to the EC (tropical beverages, vegetable oils). These products are not produced within the EC, but preference margins are very low if not zero.
2. Products imported from ACP countries which are covered by the CAP (fruit and vegetables). These products receive a product-specific and rather low preference margin which is usually offset by levies or charges which render the system redundant, at least in situations where there are surpluses.
3. Products covered by special trade arrangements which offer sizable preferences for some or all ACP exporters. These products are either CAP products such as sugar and beef or non-CAP products such as bananas and rum.

The EC sugar protocol, which was negotiated for Lomé I, was accorded special status insofar as no period of validity was specified (for details, see Gruber, 1987a, p. 84 and Koester and Herrmann, 1987, p. 35). There are 21 eligible countries/territories with a total import quota of 1.3 million tonnes of white sugar equivalent. This quota amounts to about 12 per cent of total EC consumption and was equivalent to an import share of about 75 per cent in 1987–8. For this quantity suppliers receive at least the EC guarantee price which is fixed annually by the council of ministers (see Section 16.1.1 above). This quasi indexation of a raw material price is a unique element in North–South trade relations. The allocation of the total quota to countries with preferential status was extremely lopsided. In 1979 ten countries received about 95 per cent of the total, of which five of the ten countries together held 91 per cent.[9] Nonetheless such quotas have been important for individual countries. Four countries were allowed to sell 50 per cent or more of their total output on EC markets, and Mauritius was allowed over 70 per cent.

In addition to some GATT quotas for frozen beef, live cattle and 'Hilton' beef (see Section 16.1.2 above), the EC allocated special export quotas for beef to five ACP countries (Botswana, Kenya, Madagascar, Swaziland and Zimbabwe). Imports from these countries are exempt from duty except for a surcharge of 10 per cent of the regular import levy. Preferences are granted on the condition that the exporting countries charge a duty on exports amounting to 90 per cent of the levy and that the proceeds from this duty are used to promote the domestic cattle industry (Schnoor, 1989, p. 19). The total quota was set at 38 100 tonnes in 1988. The main beneficiary was

Botswana with a quota of nearly 19 000 tonnes. The share of ACP imports in total EC beef imports fluctuates between 3 per cent and 5 per cent and that in EC consumption is around 0.4 per cent. However the share of the quotas in production and exports of the eligible countries has large annual fluctuation and it frequently exceeds 50 per cent (Schnoor, 1989, p. 51; Koester and Herrmann, 1987, p. 43).

Bananas are an important export item for quite a few countries, and for some they are the only export commodity. The CCT for bananas is 20 per cent *ad valorem* including a 100 per cent preference for ACP countries. However to date this is applied only by the Benelux countries. There are also separate trade regulations for individual EC countries with historicalities, such as Germany, France, Italy and the UK. The main suppliers of the UK are the Windward Islands, Jamaica and Belize; those of France are Martinique, Guadeloupe, Ivory Coast and Cameroon. Italy imports mainly from Somalia, and Germany is supplied by (non-Caribbean) Latin American producers (Noichl, 1985, p. 64; Cable, 1989, p. 5). The legal background for this market separation is provided by Article 115 of the Treaty of Rome, which allows a restriction on the free circulation of goods, and by the Banana Protocol of the Lomé convention. The latter guarantees that 'no ACP state will be placed, as regards access to its traditional markets and its advantages on these markets, in a less favourable situation than in the past or at present' (Protocol 4, Article 1). In accordance with the completion of the common market in 1993 a dismantling of internal market restrictions within the EC has to be accomplished. This is likely to have serious repercussions for the traditional exporters to France and the UK unless new measures to protect these producers are implemented by the EC.

ACP rum exports to the EC are governed by Protocol 7 of the Lomé Convention, which provides for duty-free quotas on the basis of the largest quantities imported over the previous three years. Over and above this it allows for yearly increases of 40 per cent in the UK and 18 per cent in the other member countries. The ACP countries were frequently unable to fill their quotas (Koester and Herrmann, 1987, p. 32; Weinmüller, 1984, p. 114).

16.1.3.3 Agreements with Mediterranean countries

The common thread running through the basically bilateral agreements[10] which resulted from the 1972 EC plan for a global Mediterranean policy is free access to EC markets for manufactured exports

(Chapter 17.4) and some concessions for agricultural commodities (for details, see Pomfret, 1986). The latter have been negotiated by the Mediterranean countries (and conceded by the EC) to protect their traditional export markets in the EC, which were increasingly endangered by the CAP. The commodities of particular importance were fruit and vegetables, some of which have quite a high share in the total exports of some countries, as the following data show (Musto, 1988, p. 64): citrus fruit – Morocco 7.3 per cent, Israel 7 per cent; olive oil – Tunisia 8.9 per cent; tomatoes – Morocco 3.6 per cent.

The EC concessions mainly comprise reductions in customs duties of between 30 per cent and 80 per cent – some minor non-competing products such as spices are zero-rated (Weinmüller, 1984, p. 126; Musto, 1988, p. 62). Since the normal EC market regulations (the reference price system, a licensing system and the option of temporary import restrictions) nevertheless apply (see Section 16.1.2 above), a clear advantage for producers from member countries has been maintained. This became particularly important after the expansion of the EC, when important producers like Spain gained membership. The anticipated trade diversion on the markets for fruit and vegetables, with potentially severe consequences for Mediterranean non-member countries (listed in Note 10), led to adapted trade and cooperation agreements with those countries (apart from Malta and Syria) These agreements were signed on 1 September 1988 (EG-Kommission, 1989, p. 127). The main new element was the introduction of duty-free import quotas determined on the basis of average previous exports calculated for a number of representative years (Musto, 1988, p. 74). Since the regulations of the EC market order have not been changed however, the extent of trade diversion caused by these agreements will depend mainly on the price policy pursued by the EC. Preferential treatment of Mediterranean countries will nonetheless have a detrimental effect on the export of fruit and vegetables by other suppliers to the EC, in particular the US.

16.2 IMPACT ON DEVELOPING COUNTRIES

16.2.1 The CAP and the level and volatility of world market prices

Since the main objective of the CAP is income protection for farmers – for which price protection is still the main instrument – the most important direct and indirect effects on trading partners – compared to a reference system outside the CAP – are as follows:

- The EC net exports (net imports) of agricultural commodities are higher (lower). The magnitude of this depends, in addition to supply and demand conditions, on the nominal (for consumers) and effective rates (for producers) of protection, which vary widely between commodities and over time. Since these rates are about zero for grain substitutes the trade effects have the opposite direction in this case.
- World market prices for agricultural commodities are depressed as a result of the policy-induced reversal of trade flows.

Lower world market prices lead in the first round, and under *ceteris paribus* conditions, to welfare gains for net importers and to losses for exporters of agricultural commodities. However this general theoretical result is difficult to verify empirically, as was pointed out in the methodological remarks. There are numerous partial and general equilibrium studies of the distortionary effects of the CAP,[11] but all suffer from methodological shortcomings concerning commodity and policy coverage or the modelling of linkages among different markets and policies. For this reason the following assessment is concentrated on a few, but often cited, estimates.

One of the most detailed ones for the agricultural sector, multi-country models for which frequently updated simulation results are presented, is that of Tyers and Anderson.[12] This involves 30 countries or country groups and differentiates among seven major commodities accounting for about one-half of the world food trade. Not included are soybeans and other grain substitutes – this is a shortcoming in view of the important intrasectoral distortions in the protection structure of the EC. The model has dynamic elements and is partly stochastic as production uncertainty is included. Policy is to a certain extent endogenised; the same is true for stockholding. Another shortcoming and a potential reason for underestimating the welfare gains of developing countries is the omission of certain tropical commodities (Valdés, 1987, p. 583).

The major effects on world market prices, trade and welfare derived for a phased liberalisation of the EC policy have the theoretically expected direction. World market prices would increase because EC net exports decline. The net welfare gain for the EC per year (average of 1980–2) would amount to $8.9 billion (1985 price). The magnitude lies within the range of other estimates of welfare losses caused by the CAP,[13] but there should be a definite underestimation insofar as, for example, only price protection is abolished[14] and important commodity groups such as grain substitutes, fruit and vegetables are not included. The aggregated impact on developing countries is a welfare loss of $2.3 billion (1985 price), which could be higher for the same reasons. Liberalisation of the CAP entails welfare losses for developing countries because importers stand to lose more than exporters gain as the result of first-round price effects. If one rates an isolated liberalisation by the EC as implausible[15] and runs simulations for a liberalisation of the agricultural policy in all industrial market economies, the result for developing countries is again a loss of $2.3 billion (1985 price). However the world as a whole would gain about $16.2 billion which would allow for compensation. The reason for the unaltered result for developing countries is the level and structure of protection applied by other important exporters and importers, that is, the US and Japan. Since the main welfare losses for developing countries are brought about by increasing world grain prices, the effect from the inclusion of the US is very small because US protection rates are low and are combined with supply restrictions (set-aside programmes).

Estimates by other authors with comparable models have yielded similar results. A liberalisation of the CAP would bring about small losses for developing countries as a group (Matthews, 1985). The results vary, depending on assumptions made with respect to supply and demand reactions. Although small on average, the losses or gains for individual countries can be substantial. Lomé countries, being major beneficiaries of preferential import regulations for beef and sugar, would lose their advantage with the termination of EC price protection. Other examples of 'losers' following a CAP liberalisation are the exporters of manioc, Thailand in particular. Because of the dramatic increase in EC demand caused by the CAP, the net income gain for this country was estimated at $110 million for 1980 (Nelson, 1989, p. 60).

To evaluate these general results for developing countries, three aspects should be discussed in greater detail.

First, a liberalisation of the CAP would have to start from a situation characterised by seriously depressed world market prices as a consequence of protectionist policies in industrial countries and even newly industrialised countries. Because of a long period of adjustment to low world market prices for food commodities, production and self-sufficiency are much lower in developing countries than they would be under liberal market conditions. This situation is frequently aggravated by the indirect effect that other import substitution policies in the non-agricultural sectors have on the agricultural sector (Krueger et al., 1988). Such non-agricultural policies imply a tax on the agricultural sector, in particular the exporting branch, and lead to negative effective protection. Whether this policy regime has been encouraged by low world market prices, and therefore low returns to agriculture, is not clear. In any case low food production is the cause of the calculated welfare losses for developing countries as the result of a liberalisation of the CAP. Increasing world market prices could however stimulate food production in food importing countries and bring about a reversal of food trade flows for many countries (Hartmann and Schmitz, 1987, p. 346), which would be even more pronounced if detrimental policies pertaining to other sectors are corrected. What follows is a likelihood of overestimating the negative impact of food price increases for developing countries when only first-round effects are accounted for. Similarly an analysis which includes in addition a liberalisation of developing countries' policies but is limited to agricultural policies, would not give reliable results (Valdés, 1987, p. 582).

Second, another reason for biased welfare estimates with respect to a CAP liberalisation is the effect of the CAP on price instability. As will be argued below, more stable world market prices could be expected. These would reduce risk for producers directly or would make national or international stabilisation schemes, which incur some cost, at least partly unnecessary. Hence greater price stability is *ceteris paribus* likely to reduce costs and increase production, reduce world market prices and increase global welfare. Although these effects are widely accepted among analysts, the quantitative dimension of price stability is difficult to measure and is therefore not usually included in welfare estimates.

Third, the most important shortcoming of the models discussed so far is their lack of interface with the rest of the economy. A pronounced efficiency and income gain within the EC should also give secondary benefits to trading partners. These would arise from an increased demand for imports as well from higher internal production and exports by the EC having favourable terms of trade effects on non-EC countries. These macroeconomic dynamic effects of liberalisation is more important now that the protection system of the EC has been shifting from simple border protection to numerous internal interventions.

Very few modelling efforts have been undertaken to date which attempt to incorporate all the intersectoral and international relationships necessary to trace the above effects. In their internationally-linked general equilibrium model, Burniaux and Waelbroeck (1988) basically confirm the effects of a liberalisation of agricultural markets derived from other modelling efforts. In addition they analyse the macroeconomic linkages and arrive at the conclusion that even developing countries would achieve net income gains on aggregate were the agricultural policy to be liberalised in Europe. This result is not supported by simulations using the IIASA food model (Parikh et al., 1988), where developing countries continue to lose as a group. Although this modelling effort comprises internationally-linked models with detailed agricultural sectors, the dynamic macroeconomic effects of a CAP liberalisation might not be adequately captured since the non-agricultural economy is aggregated to only one commodity. In addition both arguments mentioned earlier, which suggest an underestimation of the welfare increases, seem also to be valid. However the IIASA work concentrates on distributional aspects within developing countries, which is outside the area of this study.

Finally, a dismantling of the CAP system with variable levies and export restitutions respectively would lead to more stable world market prices since shortages and gluts could be smoothed out by a much larger number of agents. This result is theoretically plausible and unanimously supported by empirical studies (Winters, 1987, p. 41). However some reservations must be made. First, governments could have eliminated, or at least reduced, the detrimental effects of the CAP trade system on the stability of world market prices by discretionary stock and trade policies. Secondly, the slowness of producers to react to price changes could lead to the cyclical price patterns which were, for example, observed on the world sugar market. An unhindered reaction of EC producers to world market prices could have increased cyclical price fluctuations (Schrader, 1982). Nevertheless the results from adequately formulated empirical analyses show significant destabilising effects of the CAP in *ex post* simulations, which have been particular strong on the markets for wheat, and beef (Tyers and Anderson, 1988, p. 207).

16.2.2 Special trade arrangements

In this section the likely impact of some special EC measures for developing countries will be analysed. The approach taken is essentially partial, that is it does not try to work out all the interdependencies of the real world. This should be kept in mind when assessing the results from various studies.

The concession granted under the Lomé sugar protocol, that is imports of 1.3 million tonnes of sugar (white sugar equivalent) per year free of duties or levies from ACP countries at EC intervention prices, could basically be understood as a product-tied income transfer to eligible countries. In fact this transfer could become negative should the EC sugar price fall below the world market level since the regulations include an obligation to deliver. The magnitude of the transfer by country depends on the multiple of the quota allocated and the price differential between the EC and the world market prices (which fluctuate widely). The cost of freight, loading and insurance have to be subtracted in order to arrive at the net transfer value. As long as one assumes that global production and consumption remain unchanged by the protocol, calculation is straightforward. The maximum total transfer calculated along these lines has been estimated at nearly 200 million ECU for 1981–2 (Koester and Herrmann, 1987, p. 41) which could be considered a 'normal' year with respect to price differentials.

The distribution of quota rents between beneficiaries is extremely uneven, not only in absolute terms but also per capita and in relation to income measures such per capita GNP. Mauritius and Malawi may serve as examples. Mauritius had a per capita GNP of 1255 ECU in 1981–2 and received an income transfer of 79.8 ECU per capita, while the much poorer Malawi (with a per capita income of 201 ECU) had received just 0.5 ECU per capita in the same year (Koester and Herrmann, 1987, p. 41). Such distributional effects cannot be justified given that the goal of official development policies is to help the poor.

The sugar policy does incur costs, even under the assumption of unchanged production and consumption. The costs of the arbitrary shipments of sugar initiated by the regulations have to be covered on a global scale. Moreover the assumption of unchanged production in eligible countries seems unjustified since several governments pay producers prices that are above their shadow price (world market price). The additional production caused by this policy depresses world market prices and incurs detrimental effects on non-eligible sugar exporters in particular (World Bank, 1986, p. 143). However the allocative effects of the sugar protocol have to be judged with caution. It is difficult to assess what the EC internal sugar (price) policy would look like if there was not an obligatory importation of

1.3 million tonnes of sugar per year. Generally speaking it is safe to state that quantitative restrictions of trade will always distort the allocation of production and consumption between countries and cause a reduction in efficiency.

An economic evaluation of the preferential beef import quotas for Botswana, Kenya, Madagascar, Swaziland and Zimbabwe can be carried out along the lines of the analysis of the sugar protocol.[16] The preferences reflect attempts by the EC to mitigate the detrimental effects of its protectionist policy on some of the poor beef-exporting countries in Africa. Quota rents are determined by price differentials between EC and world markets, and by the quantities exported and related shipping costs. Since most of the allocated quotas have not been fully used,[17] effective economic rents are significantly smaller than potential ones, which were estimated at just over 40 million ECU for all four countries together in 1979 (Koester and Herrmann, 1987, p. 44). The main beneficiary is Botswana with a share of 50 per cent of the total quota. As is the case for ACP sugar exporters, it has been shown that beef producers can obtain part of their quota rent through raised prices, which has consequences for factor allocation. Although it can hardly be doubted that quota-owning countries benefit from the regulation, it is very difficult to establish their net welfare position under a liberalised EC beef policy. Estimates indicate that beneficiaries are better off with the present regulation, but they could easily be compensated by other beef exporters who stand to gain from a liberalisation[18] (Massow, 1984, p. 137). What makes things worse is the fact that – as with the sugar protocol – the distributional consequences of the EC policy among and within developing countries are arbitrary.

16.3 THE CAP AND THE URUGUAY ROUND

In previous GATT negotiations on the liberalisation of trade, agricultural trade was more or less omitted, but this issue has figured prominently on the agenda of the Uruguay round. The reason for this was a growing awareness of the damage caused by bilateralism to traditional food exporters in particular and to the international trading system in general, and by specific trade practices developed by the EC and the US which are frequently characterised as a trade war.

Consensus was not reached at the mid-term review meeting in Montreal (December 1988), and the participants in informal consultations in Geneva in early 1989 only reached agreement on some fairly general declarations and objectives. According to OECD (1989, p. 65): 'Agricultural policies should be more responsive to international market signals in order to meet the objective of liberalization of international trade and that support and protection should be progressively reduced and provided in a less distorting manner'. Also 'a reform process should be initiated through the negotiation of commitments on support and protection and through the establishment of strengthened and more operational GATT rules and disciplines'.

However to date no way has been found to realise the commonly agreed reduction of protection and the liberalisation of trade. Several academic proposals[19] on an adequate calculation and stepwise reduction of producer and consumer subsidy equivalents, or the transformation of all kinds of protectionist measures into tariffs, have not been adopted. The reason for the deadlock in the GATT negotiations was rooted mainly in the still controversial positions of the EC and the US.[20] The US recently (*Agra-Europe*, no. 44, 1989, p. 9) returned to an earlier position which opts for free trade after a transition period of 10 years, and the abolition of export subsidies within five years. After the transition period only those internal measures – such as direct income payments or environmental protection programmes – that have a minor impact on production and trade should be allowed. The EC on the other hand is very reluctant to provide any indication of the protection level it is striving for (*Agra-Europe*, no. 51, 1989, p. 14). Although the EC has agreed to a certain reduction in internal price support and the tariffication of some non tariff measures, it remains unclear as to how these changes are to be implemented. Moreover the EC proposes to provide special treatment for developing countries. This is in accordance with the wishes of the members of the Cairns Group who have requested that compensatory measures be extended to net food importers among developing countries. This suggestion has to be viewed as a compromise since several developing countries (for example Brazil and Thailand) are members of this group, which otherwise represents the interests of important food exporters. As food exporters are suffering because of the escalating export subsidies paid by the EC and the US, their negotiating stance is close to the US free trade position.

The chance that the negotiations will lead to a significant reduction in protection levels and a reorientation towards multilateral GATT rules seems remote. The massive agricultural lobby within the EC determines the negotiating position of the EC and is supported by other countries with high rates of agricultural protection, such as Japan, and quite a number of developing countries who benefit from special EC import regulations or are traditional net food importers. The consideration that potential winners of a liberalisation of agricultural trade could easily compensate potential losers does not seem to be a sufficient condition for achieving free trade in agriculture.

Notes and references

1. For a detailed presentation and discussion of the EC market regulations for agricultural products, see OECD, 1987; BAE, 1985; *Agra-Europe*, no. 27, 1985 and no. 44, 1985.
2. For several products the common external tariff is applied. For others (for example bran) an import levy or a tariff quota combined with a VER (manioc) is introduced.
3. Reference prices are calculated on the basis of EC production costs. They are fixed for each marketing season of each individual product. The products covered are (1) cherries, cucumbers, zucchinis and plums, and (2) peaches, pears, apples, table grapes, oranges, mandarins, lemons, tomatoes, cauliflowers (since 1982–3), apricots and aubergines. Whereas the first group belongs to the third category of commodities mentioned above (external protection only), for the latter group (category 2), which is considered of particular importance to producers, 'base' prices and 'buying in' prices are fixed. The base price represents the price that producers should normally be able to obtain on the market. The buying in price ranges from 40–70 per cent of the base price depending on the commodity.
4. In addition to these subsidies there is an external customs duty of 20 per cent (*ad valorem*) bound in GATT.
5. Policies that lead to an increase in farmers' income without raising production are theoretically possible in two ways. First, paying direct income transfers to farmers provides them with little incentive to increase production. This kind of policy, which has been heavily debated among agricultural economists for decades, entered the debate in the GATT negotiations under the term 'decoupling', that is, decoupling prices and income policy. Although several instruments that could have a reduced impact on production compared to price policy are known and sometimes even applied, transfers to farmers that are neutral with respect to production are not known in practice. Second, as the major instrument has up until now been the producer price, combining this with production quotas is a straight forward way of limiting production increase and their resultant trade effects. Leaving aside negative internal allocative and distributional effects, a precondition for efficient application is the controllability of supply, which is given for only a few commodities.

6. As discussed above, there are several products where both a variable levy and a customs duty apply, for example live cattle, beef, fruit and vegetables. The definition of 'levy-systems' might not be unequivocal since, for example, the system for fruit and vegetables is frequently not included. But even if the 'countervailing charge' levied on imports is not officially called a levy, it functions in the same way as the variable levies in the other markets.

7. For an analysis of, and empirical evidence for, cocoa, soya and palm oil, see Dihm, 1989. For a comparison of tariff rates for tea, cocoa and coffee and respective processed goods, see Menzler-Hokkanen, 1988, p. 94.

8. The quantities which could be exported to the EC at a 6 per cent *ad valorem* tariff were: 1982–4, 5 million tonnes p.a.; 1985–6, 4.5 million tonnes p.a.; 1986 onwards, 5.5 million tonnes p.a. The total EC customs quota for all countries for 1989 was 6.825 million tonnes (*Agra-Europe*, no. 34, 1989, part III, pp. 7–8). For details of the regulations and legal aspects (GATT), see Hartwig and Tangermann, 1987; Menzler-Hokkanen, 1988, p. 103; and Sathirathai and Siamwalla, 1987.

9. See Koester and Herrmann, 1987, p. 77; for shifts of quotas between preferred countries and the underlying regulations, see Gruber, 1987a, p. 90.

10. Cooperation agreements with Algeria, Tunisia and Morocco (Maghreb) were concluded in 1976 and with Egypt, Jordan, Syria and Lebanon (Mashreq) in 1977. Association agreements have been signed with Malta (1971) and Cyprus (1973) and Turkey (1964); a free trade agreement was signed with Israel in 1975 and a special cooperation agreement was signed with Yugoslavia in 1980.

11. A review of more recent empirical work can be found in Winters, 1987; Demekas et al., 1988; Valdés, 1987.

12. Here the version described in Tyers and Anderson, 1988, is discussed.

13. Conservative estimates of the economic costs of the CAP point to a range of $11 billion ECU in 1978 (BAE, 1985, p. 107) to $24 billion (1985 price) (Tyers and Anderson, 1986). A more recent estimate from the same authors for the average for 1980–2 arrives at $8.9 billion (1985 price) (Tyers and Anderson, 1988, p. 211). These estimates differ widely because of: (1) annual fluctuations in world market prices and the exchange rate of the dollar; (2) differing commodity and policy coverage; (3) differing types of models, assumptions and methodology. For a more thorough discussion, see Winters, 1987 and Demekas et al., 1988.

14. Realizing that not only price policy but also structural, agricultural, social, and even regional policies have distorting effects on the allocation of resources, the OECD publishes yearly estimates of producer and consumer subsidy equivalents as a more comprehensive indicator for distortions in the agricultural sector of OECD countries (see OECD 1989). On the concept of subsidy equivalents, see OECD 1987, and Tangermann et al., 1987.

15. Isolated liberalisation might even have detrimental effects. For a discussion of 'disharmonies' between US and EC agricultural policies, see Koester et al., 1988.

16. For a detailed evaluation of beef import quotas, see v. Massow, 1984; Gruber, 1987b; Schnoor, 1989.
17. For details of likely causes, see Schnoor, 1989, p. 42.
18. Koester and Herrmann, 1987, p. 45, argue that Kenya would be better off with free trade.
19. For an overview and the discussion of technical and political problems, see Wissenschaftlicher Beirat, 1988, p. 30.
20. For a discussion of a possible coordinated liberalisation of agricultural trade and its advantages, see Tangermann, 1988 and Koester, 1988.

17 Trade Preferences for Processed Goods from Developing Countries[1]

Volker Stüven

17.1 THE EUROPEAN COMMUNITY'S GSP SCHEME

The European Community's generalised system of preferences (GSP) was introduced in 1971 (for details, see Weston et al., 1980, and Weinmüller, 1984, p. 83). In determining the eligibility of a country for the scheme the EC has regarded that country's membership in the Group of 77 as the main criterion. But apart from this group, generalised preferences were also granted to Romania in 1974 and to the People's Republic of China in 1980. Applications from dependent territories were approved if their customs departments were authorised to issue certificates of origin. In 1984 a total of 149 developing countries were eligible for the GSP (Borrmann et al., 1985, p. 29).

From the beginning the product coverage of the GSP for semi-manufactured goods and manufactured good has been very comprehensive. The EC offered preferential treatment for about 96 per cent of all semimanufactured and manufactured products – the remaining 4 per cent were excluded mainly to protect the interests of competing suppliers from the ACP countries. This is in sharp contrast with the number of processed agricultural products covered by the GSP. Even with the increase from 145 products in 1971 to 338 in 1983, this coverage represents only 74 per cent of all items imported. In addition imports of processed agricultural products under the GSP can be restricted by a general escape clause which is also intended to protect competing ACP suppliers, as mentioned in Chapter 16.1.3.

However semimanufactured and manufactured products are also subject to a considerable number of a priori limitations that restrict the quantity of preferential imports to the EC.[2] For each GSP item a ceiling is calculated annually on the basis of past trade flows. The sum of all ceilings indicate the annual GSP offer. In principle, an import that has exceeded its ceiling faces the MFN tariff, but ceilings can be enforced either automatically, or on a discretionary basis, or not at all, depending on the category into which a particular product falls. The EC divides imported products into two categories: non-sensitive and sensitive, depending on the extent to which imports from GSP beneficiaries are likely to threaten domestic production and employment in the member states. In practice duty-free treatment for non-sensitive items is open ended provided that administrative conditions (origin rules and so forth) are met, and that the importers apply for GSP treatment.

For sensitive items – comprising those goods which compete strongly with domestic substitutes – ceilings take the form of tariff quotas. Imports that exceed a quota automatically face MFN treatment. In addition to this a further restriction is introduced. The tariff quota for each sensitive item is divided into fixed shares for each member state. As soon as a member state's quota has been filled it applies MFN tariffs on further imports of that item from GSP countries, and additional preferential imports of items are only possible via another member state whose share has not yet been used up. In practice indirect imports are made frequently, not only because of the GSP, but also because of short-term adjustments to changing market conditions. In fact the free circulation of goods within the EC makes member-state shares costly to administer and ultimately useless. Since the mid-1970s an EC reserve has allowed for some intermember-state reallocation of import shares. For another category of so-called 'hybrid' products the EC imposes the same strict tariff quotas as it does for sensitive products, but these quotas are not divided into shares for individual member states.

Since 1981 tariff quotas for sensitive products have been combined with special restrictions for individual countries. Some of the developing countries that were regarded as very competitive have been granted identical tariff quotas each, not as a percentage share but in absolute amounts. These amounts are again subdivided among member states and are strictly obligatory. When a supplier has exhausted his quota in a member state, imports to this country face MFN tariffs. For the other countries which receive GSP treatment and export very sensitive items, fixed quotas also exist in absolute amounts for each country, but these quotas are not divided between the member states. Thus MFN tariffs are only imposed on a country's exports after its EC quota has been exhausted.

Obviously the discriminatory treatment of developing countries' exports implied by the GSP scheme requires extensive administrative control and certificates of origin are necessary. Apart from being a general administrative barrier for exports from developing countries, these origin rules can also be used to impede the importation into the EC of specific items by applying local content requirements.[3]

17.2   ESTIMATING THE TRADE EFFECTS OF THE GSP

The trade effects that arise from a preferential tariff reduction are similar to those resulting from the formation of a customs union. Commonly the GSP is characterised by the effects it has on trade creation and trade diversion. Trade creation results if tariff cuts lead to a price reduction for the beneficiaries' imports and thus induce consumer demand to shift from domestic substitutes to imports. In Addition the tariff reduction may change the price ratio between imports from beneficiary and non-beneficiary countries in favour of the former and lead to a corresponding shift in demand. This effect is called trade diversion. For those developing countries that receive preferential treatment for their exports the sum of both effects represents the total benefit gained from the preference system. But for the donor country only trade creation leads to an increase in its welfare because resources are moved from inefficient import-competing sectors into more productive areas, whereas the trade diversion effect implies a welfare loss, since imports are diverted from more efficient to less efficient suppliers.

The empirical evidence of the effects of the GSP scheme in the 1970s is not clear,[4] but the highly disaggregated study by Langhammer (1983) indicates that the effect of GSP treatment on trade flows was negligible. However, the strong impact of the complex quantitative limitations to preferential tariff treatment that are incorporated in the GSP scheme suggest a further approach, based on plausibility considerations, could be adopted to analyse the trade effects of the preference scheme. This should refer to the actual amounts of imports of GSP items with and without preferential treatment, that is, GSP-receiving versus GSP-covered imports, and discuss whether it is reasonable to expect significant trade effects under this form of partial preferential treatment. The approach draws on an assumption advanced by Cooper (1972) that there is no trade effect at all in the case where imports exceed the preference quotas. This assumption is based on the reasoning that marginal imports are important for trade creation and trade diversion and that in the case of beneficiaries' imports exceeding the tariff quota these suppliers must be regarded as being competitive even without the help of preferences.

A comparison between the imports of the EC countries, other industrialised countries and (GSP-receiving) developing countries opens our discussion on the development of imports to the EC under the GSP scheme. EC imports originating from industrialised countries increased from 90 463 million ECU in 1978 to 201 400 million ECU in 1987, an overall growth of 222 per cent (EUROSTAT, Cronos Data Bank: FRIC – Foreign trade of the European Community). Imports from developing countries grew by only 138 per cent, from 78 650 million. ECU in 1978 to 108 490 million ECU in 1987. The weaker performance of the GSP beneficiaries was due mainly to the sharp decline in the price of oil and commodities after 1985 that hit developing countries much harder than it did the industrialised countries. In other product categories such as food, beverages and tobacco (SITC $0 + 1$) and manufactures (SITC $5 - 9$) imports from the GSP countries in 1978–87 grew at a faster rate than imports from the industrialised world.

Table 17.1 provides the base for a more detailed analysis of GSP countries' exports to the EC in the different product and sensitivity categories embodied in the GSP scheme. It records EC imports from GSP beneficiaries that actually received preferential tariff treatment and the respective shares of these imports in total GSP-covered imports of the items. This allows assessment of whether the export performance of GSP suppliers has been influenced by the degree of preferential treatment received. Furthermore the breakdown of EC imports to single member countries makes it possible to take country-specific developments into account.

Looking at total EC imports of agricultural product, manufactures and semi-manufactures it can be seen that the GSP suppliers steadily increased their GSP-receiving exports from 1981–7 after an initial jump in the period from 1978 to 1981. However the ratio between GSP-receiving and GSP-covered imports stayed at a fairly constant 33 per cent, with a once-only drop in 1984. This is the first indication that GSP beneficiaries have been competitive on the EC market even without GSP treatment of their exports. The favourable performance of these countries has not been supported by a relative increase in preferential treatment. The growth rates of GSP-receiving and non-GSP-receiving imports to the EC have been similar.

The 1984 drop in GSP-receiving import shares was caused by a fall

Table 17.1 GSP-receiving imports in million of ECU and percentage share[a] in GSP-covered imports from GSP beneficiaries, 1978, 1981, 1984, 1987, by GSP categories and member countries of the EC

Country	Year	Sensitive industrial products (except textiles)[b]	Non-sensitive industrial products (except textiles)	Sensitive textiles	Semi-sensitive textiles[c]	Non-sensitive textiles	Sensitive agricultural products (tobacco type Virginia, cocoa butter, canned pineapple)	Semi-sensitive agricultural products (raw tobacco)	Non-sensitive agricultural products	Total agricultural products, semi-manufactures and manufactures
EC[d]	1978	929.5 (27.4)	1278.9 (37.0)	153.3 (8.0)	212.4 (51.0)	73.1 (67.0)	180.9 (40.0)	14.8 (57.0)	727.4 (54.0)	3570.2 (33.0)
	1981	3437.4 (38.2)	2722.8 (36.2)	448.6 (9.5)	266.7 (37.9)	85.1 (71.3)	259.6 (34.5)	22.6 (10.4)	1238.9 (44.1)	8481.5 (32.8)
	1984	4551.2 (32.8)	3499.4 (26.7)	988.8 (14.1)	–	139.8 (71.5)	350.5 (27.8)	23.0 (8.0)	1811.2 (34.9)	11364.0 (27.8)
	1987	5757.7 (39.9)	4464.2 (34.2)	1460.8 (15.7)	–	109.5 (83.8)	482.0 (53.9)	–	3307.2 (34.8)	15583.4 (33.6)
Germany	1978	438.4 (40.1)	630.4 (61.0)	58.0 (6.0)	134.1 (71.0)	16.4 (69.0)	49.7 (52.0)	8.4 (81.0)	239.1 (62.0)	1574.6 (42.0)
	1981	758.2 (39.5)	813.3 (51.2)	143.1 (7.6)	131.3 (43.2)	11.9 (69.5)	66.7 (34.0)	7.6 (9.5)	398.0 (52.9)	2330.1 (34.6)
	1984	900.1 (36.5)	1104.6 (44.8)	443.3 (15.2)	–	17.0 (83.9)	112.0 (37.4)	8.1 (9.5)	683.0 (46.6)	3268.1 (33.7)
	1987	885.9 (32.3)	1388.0 (42.9)	551.0 (15.4)	–	14.3 (92.9)	77.7 (34.8)	–	1187.2 (49.3)	4104.1 (33.7)

France	1978	72.7 (20.7)	128.3 (34.0)	21.1 (16.0)	19.8 (50.0)	5.8 (33.0)	1.8 (19.0)	0.2 (90.0)	93.8 (53.0)	343.5 (31.0)
	1981	245.0 (12.2)	398.6 (23.9)	61.6 (12.5)	45.5 (44.5)	7.4 (48.2)	2.4 (4.2)	—	244.7 (41.7)	1005.2 (20.3)
	1984	861.1 (38.7)	343.7 (12.4)	138.2 (19.9)	—	10.5 (78.0)	6.1 (6.1)	—	272.3 (29.7)	1631.8 (24.1)
	1987	1145.9 (40.9)	551.8 (24.1)	160.0 (15.0)	—	7.2 (78.8)	4.7 (7.5)	—	399.4 (27.7)	2269.0 (29.6)
Italy	1978	84.1 (17.0)	107.7 (18.0)	—	0.4 (1.0)	2.8 (31.0)	—	0.8 (38.0)	69.3 (35.0)	265.1 (18.0)
	1981	1374.1 (62.6)	369.5 (33.1)	62.6 (17.6)	19.1 (23.2)	2.2 (27.8)	10.1 (47.7)	—	110.4 (30.3)	1948.0 (46.9)
	1984	1039.9 (27.1)	502.6 (16.7)	88.5 (15.2)	—	6.3 (42.4)	2.1 (5.3)	—	168.6 (28.3)	1808.0 (22.4)
	1987	1873.6 (59.8)	543.3 (34.5)	312.3 (32.4)	—	7.0 (90.6)	14.2 (50.3)	—	453.3 (34.5)	3203.8 (45.6)
Benelux	1978	95.6 (15.6)	156.1 (20.0)	1.0 (0.4)	0.9 (2.0)	24.4 (73.0)	2.8 (4.0)	—	137.6 (63.0)	418.3 (21.0)
	1981	562.5 (53.2)	572.2 (42.1)	39.2 (7.6)	24.8 (32.8)	40.1 (74.5)	23.8 (19.5)	8.9 (11.6)	218.4 (51.3)	1489.8 (40.4)
	1984	447.4 (31.2)	544.6 (26.8)	96.0 (12.5)	—	59.3 (61.0)	46.1 (19.6)	11.1 (10.5)	315.6 (32.4)	1520.2 (26.9)
	1987	896.1 (43.6)	730.4 (29.6)	122.0 (11.6)	—	40.5 (77.1)	49.1 (25.8)	—	562.9 (44.0)	2401.0 (33.8)
UK	1978	195.2 (28.9)	224.2 (37.0)	58.4 (17.0)	46.6 (49.0)	20.5 (93.0)	115.3 (40.0)	2.2 (34.0)	168.6 (50.0)	831.1 (36.0)
	1981	416.2 (26.4)	499.5 (35.7)	127.9 (9.7)	40.2 (33.6)	19.5 (98.6)	145.2 (46.1)	4.6 (22.9)	243.0 (39.7)	1496.1 (27.8)

continued on p. 244

Table 17.1   continued

Country	Year	Sensitive industrial products (except textiles)[b]	Non-sensitive industrial products (except textiles)	Sensitive textiles	Semi-sensitive textiles[c]	Non-sensitive textiles	Sensitive agricultural products (tobacco type Virginia, cocoa butter, canned pineapple)	Semi-sensitive agricultural products (raw tobacco)	Non-sensitive agricultural products	Total agricultural products, semi-manufactures and manufactures
	1984	1197.7 (33.8)	858.6 (35.1)	189.0 (10.8)	–	42.3 (95.5)	168.1 (32.6)	1.3 (5.1)	335.8 (30.0)	2792.8 (29.6)
	1987	676.0 (25.6)	937.5 (43.2)	256.1 (12.3)	–	35.1 (98.6)	309.6 (124.3)	–	358.5 (34.9)	2582.7 (31.4)
Ireland	1978	6.7 (28.5)	7.2 (48.0)	0.6 (29.0)	0.3 (11.0)	0.5 (57.0)	4.3 (62.0)	–	1.1 (27.0)	21.0 (35.0)
	1981	10.7 (19.1)	17.5 (58.2)	2.6 (10.9)	0.4 (25.2)	0.6 (100.0)	4.8 (34.3)	–	8.1 (98.1)	44.8 (33.3)
	1984	24.6 (25.7)	36.6 (30.4)	5.6 (11.3)	–	–	9.6 (44.5)	–	2.1 (30.3)	78.5 (26.6)
	1987	13.6 (22.9)	27.8 (29.8)	5.4 (9.7)	–	–	4.5 (59.4)	–	2.7 (36.2)	54.0 (24.2)
Denmark	1978	36.9 (37.1)	24.9 (68.0)	14.1 (28.0)	10.3 (69.0)	2.6 (85.0)	6.7 (87.0)	3.2 (91.0)	17.9 (85.0)	116.5 (49.0)
	1981	70.5 (43.9)	47.6 (61.8)	11.5 (8.7)	5.4 (31.9)	3.2 (95.6)	5.9 (47.6)	1.5 (15.3)	16.0 (38.5)	161.6 (35.5)

1984	74.7	93.0	26.9	–	3.6	2.8	1.9	25.8	228.6
	(40.5)	(58.7)	(12.5)	–	(95.5)	(15.8)	(10.2)	(34.7)	(34.0)
1987	92.2	99.4	31.6	–	1.5	9.0	–	81.8	325.5
	(38.2)	(50.3)	(11.1)	–	(94.5)	(33.8)	–	(58.0)	(35.7)
Greece									
1978	–	–	–	–	–	–	–	–	–
	–	–	–	–	–	–	–	–	–
1981	0.3	4.5	0.1	–	0.2	0.7	–	0.2	6.1
	(0.8)	(1.7)	(0.5)	–	(13.4)	(5.1)	–	(1.4)	(1.7)
1984	36.1	15.7	1.4	–	0.9	3.8	0.5	8.1	36.1
	(12.0)	(13.8)	(3.3)	–	(47.9)	(11.3)	(93.7)	(21.4)	(12.0)
1987	61.8	26.4	1.9	–	1.1	2.7	–	48.1	142.1
	(46.4)	(7.7)	(4.5)	–	(81.4)	(5.8)	–	(45.2)	(21.1)

Notes: a. Percentage share in brackets.
b. Including semi-sensitive products in 1978. This category was abandoned in 1981.
c. Abandoned in 1983.
d. EC-9 in 1978; EC-10 in 1981, 1984; EC-12 in 1987.

Source: Microfiches provided by EUROSTAT.

in the preferential shares of imports to Germany, Italy and the Benelux. However this did not impede a further increase in absolute GSP-receiving imports and an even stronger increase in GSP-covered imports to France, where the preferential share had dropped in 1981. This was also true in the case of GSP-receiving imports to the UK, which doubled from 1981–4 when there had been no strong increase in the preferential share, indicating an equally high growth of GSP-covered imports.

The development of sensitive and non-sensitive industrial imports to the EC shows the same pattern as total imports. Only the share of GSP-receiving imports of sensitive industrial products increased from 27.4 per cent in 1978 to 38.2 per cent in 1981 and remained at this higher level, again with a drop in 1984. For non-sensitive industrial products the GSP-receiving share of 37 per cent in 1978 was also higher than for total imports, but it then declined to nearly equal the average in 1987. Periods of booming preferential exports in line with rising shares of GSP-receiving trade can be identified for sensitive and non-sensitive industrial products in Italy and the Benelux during 1978–81, and for French and Italian imports of sensitive industrial products during 1981–4 and 1984–7 respectively. Imports to Germany increased steadily over the whole period however, whilst preferential import shares declined. Mixed evidence regarding the effectiveness of the GSP scheme also arises from the sharp decline in GSP-receiving shares for sensitive industrial imports to Italy and the Benelux in 1984 that did not result in an equally pronounced reduction in GSP-receiving trade.

With sensitive and non-sensitive industrial products representing the most important export categories of the GSP beneficiaries, the third place is held by non-sensitive agricultural products. EC imports in this category recorded slower growth rates from 1978–84 but gained momentum after 1984. The shares of GSP-receiving imports declined up to 1984 and then stabilised at well above 30 per cent. The relationship between the degree of preferential treatment and export performance in this product category is rather mixed. For all the major importers (Germany, France, Italy, Benelux and the UK) the shares of GSP-receiving imports in total non-sensitive agricultural imports reduced during 1978–84. Nevertheless the GSP beneficiaries were able to increase their preferential as well as their non-preferential exports to these countries. Even in 1987, when preferential exports to these countries gained momentum, the shares of GSP-receiving imports rose only slightly, thus indicating that non-

GSP receiving exports of non-sensitive agricultural products had also grown at a fast rate.

The most favourable tariff treatment of imports is granted by the EC to non-sensitive textiles, with preferential imports accounting for more than 70 per cent of total imports. For sensitive agricultural products the preference share rose to a remarkable 54 per cent in 1987 when the category of semi-sensitive agricultural products was cancelled. Comparatively low ratios of GSP-receiving to GSP-covered imports can be observed for sensitive textiles, which are regulated by the MFA. But again a strong influence by the share of GSP-receiving imports on the development of imports is not observable. The import growth of non-sensitive textiles and sensitive agricultural products remained moderate despite extensive preferential treatment, whereas imports of sensitive textiles experienced a stronger increase with low preferential shares.

The above analysis shows that only one-third of the GSP-covered imports by GSP beneficiaries to the EC actually received GSP treatment during 1978–87. Therefore the GSP suppliers must be regarded as being competitive on the EC market even without the preferential treatment of their exports. This suggests that the trade effects of the GSP scheme were only minor. Trade creation and trade diversion occur at the margin and this trade had already taken place under MFN conditions. The limited effect of the GSP scheme is also indicated by the unstable relationship between the share of GSP-receiving imports in total imports and import growth. Stable or even decreasing shares of GSP-receiving imports in some product categories did not impede strong increases in GSP-covered exports by the beneficiaries, which in particular implied increases in non-preferential exports. On the contrary, falling shares in preferential trade did not result in a sufficiently large reduction in GSP-receiving imports to explain the fall in the share, thus indicating that the non-GSP-receiving import must still have increased.

This reasoning implies that the economic performance of the GSP beneficiaries and the development of their international competitiveness must be regarded as a major factor determining the GSP countries' export performance. Thus the domestic policies of the GSP countries and the way in which their economies adjust according to their comparative advantages should take centre stage. Furthermore it seems reasonable to expect that most GSP suppliers would benefit more from general MFN-tariff reductions than from an extension of the prevailing GSP scheme (Langhammer and Sapir, 1987, pp. 68–71,

78–9). This view is supported by the good export performance of the ASEAN countries, which are all GSP beneficiaries. During the period 1981–4 ASEAN was able to nearly double its total exports – GSP-receiving as well as non-preferential – to the EC, whereas the total GSP-covered exports from the other GSP countries only recorded a 43 per cent increase.[5]

A closer look at the mechanics of the GSP provides an explanation of why the trade effects from the GSP are unlikely to be substantial. Trade effects will occur if tariff cuts are passed on tu the consumer, thus raising demand for the products. Income instead of trade effects will arise in cases of tariff-pocketing either by the GSP supplier or by the EC importer. Tariff-pocketing means the GSP supplier has to increase the price of those exports which receive preferential treatment, or that the importer does not pass on the tariff saving. Leaving aside competitive considerations, the following argument can be advanced for both traders. The system of quantitative restrictions for GSP treatment puts both trading partners into a state of uncertainty (Langhammer, 1983). When pricing their sales neither the GSP supplier nor the EC importer can know which part of their trade will remain duty-free. Thus pricing is based on MFN tariffs. Eventual tariff savings realised during the year will accrue to the EC importer. He will regard these savings as windfall profits and may use them to subsidise marginal imports through special sales, thereby inducing additional trade. In general however, the above argument suggests that the trade creation effects of the GSP scheme are minor and that even the income effects mainly favour EC importers.

17.3   TRADE PREFERENCES FOR THE ACP GROUP

In addition to the GSP scheme, the EC grants special preferences to different groups of developing countries. Among these the ACP countries, which comprise former colonies in Sub-Saharan Africa, the Caribbean and the Pacific archipelago, form the largest group.[6] The privileged trade relations between the ACP countries and the EC are governed by the three so-called Lomé Conventions of 1975, 1979 and 1984. These supersede a number of preferential trading arrangements between EC member states and developing countries, in particular the preferences that were granted by the UK to members of the Commonwealth prior to the UK's entry into the EC. The ACP agreement grants duty-free access to EC markets for the large majority of tariff items, which are also free of quantitative restriction. The exception to this is those agricultural products that are subject to the CAP, where unilateral variable levies and quantitative restrictions can be imposed on imports. But in general ACP–EC trade does not suffer from the detrimental effects on trade creation that result from the various quantitative restrictions under the GSP scheme.

The degree of preferential treatment enjoyed by ACP exports compared to the exports from other developed countries and other developing countries depends on:

1. The level of GATT-negotiated most-favoured-nation tariffs that have to be paid by suppliers in developed countries on GSP exports in excess of the respective quotas and ceilings. A reduction in MFN rates, for example as a result of the Tokyo round, erodes the preference enjoyed by ACP countries, as well as that enjoyed by GSP-beneficiaries and other developing countries with preferential treatment.
2. The coverage of the GSP-scheme and other preferential trading arrangements. The broadening of GSP product coverage or the relaxation of its quantitative restrictions reduces the preference margins of the ACP exporters. This happened in 1977–82.
3. The imposition of unilateral variable levies and quantitative import restrictions on agricultural products which are subject to the CAP or other non-tariff regulations against ACP countries (Agarwal, Dippl and Langhammer, 1985, p. 15).

As has already been spelled out, the preference margins of the ACP group depend on the level of MFN and GSP tariffs as well as on the quantitative restrictions on GSP imports. The following section draws on the Amelung and Langhammer study (1989, pp. 44–50), where the tariff treatment of the major ACP export items has been analysed. From 1983 to 1987 the share of products in ACP exports to the EC which are subject to duty under the MFN rose from 26.7 per cent to 32.4 per cent. This shift was due mainly to the reduced share of duty-free oil exports. Thus in 1987, for at least 32 per cent of total ACP exports tariff preferences could have been effective. Besides oil, important duty-free products were diamonds, iron ore, cotton and copper; while the share of products subject to duty was dominated by coffee, cocoa and sugar. Sugar was treated as a separate case because sugar exports are governed by the Sugar Protocol of the Lomé Convention (Chapter 16.2.2). Amelung and Langhammer emphasise that the ratio between dutiable and duty-free products in ACP exports, and thus their relative degree of preferential treatment, is strongly influenced by the world market price of these few goods. Therefore the degree to which preferential tariff treatment can have an impact on ACP exports depends mainly on external factors. On balance it is concluded that the differentials between MFN, GSP and the special preference rates granted to the ACP group are not important determinants of price competition on the EC import market since the differentials are relatively small in comparison with other factors affecting import prices, for example exchange rate fluctuations.

Taking this into account, the degree to which ACP exporters can benefit from their special preferences may depend more on quantitative restrictions, either market access per se or to preferential access, that are levied on other suppliers. But ACP exports are also subject to restriction if particular products fall under CAP regulations, as discussed in Chapter 16. In this case preference only results in a transfer of resources and not in trade expansion. This is the case with beef, other meat, sugar and cereals. Since 1985–6 canned pineapples have also been regulated by the CAP.

In order to evaluate the advantage of the ACP group over the GSP beneficiaries it must be taken into account that GSP treatment is restricted by the various ceilings and quotas that limit the share of GSP-receiving in GSP-covered imports. Thus the effective preference margin of ACP countries vis-à-vis GSP exporters is actually higher than indicated by the GSP rates. From the previous discussion of the effects of the GSP it may be concluded that for competing exports from GSP beneficiaries MFN tariffs constitute the relevant basis for assessing the ACP countries' preference margins. This is because, due to uncertainty about whether specific exports enjoy preferential GSP treatment, GSP suppliers have to price their exports with reference to MFN tariffs. Therefore GSP-treatment results mainly in income effects, and so comparison of the export performances of ACP and non-ACP countries should focus on total exports of non-ACP countries and not just on GSP-receiving exports. Table 17.2 provides a breakdown of ACP and non-ACP exports to the EC according to the broad GSP categories of sensitive and non-sensitive manufactures and agricultural products. The Maghreb and Mashreq countries and Yugoslavia are excluded from the group of non-ACP countries because they receive special preferences that exceed the regular GSP treatment (Section 17.4 below).

Table 17.2 shows that in 1978–87 total exports of agricultural

Table 17.2 Structure of EC imports from ACP countries and non-ACP developing countries,[a] 1978, 1981, 1984 and 1987

GSP category	GSP-covered imports from non-ACP beneficiaries (millions of ECU, share of GSP-receiving imports in brackets)				EC imports from ACP countries (millions of ECU)			
	1978	1981	1984	1987	1978	1981	1984	1987
Sensitive industrial products (except textiles)	3493.9 (26.9)	6852.1 (46.5)	11537.9 (37.2)	12962.1 (42.6)	29.0	594.5	598.0	265.2
Non-sensitive industrial products (except textiles)	3740.8 (34.0)	5202.8 (49.2)	6173.1 (55.2)	7028.5 (61.5)	388.1	528.5	780.0	1026.5
Sensitive textiles	2130.5 (7.0)	4715.1 (8.6)	6924.8 (14.2)	9108.6 (16.0)	86.9	90.3	31.4	55.9
Semi-sensitive textiles	427.9 (50.0)	637.5 (41.0)	–	–	3.0	55.4	–	–
Non-sensitive textiles	114.1 (65.0)	119.4 (71.3)	195.5 (71.5)	130.7 (83.8)	0.4	0.1	–	–
Sensitive agricultural products (tobacco type Virginia, cocoa butter, canned pineapples)	455.2 (40.0)	510.7 (50.5)	834.2 (41.7)	603.7 (79.4)	261.7	239.1	420.8	285.6

continued on p. 252

Table 17.2 continued

GSP category	GSP-covered imports from non-ACP beneficiaries (millions of ECU, share of GSP-receiving imports in brackets)				EC imports from ACP countries (millions of ECU)			
	1978	1981	1984	1987	1978	1981	1984	1987
Semi-sensitive agricultural products	26.2 (56.0)	176.5 (12.8)	189.3 (12.0)	–	21.3	34.1	85.2	–
Non-sensitive agricultural products	1434.5 (51.0)	1888.6 (61.7)	2810.5 (61.9)	5330.5 (60.9)	372.0	1529.6	1975.3	2611.6
Total agricultural products, semi-manufactures and manufactures	11823.1 (30.0)	20109.1 (39.7)	28723.3 (38.1)	35153.4 (43.0)	1615.2	3071.7	3900.6	4244.8

Note: a. Maghreb and Mashreq countries and Yugoslavia are excluded from the non-ACP Group of 77 members (the GSP-beneficiaries).

Source: Microfiches provided by EUROSTAT.

products, semi-manufactures and manufactures from non-ACP countries grew at a faster rate than ACP exports, with an average annual growth rate of 14.6 per cent compared with 12.8 per cent for the ACP countries. Both groups saw a decline in their export growth rates over time. For ACP countries exports of agricultural products, semi-manufactured goods and manufactures declined from an average growth rate of 19.3 per cent in 1978–84 to 6.7 per cent in 1981–7. The growth rate of non-ACP total exports fell from 25.3 to 13.6 per cent, but this was still higher than the ACP growth rate. This general reduction in EC imports was mainly the result of declining demand due to lower GDP growth in the EC during the 1980s.

The better performance of non-ACP exports against ACP exports is also evident for all sensitive products, despite the fact that in these categories in particular the GSP beneficiaries suffer from quantitative restrictions. For sensitive industrial products the non-ACP export pattern is similar to that of total non-ACP exports, while ACP exports remained constant between 1981 and 1984 after a strong increase from 1978. However in 1987 ACP exports of sensitive industrial products more than halved, whilst the development of non-ACP exports remained stable.

The same picture emerges with sensitive textiles in 1984, when a heavy decline in ACP exports contrasted with the favourable export performance of the non-ACP countries. The growth in sensitive textile exports ranks first among all product categories for non-ACP countries in 1978 and 1987 (see in particular Chapter 18.2).

In conclusion it can be stated that an assessment of the ACP preferences granted by the EC does not show very favourable results. For the main categories of ACP exports preferential treatment does not seem to have had a significant impact on the performance of the ACP group. This judgement is supported by the fact that in 1987 at least 43 per cent of total EC imports from ACP countries were duty-free under MFN conditions, and thus by definition received no preferential treatment. Most of these duty-free imports were the primary commodities which represent the bulk of ACP exports. Even in those product categories where ACP suppliers receive special preferences, the preference margins only varied by around 6.3 percentage points relative to MFN treatment and 5 percentage points compared to GSP beneficiaries (Amelung and Langhammer, 1989). In order to benefit more extensively from their special preferences the ACP countries would have to shift their export composition towards manufactured products, where their preference margins against MFN and GSP suppliers are larger. Whether this change will take place depends on the economic policies in the ACP countries themselves – in the past their regulations and an overvalued exchange rate have favoured domestic market-oriented production.[7]

17.4 SPECIAL PREFERENCES FOR MEDITERRANEAN COUNTRIES

While the existence of special trade relations between the EC and the Mediterranean region dates back to the very beginning of the Treaty of Rome in 1957, the current trade agreements are the result of the 'global' Mediterranean policy formulated in late 1972. Under this unified approach the EC agreed with the Mediterranean countries on equal treatment of the trading partners despite the fact that individual bilateral agreements were still in effect. In particular the EC reached a preferential trade and cooperation agreement with the Maghreb countries in 1976 and with the Mashreq countries in 1977 (Pomfret, 1986).[8] A similar agreement was signed with Yugoslavia in 1980.

In the case of the Maghreb and Mashreq countries the trade preferences provide for the duty-free access of raw materials and all industrial products that satisfy the EC's rules of origin. The Maghreb countries enjoy a special preference whereby the production processes in individual countries enter the rules of origin on a cumulative basis (Bachmann, 1981, p. 38). However two categories are not granted duty-free access to the EC market: cork and refined petroleum products. Furthermore a general safeguard clause allows the EC to withdraw trade preferences for all products if an increase in exports causes difficulties on the EC markets (Mishalani et al., 1981, pp. 64–8). For agricultural products, tariff reductions from 20 to 100 per cent apply to most of the countries' important export products. In the case of Yugoslavia, the introduction of more extensive preferences was especially relevant for its industrial exports. Before 1980 Yugoslavia had been subject to the general GSP scheme, but in 1977 only 33 per cent of its industrial exports benefited from the GSP. However with the new preferential trade agreement Yugoslavia can expect 70 per cent of its industrial exports to enter the EC duty-free. The remaining products were either subject to duty-free tariff ceilings or to special arrangements like the MFA (Mishalani et al., 1981, p. 70). The treatment of Yugoslavia's agricultural exports to the EC is largely comparable to the agreement with the Maghreb and Mashreq countries. Again preferences were granted in relation to the importance of the respective agricultural products to the country's exports.

When one tries to rank the different preferential trade schemes of the EC according to the degree of effectively-granted preference margins, the trade agreements with the Mediterranean countries assume a middle position with the ACP preferences ranking highest and the GSP scheme lowest. In order to assess the trade effects that might have arisen from the preferential trade agreements with the Maghreb and Mashreq countries and Yugoslavia, the exports of these countries to the EC for 1981 to 1987 are given in Table 17.3. Exports are again broken down into GSP categories to allow for comparisons with ACP countries and other GSP countries (the data refer to GSP-covered exports). Although there may be quantitative limitations to preferential access it is not possible to present information on the share of preferential exports as was the case with GSP beneficiaries. However compared with the GSP scheme the restrictions on trade preferences are less important in the case of the Mediterranean countries. Therefore the general conclusions should not be seriously affected.

Table 17.3 shows that total EC imports from the Maghreb and Mashreq countries and Yugoslavia are dominated by industrial products. The Maghreb and Mashreq countries experienced dramatic fluctuations in their exports to the EC during the period in question and this can be attributed to their development of industrial, especially non-sensitive industrial, exports. Total exports of the Maghreb and Mashreq countries grew by 40 per cent per annum from 1981 to 1984, followed by an annual decline of 23 per cent over the next three years. Another severe export reduction took place with sensitive textiles. This may have largely been due to restrictions that are similar to those of the MFA. Despite the fact that the Maghreb and Mashreq countries are not contracting parties to the MFA, the EC has been able to negotiate similar restrictions with the Mediterranean countries (that is, informal agreements, notes, memoranda and 'understandings'; Langhammer, 1988, p. 206).

Yugoslav exports to the EC grew over the whole period, with a strong gain in momentum up to a 14 per cent growth rate during 1984–7, but again this growth was only brought about by non-sensitive industrial exports. Sensitive industrial exports drew to a standstill from 1981 to 1984, and to a large extent this was responsible

Table 17.3   Structure of preferential EC imports from Maghreb and
Mashreq countries and Yugoslavia, 1981, 1984 and 1987

	Maghreb and Mashreq (millions of ECU)			Yugoslavia (millions of ECU)		
GSP Category	*1981*	*1984*	*1987*	*1981*	*1984*	*1987*
Sensitive industrial products (except textiles)	1165.8	1705.0	1195.0	385.1	n.a.	4.4
Non-sensitive industrial products (except textiles)	1008.7	3719.8	1770.3	769.6	1218.9	1609.2
Sensitive textiles	546.8	5.3	14.3	4.9	23.8	61.2
Semi-sensitive textiles	33.7	–	–	4.2	–	–
Non-sensitive textiles	0.1	n.a.	n.a.	n.a.	n.a.	n.a.
Sensitive agriculture (tobacco type Virginia, cocoa butter, canned pineapple)	1.1	1.0	n.a.	1.2	1.8	2.0
Semi-sensitive agricultural products	1.0	0.6	–	5.8	6.4	–
Non-sensitive agricultural products	92.8	162.3	331.3	112.1	120.7	128.0
Total agricultural products semi-manufactures and manufactures	2850.0	5595.0	3310.9	1283.0	1371.8	1804.8

Note: n.a. = data not available.

Source: Microfiches provided by EUROSTAT.

for the weak growth of Yugoslav exports to the EC during that
period.

A comparison of the export performance of the Maghreb and
Mashreq countries and Yugoslavia with the growth of EC imports
from the ACP group and the other GSP beneficiaries (Table 17.3)
reveals the following. Over the period 1981–7 the Maghreb and

Mashreq countries' exports to the EC achieved the lowest export growth rate (3 per cent), followed by the ACP group and Yugoslavia (6.7 and 7.1 per cent respectively), while the GSP beneficiaries clearly stayed on top with 11.8 per cent. It should also be noted that the total export performance of the ACP group and the remaining GSP countries was strongly dependent on industrial exports.

For Yugoslavia it has to be stated, especially in the light of its high export growth rate in the second half of the period, that the preferential trade agreement has given rise to strong trade effects. The concentration of these trade effects on non-sensitive industrial products seems plausible because these products had been added to the list of products which could enter the EC without quantitative restriction and under preferential terms under the new agreement of 1980. For the Maghreb and Mashreq countries it is difficult to assess why the export boom in industrial products was so drastically reversed. Whilst with sensitive industrial products it may be possible that the EC took recourse to quantitative restrictions – as provided for in the agreements – this reasoning does not apply to non-sensitive industrial products. For non-sensitive products even the unilateral GSP scheme does not provide for quantitative restrictions. Therefore the strong decline in non-sensitive industrial exports by the Maghreb and Mashreq countries to the EC seems to have been caused primarily by domestic developments in the exporting countries.

Notes and references

1. This chapter draws heavily on Langhammer and Sapir, 1987.
2. With the exception of five product groups, agricultural products have not been subject to quantitative restrictions under the GSP scheme.
3. The following example illustrates the restrictive nature of origin rules. To qualify for GSP treatment a radio or television set requires first that the import content does not exceed 40 per cent of the total value, second that at least 50 per cent of the value of the intermediate parts originated in the country seeking preference, and third that all the transistors also originated in that country. The last provision especially has disqualified many products of South East Asian countries from GSP treatment since, because of large economies of scale, they import transistors from Japan and the US. It seems obvious that the EC included this provision with full knowledge of this division of labour in order to impose a brake on duty-free imports of radios and television sets (Langhammer and Sapir, 1987, p. 28).
4. See the studies by Baldwin and Murray (1977) Sapir (1981) and Langhammer (1983).

5. Data from microfiches provided by EUROSTAT.
6. For a detailed analysis of ACP–EC trade, see Amelung and Langhammer (1989).
7. For an extensive discussion of domestic policies in the ACP countries and their effect on export growth and diversification, see Agarwal, Dippl and Langhammer (1985).
8. The Maghreb countries include Algeria, Morocco, and Tunisia; the Mashreq countries consist of Egypt, Jordan, Lebanon and Syria.

18 MFA and Article 115: Two Complementary EC Non-tariff Barriers

Dean Spinanger

18.1 MFA AND EC

The EC was instrumental in launching the Multi-Fibre Arrangement (MFA) in 1974. This was viewed as an accomplishment towards bringing the ever-expanding hotchpotch of different bilateral trade restraints for textiles and textile products under one set of rules, even if this meant opting out of the GATT framework. After all, the multiplicity of trade barriers engendered throughout the reign of the Long-term Agreement (that is, since 1962) was threatening to make a farce out of the GATT non-discrimination principal upon which the international trading system was based. Thus spinning off such distorting elements into a separate organisation was viewed as a logical move to ensure that non-discrimination could be generally maintained elsewhere. Specifically it was and still is noted that it is not an expressed purpose of the MFA to protect the clothing and textile industries in industrialised countries at the expense of the same industries in developing countries. Rather the MFA was designed to ensure that the advantages to be gained from a more efficient allocation of resources are not jeopardised by ruinous international competition followed by an ensuing wave of protectionist measures that close off export markets to future as well as to existing producers. Based primarily on this line of reasoning the MFA and its predecessors have managed to survive and indeed thrive for almost three decades.

What now exists (MFA IV, 1986–92) is however hardly liberal, but rather an incomprehensible maze of tiered restrictions ranging from tight, mandatory, country-specific import quotas down to voluntary self-monitored exports (Spinanger and Zietz, 1986). Since the MFA is merely the overall framework within which bilateral agreements are reached (there are about three dozen such agreements[1]) on

259

country-by-country (that is, for ten EC countries since the Benelux countries – based on their earlier customs union – are counted as one) and category-by-category specification (that is, around 100), roughly 36 000 individual restrictions are possible. In 1987 probably well over 5000 actually prevailed; for Hong Kong alone (the EC's main supplier) more than 300 quotas and 600 items under export authorisation were in effect. Unfortunately this listing of agreements does not do full justice to the spectrum of EC restrictions on MFA products vis-à-vis developing countries. Even exports of textiles and clothing from the ACP countries – which are supposedly given free access to the EC market – become subject to restrictions when increase too rapidly (for example, see Hein, 1988, p. 9 and Lamusse, 1989, p. 27).

While official EC institutions have been creating the impression that they are serious about returning the MFA to the folds of GATT (for example communications submitted to GATT in 1985 and 1989), industrial lobbies in some EC countries have been stressing the need to maintain the MFA (see for example Wilson, 1988, p. 24). That the EC MFA-industry interests may well prevail can be deduced from anti-dumping actions taken against – among others – Hong Kong, Indonesia and Turkey in connection with denim cloth. This was the first time the EC had applied anti-dumping rules to an MFA product. The reason why it had not occurred previously was simply that the MFA was interpreted as containing guarantees for a certain import volume, with no stipulations being made about prices. Such a new interpretation of the MFA by the EC could herald a more protectionistic stance in the future.

18.2   IMPORTANCE OF TRADE IN TEXTILES AND CLOTHING FOR THE EC AND DEVELOPING COUNTRIES

Despite the amount spent by the EC, national governments and MFA industrial lobbies to maintain the protectionist stance against MFA products from developing countries, the textile and – in particular – clothing industries have been adjusting to decreasing comparative advantages. In the period 1975–85 employment in both sectors fell by about 40 per cent, amounting to a loss of roughly one million jobs. However, whereas textile production in 1987 was at 1980 levels (after falling almost 10 per cent during 1983), clothing production was almost 10 per cent below.

Concerning EC trade with MFA products, 38 per cent of clothing imports in 1986 came from developing countries (including China), compared with 34 per cent in 1980, whereas for textiles only 15 per cent was achieved, a slight reduction from the 1980 figure of 17 per cent. The degree to which the EC has actually opened up to MFA imports from developing countries can of course only be determined by referring to import penetration ratios (imports as a percentage of apparent domestic consumption). While such ratios are not easily constructed, they are subject to similar constaints across all countries and thus can be used to give an adequate overview of the success of developing countries in gaining entry to EC markets.[2] Based on OECD 1980–5 figures (1988, p. 25; includes clothing, textiles, leather and footwear) the values for Germany (1.33–7.96 per cent) and the UK (2.10–7.74 per cent) far exceeded those for France (0.11–2.08 per cent) and Italy (0.34–1.18 per cent) in the EC. These figures however were considerably below those for Sweden (4.03–18.72 per cent), Australia (2.50–11.55 per cent) and the US (1.53–11.16 per cent).

These statistics unfortunately do not fully reflect the degree of EC market penetration achieved by all developing countries since they include only Hong Kong, Taiwan and South Korea as important suppliers of textile and clothing products. Furthermore these three countries accounted for less than 2 per cent of total EC textile imports and slightly less than 15 per cent of clothing imports in 1986. Unlike the US, whose major suppliers are exclusively in the Far East,[3] the EC obtains many of its MFA imports from Mediterranean and Eastern European countries. While Hong Kong and South Korea have been the two largest suppliers of clothing to the EC since 1980 (in the years 1986–8 they accounted for over 25 per cent of non-member imports), Turkey now runs a very close third (in 1980 it ran twenty-seventh). Turkey, Yugoslavia, Morocco and Tunisia together account for roughly 25 per cent of EC clothing imports from non-member countries.

With the coming of the common internal market in 1992, and assuming that the existing preferences for the Mediterranean region remain (offshore processing agreements are very important), these countries should be able to profit all the more. Furthermore the events in Eastern Europe will undoubtedly cause a further focusing on nearby suppliers; this should prove to be especially true for West Germany whose share of MFA products from Eastern Europe is the highest in the EC.

The above regional distribution of suppliers is not the same across all EC countries. The differing sources of imports to various EC countries can be attributed to colonial ties (for example France and the UK), proximity (for example Germany) or simply the development of trading links. Together with developments in domestic economies (such as structural change or protectionism), all this not only has implications for import penetration ratios (as already noted) but also definite implications for MFA restrictions, and accordingly for the use of Article 115 (see Section 18.3 below).

With respect to the MFA the main source of the problems underlying the EC's policy can be identified as stemming from country-specific demands. That is, although the EC acts as a single negotiator, within each bilateral agreement quotas or other restrictions are set up by product on a member country basis. While the initial allocation of quotas is based on prevailing trade patterns, the EC has stipulated that 'appropriate shares' should be aimed at.[4] In reality however, the distribution of quotas within the EC rarely reflects these shares.

Exactly what this means in terms of the relative size of the quotas can best be explained by examining a specific MFA category. This is done in Table 18.1, which has specified quotas for shirts (men and boys) for selected EC countries by major suppliers (shirts make up about 10 per cent of the EC's clothing imports from developing countries). Likewise imports from the EC have also been included as a comparative disaggregation for the US. All the quotas for developing countries and actual imports for the US and the EC have been calculated in terms of pieces per 1000 population so cross-country comparisons can be made (even if income and other factors influence these figures).

The quota distribution shown in Table 18.1 clearly underlines the restrictiveness of countries like France or Italy vis-à-vis Germany or the UK. With factors of 36 between German and French imports from China, 26 for those from Korea and 5.3 for all the listed developing countries, the burden-sharing difference of 1.5 (that is, 25.5/16.5 – see note 4) has been greatly exceeded. While not all categories differ to this degree the sum of MFA quotas over all textile and clothing products from Hong Kong were 60 per cent higher for the Benelux countries, 520 per cent higher for Germany and 710 per cent higher for the UK than those for France (in 1987).

In more general terms it can be shown that for the eight most sensitive categories,[5] Germany (category 1), the UK (category 2) and Denmark (category 1) had only one case where quotas were lower than the expected shares. In the case of Spain and Greece all eight categories were lower, for France and Portugal seven categories were

Table 18.1 Per capita quotas (pcs/1000 pop.) for EC MFA category 8 (woven shirts, mens and boys) and for the US equivalent thereof[a] by major suppliers, 1987

	Germany	France	Italy	Benelux	UK	Spain	US[a]
Hong Kong	311.5	14.4	27.0	125.0	359.1	2.0	168.5
Macao	10.5	41.6	13.4	10.5	25.2	.9	10.5
China, PR	60.0	13.9	14.6	23.8	19.3	1.7	110.4
China, R	76.1	2.1	4.2	41.2	11.5	.9	182.2
Korea	274.4	10.5	20.6	255.2	48.8	4.1	316.4
Indonesia	38.2	18.0	16.7	27.5	21.2	1.2	33.9
Malaysia	21.2	33.0	3.5	9.4	5.6	2.1	30.0
Philippines	26.6	6.9	8.0	20.7	7.5	1.8	22.1
Thailand	8.0	2.9	7.1	11.6	3.6	2.0	12.4
India	153.0	27.7	69.3	124.1	163.5	5.5	68.7
Bangladesh[b]	115.8	24.8	58.6	23.7	31.4	3.0	84.1
Sum of the above developing countries	1105.3	195.8	243.0	672.7	696.7	25.2	1039.2
EC-12[b]	134.2	172.6	63.7	579.8	105.8	27.8	17.8

Notes: a. Actual imports in US categories 340, 440 and 640; almost identical with EC category 8.
  b. Actual imports.

Source: Own calculations based on MFA bilaterals, (EC Official Journal, 31.12.86: L 386, L 387 and L 389). EUROSTAT External Trade – NIMEXE 1987; Import, vol. F and US trade data (Major Shippers Report, 1988). Population data taken from World Bank, World Development Report 1989.

lower, for Italy and Ireland there were six and for the Benelux countries there were only two (categories 2 and 3). A comparison with the US also puts these figures in a more proper perspective and shows the greater openness for imports from developing countries (as noted earlier in more general terms).

18.3 ARTICLE 115 AND DEVELOPING COUNTRIES

Article 115 of the Treaty of Rome[6] clearly runs counter to one of the cornerstones of the common market, namely the principle of free movement of goods laid down in Article 9 of the treaty. Experience has shown that its application effectively closes the borders of a member state to a specific product from a non-member country (or group of countries). In order to apply this measure, the indirect importation of such products from non-member countries must be shown to be causing damage to a specific domestic industry in such a manner that the EC Commission is also convinced of the evidence. Through the 1970s – in connection with the MFA I and II-induced flood of actions – it was relatively easy to obtain such permission. At the turn of decade however conditions were tightened and it was stated that attempts would be made to ensure that such actions would be rolled back over time.

The annual frequency of application of Article 115 during the period 1981–8 varied considerably, with the peak in 1983 lying almost 50 per cent above the lowest value in 1986 (Table 18.2). One factor which seems to increase the number of cases is a low US dollar rate. Although basically there seems to be no recent trend (on average about 120 actions are initiated each year), the actual impact has nonetheless grown considerably larger. First of all, the length of time-restrictions applied in 1987 and 1988 lies about 10 per cent above that of the early 1980s. Whereas in 1981 and 1983 Article 115 restrictions lasted 156 days on average, in 1987 and 1988 they lasted 172 days. Secondly a greater number of actions are applied in the first half of the year (in 1981–5, 49 per cent as opposed to 61 per cent in 1986–8) thus more effectively cutting off supplies. As for the structure of the Article 115 cases, a definite shift away from MFA products toward other manufactured products can be detected. For example in 1988 other manufactured products accounted for 33 per cent of all Article 115 cases, up one-third from this category's relatively constant rate during the period 1981–6.

With respect to the MFA products, an examination of the initiating-country structure of Article 115 cases reveals quite clearly an increased concentration on France and Ireland (Table 18.2). That is, they accounted for over 85 per cent of the cases from 1986–8 as opposed to roughly 65 per cent in 1981 and 1983. The story is different however for other industrial goods, where Italy has long been one of the major initiators of Article 115 cases. As opposed to MFA products, 1988 marks the highest year on record for actions on non-MFA manufactured items. This upsurge was primarily the result of actions taken by the new member, Spain. These 'other countries' have now surpassed Italy, which was the major initiator in 1986, and France, the major initiator in 1987.

Turning to the countries being hit by Article 115, Table 18.3 underlines the dominance of developing countries in the Asia Pacific

Table 18.2 Distribution of Article 115 actions by product groups and initiating countries, 1981–8 (in per cent)

Product group/ initiating country	1981	1983	1985	1986	1987	1988
By product group affected:						
Agricultural goods	1.8	3.1	5.3	1.9	1.5	7.2
MFA products	74.6	74.4	70.2	74.1	69.5	59.5
Other industrial goods	23.7	22.5	24.6	24.1	29.0	33.3
Total (actual)	114.0	160.0	114.0	108.0	131.0	111.0
By country initiating action against MFA products:						
Benelux	17.6	12.6	2.5	0.0	1.1	1.5
France	37.6	27.7	38.8	55.0	45.1	40.9
Ireland	27.1	38.7	36.3	37.5	42.9	42.4
Italy	7.1	6.7	8.8	3.8	8.0	15.2
UK	9.4	10.9	13.8	3.8	1.1	0.0
All others	1.2	3.4	2.3	0.3	2.1	0.0
Total (actual)	85.0	119.0	80.0	80.0	91.0	66.0
By country initiating action against other industrial goods:						
Benelux	3.7	11.1	3.5	0.0	0.0	0.0
France	37.0	27.7	35.7	26.9	36.8	37.8
Ireland	11.1	5.6	7.1	7.7	7.9	0.0
Italy	40.7	47.2	35.7	61.5	28.9	21.6
UK	7.4	8.3	14.3	0.0	0.0	0.0
All others	0.0	0.0	0.0	3.8	26.3	40.5
Total (actual)	27.0	36.0	28.0	26.0	38.0	37.0

Source: Own calculations based on EC official registry.

region (PACRIM). With 75 per cent of the Article 115 cases in the area of MFA products, and over 80 per cent in 'other products' in the most recent period, the PACRIM countries have been subjected to a far larger share of Article 115 actions than the EC imports of the respective product categories from these countries (roughly speaking, the Article 115 shares exceed import shares by over 100 per cent). Furthermore the discrepancy between the share of Article 115 cases versus the share of imports becomes even larger when individual countries are examined. Thus Hong Kong, which accounted for about 14 per cent of the EC's non-member clothing imports in 1985, was hit with 37 per cent of Article 115 actions on clothing that year.

In addition to the overall dominance of the PACRIM countries as

Table 18.3 Number of Article 115 cases[a] by regions/countries affected by MFA and non-MFA products, 1981–5 and 1986–8

Region[b]/country	1981, 1983, 1985				1986, 1987, 1988			
		MFA				MFA		
	Total	Total	Clothing	Other	Total	Total	Clothing	Other
PACRIM	64.6	62.0	62.6	72.4	77.0	75.6	78.8	80.3
E-Asia	58.2	54.1	56.5	70.7	70.5	66.1	70.3	80.3
China, PR	9.2	7.6	3.1	13.8	12.3	12.8	8.1	11.2
China, R	11.8	11.1	11.1	13.8	15.0	13.4	14.7	18.4
Hong Kong	17.5	21.2	29.4	6.5	19.1	27.7	35.1	
Japan	7.7			30.9	11.7	0.3		36.8
Korea	10.0	11.4	9.5	5.7	11.3	10.1	10.0	13.8
SE-Asia	6.3	7.9	6.1	1.6	6.6	9.5	8.5	
Philippines	2.6	3.3	4.6	0.8	0.8	1.2	1.5	
Thailand	2.0	2.7	0.8		5.1	7.4	5.8	
S-Asia	8.4	10.6	10.3	1.6	9.2	13.4	13.1	
India	4.7	6.0	5.7	0.8	5.7	8.3	10.0	
Pakistan	3.7	4.6	4.6	0.8	3.3	4.8	2.7	
Other countries	27.1	27.4	27.1	26.0	13.7	11.0	8.1	19.7
Total (actual)	491.0	368.0	262.0	123.0	488.0	336.0	259.0	152.0
percentage of total	100.0	74.9	53.4	25.1	100.0	68.9	53.1	31.1

Notes: a. Based on number of BTN 4 digit product groups affected by individual cases instituted by EC countries; not comparable with other tables.
b. Regions include data on countries not listed.

Source: Own calculations based on EC official registry.

well as their growth over time, two other important trends have
become evident. First of all the vulnerability of PACRIM countries
to being hit by Article 115 in the MFA area increased relatively more
than in the 'other product' category. Second, the shift of Article 115
actions to non-MFA products (as described above and as initiated
primarily by the new EC members) is evident for Taiwan and the
Republic of Korea, but not for Hong Kong.

A glance at the more specific product structure of Article 115
actions shows that within the MFA products, clothing maintained a
relatively constant and high share throughout the entire period. Shifts
into more capital-intensive (for example textiles) areas have not (yet)
taken place, or at least are not revealed at this level of aggregation.
With respect to non-MFA products, one can detect a move into less
traditional products or rather into products which demand more skill
and technology inputs (see Spinanger, 1989, Table 5). In other
words, inroads are being made into areas where EC countries had
previously been alone.

Despite the widespread use of Article 115 in numerous EC countries,
as well as its longevity, it is nonetheless often contended that the
Article is of only minor importance with respect to the actual amount
of trade affected and/or the price impact. Calculations on this were
carried out for MFA products imported into France (Table 18.4).
The four 4-digit BTN categories selected for Table 18.4 were among
the hardest hit by Article 115, and covered about 60 per cent of
developing countries' exports of clothing to France in 1985. More
specifically they accounted for 76 per cent of Hong Kong's (HKG), 55
per cent of Korea's (ROK) and 46 per cent of Taiwan's (ROC)
clothing exports to France. In light of this information the 4-digit
BTN categories listed for Hong Kong and Korea cannot be viewed as
insignificant compared with their exports. What was insignificant in
most cases however was the amount imported from a non-member,
non-industrialised country when compared to imports of the same
product from EC or other industrialised countries. This was particularly the case for Taiwan, whose minuscule, albeit increasing, share in
France's total clothing imports still prompted punishment by Article
115 early on. Such actions are indicative of France's extreme protectionist stance against the importation of MFA products from non-EC,
non-OECD countries.

Concerning price effects, it should be pointed out that developments in this connection tend to favour those exporting countries
whose ownership of quotas puts them into a quasi-oligopolistic

Table 18.4 Values and unit values of selected imported MFA products from major PACRIM suppliers affected by Article 115[a] in France, 1981–5

BNT	Value (millions of ECUs)[b]						Unit value (ECU[b]/kg)					
	HKG	ROC	ROK	DCs	ICs	EC	HKG	ROC	ROK	DCs	ICs	EC
1981:												
60	16.4	3.5	38.0	197.5	137.0	786.8	–	–	–	–	–	–
6005	7.5*	1.1*	9.4	95.4	60.8	427.9	24.35	12.87	17.29	16.50	15.92	25.12
61	22.2	2.7	28.2*	341.2	113.6	533.8	–	–	–	–	–	–
6101	8.4	1.1	16.5	134.5	56.6	217.0	13.56	10.31	13.41	10.69	17.96	19.09
6102	7.6	0.2	7.9	117.7	25.9	228.5	18.90	17.77	17.03	19.84	24.17	31.23
6103	2.4	0.1*	1.6	60.2	15.3	20.8	15.29	12.44	18.73	15.79	13.99	25.19
1983:												
60	19.3	2.9	33.2	217.5	165.7	986.6	–	–	–	–	–	–
6005	9.5	1.0*	8.8	105.8	79.9	512.6	22.68	13.75	17.56	17.36	16.93	28.69
61	26.8	3.0	23.1	398.9	157.3	708.0	–	–	–	–	–	–
6101	9.2	1.4	11.7	155.9	79.1	293.1	12.95	14.74	15.17	11.74	19.45	23.25
6102	10.7	0.3*	8.9*	137.3	41.1	303.7	21.05	22.21	19.91	20.93	25.80	37.94
6103	2.7	0.0	1.5	75.7	19.2	30.3	15.00	15.00	23.41	17.55	18.05	30.79
1985:												
60	31.6	3.8	46.2	308.2	250.6	1265.6	–	–	–	–	–	–
6005	15.4	1.8	11.6*	170.8	136.8	707.9	29.68	17.42	18.50	20.06	19.52	34.18
61	46.0	2.6	36.8	538.4	219.8	829.3	–	–	–	–	–	–
6101	17.8	0.4	22.3	218.0	94.1	290.9	21.01	16.72	18.90	15.27	23.18	30.68
6102	17.7	0.3	10.3	178.9	70.7	384.8	26.32	15.06	21.27	19.26	28.47	43.42
6103	4.5*	0.0*	2.5	97.3	32.3	41.6	25.16	15.00	22.89	22.63	17.05	34.72

1987:												
60	35.9	8.7	54.3	497.3	124.6	1761.1	–	–	–	–	–	–
6005	19.9*	4.9*	17.2*	293.9	49.3	1086.4	23.87	15.66	15.65	16.68	20.81	28.29
61	57.6	9.4	58.5	829.1	144.1	1136.6	–	–	–	–	–	–
6101	19.8*	2.8	33.1	366.6	55.8	421.0	16.24	13.70	17.63	13.71	21.36	27.64
6102	24.5*	1.4	17.4*	271.8	50.6	509.4	23.18	15.15	17.49	19.31	21.79	39.53
6103	5.5*	0.3*	3.1*	123.4	17.6	76.5	20.36	19.47	20.76	19.55	14.91	28.96

Notes: 60 – Mainly knitted clothes
6005 – Outer garments, etc. knitted
61 – Other clothes
6101 – Men's and boy's outer garments, woven
6102 – Women's, girl's and infant's outer garments, woven
6103 – Men's and boy's under garments, woven

a. A* designates Article 115 actions in given year. HKG was also hit in 1986 in all four categories and in 1988 in all but 6101; the ROC was hit in 1986 in 6103 and in 1988 in all but 6103; the ROK was hit in all four categories in 1986.
b. ECUs/$US rates as follows: 1981 = 0.896; 1983 = 1.123; 1985 = 1.310; 1987 = 0.866.

Source: Own calculations based on EC foreign trade statistics.

position, from which they can increase their welfare – under certain conditions – over free trade arrangements. Therefore, whereas the MFA, VERs and Article 115s restrict entry to outsiders, these same quantitative restrictions force upgrading and engender benefits via quota rents. It is generally assumed that increases in unit values reflect such movements. Unit values will therefore increase faster as the quotas become more restrictive and the rent-taking share grows and reinforces upgrading.

While the evidence on price increases for Hong Kong products in all four categories does not point to greater price increases (or rather upgrading) relative to the totals for developing countries or industrialised countries, this can be established for two categories (that is, 6102 and 6103). Similar conclusions can be made for Taiwan and Korea. The fact that the unit price increase is the largest for Hong Kong in category 6103 fits well into the picture drawn above about the relative degree of restrictiveness of the four product groups. Further substantiation that more-restrictive quotas induce larger price increases (and higher prices) can be found when comparing Category 8 (that is, within BTN 6103 – see Table 18.1) developments in France with those in Great Britain. It should be remembered that quotas for imports from Hong Kong are 26 times higher in Great Britain than in France. Unit values for Category 8 increased by 55 per cent, 41 per cent and 73 per cent for imports from Hong Kong, Korea and Taiwan respectively from 1981–7 in France; in Great Britain the corresponding figures were 21 per cent, 3 per cent and 9 per cent.

It should also be underlined that unit values for Hong Kong products – apart from being higher than the unit values for all developing countries in 1987 – were in half of the cases (eight of sixteen 4-digit categories in the four years) higher than those for extra-EC industrial countries. Taiwan, on the other hand, was higher only once and Korea four times out of sixteen. In other words Hong Kong in particular is now competing with middle-range clothing rather than with that from the lower end. Although it could be assumed that Hong Kong's moving up-market would decrease France's and the rest of the EC's protectionist tendencies induced by low-wage labour-intensive clothing production, Table 18.3 revealed that Hong Hong actually received an even larger share of Article 115 actions. Moving up-market thus merely meant aggravating new competitors.

Notes and references

1. They are as follows. *Bilateral Agreements*: Argentina, Bangladesh, Brazil, Bulgaria, China, Colombia, USSR, Guatemala, Haiti, Hong Kong, Hungary, India, Indonesia, Korea, Macao, Malaysia, Mexico, Pakistan, Peru, Philippines, Poland, Romania, Singapore, Sri Lanka, Thailand, Uruguay. *Cooperation Agreement*: Yugoslavia. *Mediterranean Countries*: Egypt, Malta, Morocco, Tunisia, Turkey. *Autonomous Agreements*: Albania, Korea, Taiwan, USSR, Vietnam.
2. The figures cover imports from only six developing countries (that is, newly industrialised countries): Brazil, Hong Kong, Mexico, Singapore, South Korea and Taiwan.
3. The situation is entirely different for the US as the above three accounted for 18 per cent of textile imports and about 50 per cent of clothing imports (1986).
4. These are as follows (per cent in volume, not value terms): Germany 25.5 per cent; UK 21.0 per cent; France 16.5 per cent; Italy 13.5 per cent; Benelux 9.5 per cent; Spain 7.5 per cent; Denmark 2.7 per cent; Portugal and Greece, each 1.5 per cent; Ireland 0.8 per cent.
5. That is: cotton yarn (1); cotton fabric (2); synthetic fabric (3); T-shirts and shirts (4); pullovers (5); trousers (6); blouses (7); shirts (8).
6. Article 115 of the Treaty of Rome:
   1. In order to ensure that the execution of measures of commercial policy taken in accordance with its Treaty by any Member State is not obstructed by deflection of trade, or where differences between such measures lead to economic difficulties in one or more of the Member States, the Commission shall recommend the methods for the requisite cooperation between Member States. Failing this, the Commission shall authorize Member States to take the necessary protective measures, the conditions and details of which it shall determine.
   2. In the selection of such measures, priority shall be given to those which cause the least disturbance to the functioning of the common market and which take into account the need to expedite, as far as possible, the introduction of the common customs tariff.

19 The EC Single Market and its Effect on Developing Countries

Rolf J. Langhammer

19.1 EUROPE 1992 AND CHANGES IN THE INTERNATIONAL TRADING SYSTEM

Non-EC member countries in general and developing countries in particular have often expressed concern about the completion of the internal market by 1993. Various studies stressing the positive effects of EC integration on economic growth, structural change and import demand could not dissipate the fear that the EC would be tempted to shift parts of the adjustment burden to third countries by building a 'fortress Europe'. This fear is based on an extrapolation of past experience with EC protectionism, and it receives further support from uncertainty about the stage of integration after 1992. There are a number of valid reasons for uncertainty about the future course of EC trade policies:

- The Cecchini Report (1988) as well as the empirical studies presented in the so-called Emerson Report (CEC, The Economics of 1992, 1988) focused solely on internal effects and neglected the external dimension.
- Differences in protection levels among individual member countries are still sizeable and there are disputes about the way to achieve a common protection level.
- The effects of liberalising factor movements and trade in services are much less easily predicted than integration effects in the case of merchandise trade (trade creation and trade diversion).

Finally and most importantly, uncertainty is enhanced by the fact that parallel to 'operation 1992' three other operations have to be conducted which will determine the level of market accessibility for third countries. In principle these are independent of the completion of the single market, but they still have to be seen in the context of the integration process. The three events comprise the completion of the Uruguay round scheduled for the end of 1990, the reform of the GSP after 1990, and the negotiations on principles of trade in textiles and clothing after the expiration of MFA IV in 1991.

In the four negotiation rounds the critical parameters of competitiveness will be determined, that is the changes in relative prices between imports and domestic substitutes. The net outcome is highly speculative since the EC has not yet decided on the future shape of the single market. Therefore an evaluation of the future position of developing countries in this market can only rely on alternative scenarios. Forecasts are not possible given the fact that the core of EC integration will be the liberalisation of services and very little information is available on the initial amount and structure of intra- and extra-EC trade in services.

19.2 EFFECTS OF THE INTERNAL MARKET ON INCOME GROWTH AND IMPORT DEMAND

19.2.1 Income growth

The removal of all physical barriers to intra-EC trade in goods and services, as well as the scale effects of a large single market, are expected to result in added economic growth. Estimates range between an optimistic 4.5 per cent over a five year period (CEC, Economics of 1992, 1988, Part A) and just 2.3 per cent over the same period (Bakhoven, 1989). The only thing these estimates have in common is that they fail to consider the dynamic effects of structural change after 1992 and instead focus on cost reduction only (process innovation). For this reason, 1 per cent added growth per year can be regarded as a rather conservative estimate which may actually be exceeded. 'Normal pattern' estimates arrive at similar results. They measure the relationship between sectoral value added as a dependent variable and per capita income and population as independent variables in a cross-country regression. The difference between the sum of the estimated value added for individual EC member countries and the theoretical value for the EC as a single entity is taken as a proxy for scale-induced added growth. Using a sample of 61 OECD and middle-income developing countries this relation can be described as follows:

$$\log V = -1.146 + 1.033 \log y + 1.178 \log P$$

where V is gross manufacturing value added, y is per capita income and P is population (prices and data of 1986). Inserting data for all individual EC member countries yields a total of \$552 billion compared with \$910 billion for the EC as whole. The difference amounts to 11 per cent of the 1986 GDP of the 12 EC countries or 1.3–1.5 per cent of the estimated annual GDP of the 12 EC countries between 1987 and 1992.

19.2.2 Import demand for manufactures from developing countries

The increase in economic growth following the completion of the internal market is expected to fuel import demand. An empirical assessment of this demand effect should however take into account the fact that demand elasticities significantly differ by product and by supplier. In particular the elasticities estimated for all developing countries differ from those measured for individual countries and sub-regions as a result of differences in the economic policies adopted by these countries and/or the product mix. Artificial market segmentation, such as preferences, may cause a further increase in demand elasticity. There is reason to assume that the demand elasticities estimated for developing countries' products are higher than those for all extra-EC suppliers. This hypothesis is based on the observation that developing countries in general and some countries in particular (for example South Korea) succeeded in raising their share in apparent consumption of all OECD countries during the 1970s and 1980s (OECD, 1986). This holds true for those countries which achieved rising shares of non-traditional products in their export supply, such as the Asian newly industrialised and nearly industrialised countries.

As a yardstick for integration effects, EC and US import demand functions have been estimated for manufactures exported by developing countries (for details see Langhammer, 1990). The US estimate is to capture the effects of a large internal market comparable to the one now being formed by the EC. What matters for the assessment of growth effects on import demand are the income elasticities. The estimates show that they do not differ significantly between the EC and the US and that they are in the range of 5–5.5, with the higher value attributed to the EC. This would mean that – assuming 1 per cent added growth in the EC – real manufactured imports would rise by 5.5 per cent annually, that is by \$2 billion in current prices or – in terms of world manufactured exports of developing countries in 1986 – by slightly more than 1 per cent.

However this growth effect does not take into account estimates of the static trade effects due to a once and for all change in relative prices between domestic supply and imports. The Emerson Report (1988, pp. 180–2) estimates that there will be a fall in relative prices as a result of the removal of internal trade barriers, and that this fall will lead to a trade diversion effect in the range of 10 per cent of the initial level (extra-EC imports in 1985). Related to EC manufactured imports from developing countries and compared with the growth-induced additional import demand, the once and for all reduction of imports from developing countries would amount to approximately \$2.3 billion, that is, slightly more than the value estimated above of additional import demand for *one* year. Therefore over a period of five years additional import demand is expected to exceed the trade diversion effect by more than fourfold.

Of course such estimates merely capture past reaction patterns to the extent that the internal market reacts or rather shifts over time because of other reasons, so their validity for the future must be viewed with caution. Although the comparison of income elasticities between the US – as an already completed single market – and the EC does not suggest major changes for developing countries, this does not exclude temporary shifts between domestic and foreign supply in the early stage of the EC single market. The question arises of whether there will be a constant or increasing import propensity or whether a declining import propensity will offset the growth-induced increased import demand. To answer these questions, scenarios of likely changes in the production structure of the EC after 1992 are required.

The following alternatives come to mind. First, the sector which receives the largest benefits from intra-EC liberalisation is the service sector. This sector would expand much more than predicted by long-term trends (3-sector hypothesis). The US, which has already liberalised its services' markets, may serve as a reference for the extent of expansion. Input–output analyses show that the import propensity of final demand for services is generally lower than the import propensity of final demand for commodities and manufactures. If this holds true, the import propensity of the EC could decline.

Second, there may be a countervailing effect in the sense that the income elasticity of demand for some consumer services (tourism, passenger transport, non-commercial insurances, banking) is higher than for manufactures and tends to increase with rising income. Some of the more advanced developing countries which have already proven themselves competitive in supplying services to EC consumers in aviation, maritime shipping and travel could draw benefits from rising incomes and high demand elasticities. For these countries, import market penetration could accelerate.

Third, the completion of the internal market requires an enhanced integration of the two new EC members which have the strongest similarities in relative resource endowment with developing countries. Spain and Portugal will have to pass through the three stages of integration (free trade area, customs union, common market) much more rapidly than did the older members. Increasing investment flows into these new member countries reflect the progress of integration into the heart of the EC, but they also contribute to the establishment of new production capacities, replacing import of the old members from non-member countries (trade diversion). Furthermore the Spanish and Portuguese currencies may appreciate in real terms because of the capital inflows, thereby improving the competitive position of suppliers from developing countries on domestic and international market vis-à-vis Spain and Portugal. As new members of the European Monetary System (EMS), Spain and – probably soon – Portugal will not be able to autonomously realign their exchange rates. Claims for protection against developing countries are therefore likely to become more rigorous and this may mean that part of the adjustment burden faced by the new member countries will be shifted to developing countries. Here a 'fortress Europe' of some sorts could materialise and lead to declining import propensities, at least for some industries.

Fourth, the creation of the internal market may attract investment from non-member countries which otherwise would have been aimed at developing countries. Investment diversion may impede the transfer of technology to developing countries and this may affect the supply capacity of these countries. The exchange rate effect also has to be taken into consideration. As a result of massive capital inflows the ECU would appreciate in real terms and this would improve the competitive position of those developing countries pegging to non-ECU currencies.

Fifth, stronger competition, economies of scale and the harmonisation of standards by law (ex ante) or by competition (ex post) within the EC will give rise to innovations which accelerate labour-saving technological progress. As a result the capacities of some industries may be relocated to the EC. Episodical evidence in the clothing industry, for instance, highlights this possibility (Mody and Wheeler, 1987; Jungnickel, 1989). In the short term, shifts in investment back to the EC could hamper developing countries' exports in those industries which are vulnerable to labour-saving techniques. On the other hand there must be other manufacturing sub-sectors which EC suppliers will have to leave because of rising wage levels and structural change.

Sixth, technological progress in the internal market will not only be labour-saving but also resource-saving and less polluting (Siebert, 1989). Demand for fossil fuels and for mineral commodities could be increasingly de-linked from economic growth. Commodity exporters among the developing countries could become seriously affected as the short-term demand effect for commodities would be overshadowed by the medium-term effect of economising on commodities. Countervailing effects are possible in the agricultural sector if the EC reduces its degree of market intervention in the agricultural sector under international pressure and budget constraints. However in principle the reform of the CAP should be dealt with separately from the internal market.

To summarise, there is no ready answer for changing import propensities after 1992. Effects will differ by countries affected as well as by product. All one can say is that a short-term decline in import propensity would remain a transitory problem if the transmission process between EC internal prices and international prices is allowed to run via flexible exchange rates as well as liberal trade policies.

19.3 REMNANTS OF NATIONAL SOVEREIGNTIES IN TRADE POLICIES: POSSIBLE CONSEQUENCES FOR DEVELOPING COUNTRIES

The completion of the internal market requires that remnants of national quantitative restrictions are fully abandoned. This condition has not yet been met, as has been shown in previous chapters. In 1988 about 1000 national quotas still existed outside the textile industry, but only 4 per cent of these were made effective by invoking Article 115 of the EEC Treaty in order to control intra-EC trade in such products (Bundesverband, 1988, p. 7). This low share suggests that most national quotas are redundant and will be removed after 1992 (for example see Ab1, L 2429/89 of 28 July 1989). Yet a hard core of national quotas exists in textile, clothing, entertainment electronics and – the major stumbling block to a common trade policy – in the car industry. Chapter 18.3 provided a survey on measures under Article 115, mostly invoked by Ireland and France against Asian countries and newly industrialised countries. In the agricultural sector, national quotas are still relevant for some tropical products like bananas, while excise taxes in some member states on products such as coffee are looked upon as a further national barrier to imports (Chapter 16).

One test case of whether remnants of national sovereignty in trade policies will be abandoned after 1992 is the car industry and the common treatment of Japanese car exports to the EC. Consensus is hampered by the different character of national measures. These comprise strict per unit quotas (Italy, Spain and Portugal), the surveillance of ceilings in terms of upper limits in percentage shares of imports for newly registered cars (France), privately organised VERs between importers and exporters (UK) as well as progressive national sales taxes (Denmark and Greece). It is very likely that controversies among EC member countries on a common policy in the car industry will affect advanced developing countries in the future. This may occur either directly if low-cost suppliers like South Korea and Malaysia try to penetrate EC markets and then face local content requirements, or indirectly if suppliers of car components in developing countries suffer from barriers against Japanese investments outside Japan.

Furthermore developing countries' exports have mainly fallen into product categories which have hitherto been subject to national quotas in all national markets, but were quotas are controlled either liberally or restrictively. Cases in point are the sensitive categories of the MFA. Just how differently individual EC members have handled their quotas in the past has been nicely demonstrated by Hamilton (1986, cited in Winters, 1987) who estimated tariff equivalents of national quotas for Hong Kong exports of jeans to the EC. Estimates ranged from 32 per cent for the UK to 11 per cent for France and 0 per cent for West Germany, which did not enforce its quota.

Where such remnants of national sovereignty exist, there are three scenarios for possible changes to comply with the 1992 target. First, under a *pessimistic* scenario national competence in sensitive sectors (clothing, cars) cannot be abandoned until 1992. This scenario includes the replacement of national quotas by national escape clauses and safeguards which are likely to make things rather worse than better. Second, under a *neutral* scenario national quotas would be replaced by a common quota. Third, under an *optimistic* scenario national quotas would be abandoned without any substitute.

A realistic assumption for the neutral scenario would be the introduction of a common quota being the sum of national quotas. Assuming quotas would have been applied by all members in the same way, the import volume would not change after 1992. The political economic background of consensus-building suggests a gloomier result though. Restrictive partner countries are expected to agree to a common quota only under the binding commitment of all members to apply the quota strictly. Such commitment could mean that relatively liberal members would be disciplined under a common administration of quotas whereas in the past they were free to lift national quotas by 'revealed preference'. Under such a scenario, strict control of a common quota would reduce market access compared to the side-by-side implementation of less restrictive and more restrictive national procedures.

The extent to which national quotas are differently applied is evident in Tables 18.1 and 18.2 (Chapter 18). As quotas were politically negotiated on a case-by-case basis, low and strictly controlled quotas for countries like France and Ireland provided an incentive to exploit the potential of price arbitrage and to shift imports from open markets to restrictive markets. To discourage this the latter countries invoked Article 115 and thus prevented prices from falling in their markets. Under a common quota prices would be expected to fall in the restrictive markets and to rise in the relatively open markets. This would affect the export earnings of developing countries from individual EC member countries.

Apart from income effects which arise from changing export earnings, a common quota may become important for suppliers acting under oligopolistic competition. The segmentation of EC markets due to national quotas, and the scope for price discrimination, may have enabled foreign suppliers to exploit the consumer surplus more fully than they could have done under a common quota. In this respect a common quota could be instrumental in eroding economic rents in the formerly restrictive markets and intensifying the competition between established suppliers and new comers, but also in creating new rents in the formerly open markets.

A transitory common quota seems to be preferred by EC officials

Table 19.1 Static trade effects of removing national quotas against developing countries

Exogenous parameter		Relevance of national quantitative restrictions[a]	Estimated trade creation (TC)[b] in millions of ECU under		Estimated trade diversion (TD)[c] in millions of ECU under	
			MFN rate	GSP rate	MFN rate	GSP rate
Average MFN tariff for semi-manufactures and manufactures from developing countries (in per cent)	7.1	FRG	0.1	1.1	1.2	1.0	1.0
		France	10.8	65.1	69.1	43.2	45.9
		Italy	6.1	35.9	38.1	24.2	25.7
Average GSP rate (in per cent)	0.9	UK	12.3	104.1	110.5	89.9	95.5
		Benelux countries	0.6	4.0	4.2	3.3	3.5
Tariff equivalent of national quota (in per cent)	10.0	Denmark	5.2	3.6	3.8	6.9	7.4
		Ireland	2.2	0.6	0.7	0.6	0.6
Price elasticity of import demand	-0.96	EC-9	–	214.4[d]	227.6[d]	169.1[d]	179.6[d]

Notes: a. Imports from developing countries subject to national quantitative restrictions as percentage of total EC member country imports of semi-manufactures and manufactures (CCT 25–99) from developing countries (excluding fuels), 1978 in per cent.

b. Estimated as follows: $TC = M_E \cdot \Delta t_Q/(1 + t_Q) \, (1 + t) \cdot e_m$

Where M_E = initial imports according to note (a) in 1987.

Δt_Q = reduction of tariff protection by the tariff equivalent of quota t_Q.

t = tariff rate without the average tariff equivalent.

e_m = price elasticity of import demand.

c. Estimated by using the so-called non-restrictive Verdoorn concept: $TD = M_E \cdot [a(e_s - e_m)] \cdot \left[\dfrac{\Delta t_Q}{(1 + t_Q)(1 + t)} \right]$

Where a = share of extra-regional imports from non-developing countries (M_{NE}) in total imports of the EC from no members ($a = M_{NE}/M_E + M_{NE})$ and e_s = elasticity of substitution between imports from developing countries and non-developing countries. This elasticity is assumed to be -2.0. See for the various assumptions underlying the estimates of trade diversion Sawyer and Sprinkle (1989).

d. The sum of trade creation and trade diversion amounts to 0.8 per cent (MFN rate) and 0.9 per cent (GSP rate) of EC-9 imports of semi-manufactures and manufactures from developing countries in 1987.

Sources: Langhammer, 1981, Table 1; Borrmann et al., 1985, Table 37; EUROSTAT, Foreign Trade NIMEXE 1987; own calculations.

for those products in which quota markets and non-quota markets still exist side by side (Krenzler, 1988). As far as MFA products are concerned, MFA IV (1986–92) already includes some adjustment measures, for example the lifting of non-utilised quotas or the partial transferability of quotas among member states (Neundörfer, 1987, pp. 49–54). Yet individual VERs between the EC and developing countries still include national quotas for sensitive products and these will remain in effect until the end of 1992, or rather until agreement is reached on what is to happen to Article 115. Therefore there is reason to assume that in such cases some EC members will insist on a transition period.

The optimistic scenario assumes that national quotas will be abandoned without any substitute. A possible compromise would be a transitory rise in the common external tariff by the tariff equivalent of a common quota. The possible static trade effects of this optimistic scenario are presented in Table 19.1. The magnitudes of trade creation and trade diversion depend mainly on the importance of national quotas in individual EC member countries, and thus imports are expected to increase in particular in France, the UK and Italy. Yet, as in all empirical studies on static trade effects, the magnitudes in terms of total trade are marginal because of both low tariff equivalents and low price elasticities of demand. This holds for trade creation (replacement of domestic production by imports) as well as for trade diversion (replacement of imports from OECD countries outside the EC by imports from developing countries), both of which are once and for all effects. Compared with the income-induced increase of import demand, the price-induced increase of imports due to the dismantling of national quotas is estimated to be much lower. Yet, compared to the neutral scenario, the optimistic one would offer a unilateral improvement of market access and a true step towards a single market.

19.4 DISCRIMINATION BETWEEN DEVELOPING COUNTRIES: WILL UNEQUAL TREATMENT BECOME REDUNDANT AFTER 1992?

The EC tradition of discrimination is deeply rooted as the EC itself is a preferential trading arrangement. There is no other actor in the international trading system who has deviated so widely from the principle of unconditional MFN as has the EC. Special treatment of developing countries under the GSP and the special Lome' and Mediterranean Preferences, special treatment of Eastern European countries, political preferences for sectoral arrangements and safeguard protection on a selective basis within the GATT framework bear witness to this statement. With respect to developing countries, the EC has tried to use trade policies as a vehicle for resource transfer (by allowing developing countries to raise their export prices by the amount of tariff revenues foregone).

Criticism (Patterson, 1983; Wolf, 1987) as well as discouraging results (Chapters 16 and 17) have spurred reform within the preferential trading arrangements, but there has not been a move to separate trade policies from aid policies and return to MFN treatment. Whether this will take place after 1992 cannot be answered because the outcome of the other four major negotiating rounds concerning the international trading system are still pending. Nonetheless the following hypotheses can be advanced.

First, the EC will not abandon the principle of unequal treatment of different groups of developing countries, mainly in order to avoid an erosion of the preference margins of the ACP countries. Second, within the ACP framework the trend away from largely ineffective trade preferences toward the transfer of resources will continue. Should the trade performance of ACP countries on EC markets deteriorate further – *inter alia* as a result of the integration of Spain and Portugal into the EC – additional transfers are likely to be granted as a substitute.

Third, Mediterranean countries will receive special attention by the EC as their export structure shows a stronger overlap with that of the new member countries than that of ACP countries and the new entrants. Thus the full integration of Spain and Portugal is likely to have a short-term negative impact on the Mediterranean countries and will require compensation payments if their earlier status is to be maintained. Nonetheless, should the currencies of the applicant countries appreciate in real terms because of rising unit labour costs and massive capital inflows, Mediterranean countries could improve their relative competitive position vis-à-vis Spain and Portugal.

Fourth, advanced developing countries, and especially the small group of Asian newly industrialised countries, will be graduated after 1992. This means that preferential treatment of their exports will not be improved but 'frozen', perhaps even diminished as a kind of 'admission fee' levied by the EC for allowing access to a large single market (Krenzler, 1988). Fifth, tariff preferences, regardless of whether they are general or region-specific, will become less relevant simply because of MFN tariff cuts in the GATT framework. However in those trade policy issues where decisions have to be negotiated the EC will continue to prefer bilateral over multilateral negotiations whenever possible.

What matters even more for developing countries is the question of when the EC will pay tribute to the ongoing globalisation of production and new assembly methods in manufacturing (just-in-time-procedures, module-type assembly). Both trends render traditional trade policy discrimination (and its implementation by rules of origin) largely ineffectual. Controversies between the EC, individual member states and private investors on minimum local content requirements (such as in the Nissan case of cars produced in the UK and exported to France) support concerns about future disputes challenging the EC and the European Court. The same holds true for the recent decision of the EC to link free intra-EC trade in chips to the location of a specific production stage within the EC (diffusion process).

The legal framework for traditional EC trade policies fails to provide guidelines for settling such disputes between investors operating world-wide and the EC authorities trying to enforce the fiction of an EC-originating product or – with respect to investment – of an EC-based company. Three factors however provide reason for hope that the EC will refrain from intervening excessively in flows of investment in order to keep specific investors out of the single market. First, there exist a large number of legal and illegal options to circumvent control on local content and rules of origin. Second, the possibility of retaliatory action by Asia–Pacific and the US is strong. And third, challenge and response games between investors and the EC are limited by EC budget constraints.

19.5 EXTERNAL EFFECTS OF LIBERALISING INTRA-EC TRADE IN SERVICES

As mentioned above, the liberalisation of services is one of the key tasks of the 1992 operation. It is strongly linked to the liberalisation of intra-EC capital transactions as there will be no free trade in financial services without free movement of capital.

As trade in invisibles frequently escapes statistical registration (Langhammer, 1989a, 1989b), there is only very skimpy information on the competitive strength of developing countries as suppliers of services. Tourism, passenger transport (aviation), as well as merchandise transport emerge as those broad categories of services in which a large number of developing countries have improved their international competitiveness. Construction activities, engineering and financial services are relevant for only a few advanced developing countries.

Irrespective of the speculative nature of this issue, a number of hypotheses can be advanced. Concerning tourism, relative prices of tourist services inside and outside the EC are expected to be influenced by two countervailing aspects of the EC single market. Internal prices will fall because of intensified competition in the aviation market and international mergers of travel agencies. On the other hand, internal prices may rise once and for all if a VAT of 6.5 per cent is levied on intra-European travel as well as if a fuel tax is imposed on intra-EC shipping. Finally, airport companies may try to raise their fares in order to compensate for the loss in earnings from duty-free shops, which will become redundant in the single market.

The net effect of both price movements is uncertain as changes in the real exchange rates of the European tourist resort areas have to be taken into account. With rising unit labour costs in the Mediterranean member countries there is room for the assumption that the ratio between internal and extra-EC prices for tourist services will increase, thus providing a chance for developing countries to attract tourists.

The aviation market is of considerable export interest to low-cost carriers in developing countries. This market is characterised by an extremely high degree of bilateralism, and though the Commission has subjected aviation to the competition rules of the Rome Treaty, there will be no common policy until 1992. Capacities have been expanded because of lowered barriers to entry, but price competition is still very restricted because of the so-called group exemption in the competition articles through which pool arrangements are sanctioned. As long as other member countries still have the right to protect their national flag carriers (for example France and Germany), price competition will be confined to a few routes within the EC. The recent nationalisation of private carriers in France does not support the optimistic view of enhanced competition between newcomers and national flag carriers in the context of 1992.

Developing countries are interested in the EC aviation market mainly with regard to the concentration issue. Should intensified competition among EC carriers lead to a concentration process with few remaining mega-carriers, negotiations on landing rights and slots are likely to become more difficult than under current circumstances because of changes in relative bargaining power (Mathew, 1989). 'Fifth freedom rights' are expected to be guaranteed for the period beyond 1992 so that the definition of intra-EC transport as 'domestic' transport would not mean denying third countries the right to supply transport services as they did in the past.

Unlike the aviation market, the Commission has gained a mandate in maritime transport to act against third country suppliers if they are accused of unfair pricing. In a case decided in early 1989 the Commission imposed for the first time a countervailing duty on an external supplier of services, a South Korean shipping company operating a liner service between EC ports and Australia (Ab1, 15/89, L 4, 4 January 1989). This company allegedly received subsidies and thus was able to undercut European companies, who requested that the 'unfair pricing' regulation be imposed by the Commission. This regulation can be regarded as the nucleus of a common policy in maritime transport against third countries. A common policy is facilitated by the fact that most EC shipping agencies already act jointly in liner conferences and have established common institutions to lobby in Brussels.

In banking and insurance, third countries are confronted with the reciprocity clause in the so-called Second Banking Draft Directive. Banking licences, which are necessary when providing services in the single market, are issued if EC banks and insurance companies do not report discriminatory actions against their own business in the third country. The debate on the reciprocity clause became heated because of the vague definitions set in the first draft, but passions seem to have subsided with a new draft, through which licences are issued bona fide rather than after an examination of the conditions in the applicant country. For the majority of developing countries, the reciprocity clause will be ineffectual since their banks have only established funding offices or financing agencies for merchandise trade in EC countries rather than branches offering the full range of banking services.

20 European Trade and Developing Countries: Summary and Conclusions

Ulrich Hiemenz

The EC and the US have traditionally been the two most important destinations for exports from developing countries. Access to the markets of these highly industrialised countries has provided an avenue for enhancing economic development in quite a number of developing countries through integration into the international division of labour. Against this background, this study has attempted to answer two questions. First, has the EC been supporting developing countries' efforts to expand their exports by keeping EC markets open to suppliers from the Third World? And second, as the EC is poised to become a single market by 1993, will internal EC integration facilitate or impede the division of labour between developing countries and the EC?

The answers to both questions are ambiguous. Concerning the first, the generally favourable picture of EC trade relations with developing countries is clouded by a large number of trade impediments applied by the EC and its member countries against imports of specific products from specific countries, causing considerable welfare losses to EC consumers and suppliers from developing countries. EC trade policies are characterised by a dichotomy between the commitment to liberal (GATT) trade rules and the desire to shield domestic producers against 'too much' foreign competition (already embodied in the 1957 Treaty of Rome). The result was an increasingly complex trade policy regime which is very selective on a product-by-product basis, is extremely discriminatory among countries, and has become more and more sophisticated and therefore less transparent over time. Several trends have been observed. In response to multilateral trade negotiations EC trade protectionism has shifted from tariff to non-tariff barriers under the jurisdiction of individual member governments, and – within the range of NTBs – from quantitative restrictions to measures partly outside GATT rules, such as VERs, surveillance and anti-dumping procedures. Most of these

287

trade policy instruments have been implemented against imports from other industrialised countries, but their use against competitive suppliers from both more advanced and less advanced developing countries has been on the increase, particularly in recent years.

This targeting of trade intervention went hand in hand with a de facto renationalisation of trade policy decisions. Legally, the EC applies a common trade policy, but a host of safeguards and escape clauses – as well as the availability of instruments such as private VERs, standards, government procurement and so forth, which are not even legally covered by the common policy – have provided a large measure of discretion to the governments of individual member countries. This trend seems to have been dampened a little in the late 1980s when the EC Commission began to increase its role in trade policymaking and was more restrictive with respect to granting permission for the application of the escape clauses, which led to fewer applications but not to reduction in the number of restrictions. The trade policy stance of the EC is nonetheless difficult to ascertain since member governments have to agree on a common position before the Commission can enter multilateral trade talks. Such agreements have not in the past been reached with respect to the dismantling of national NTBs, but some such policy changes will become inevitable by 1993.

Compared with trade restrictions, trade preferences granted to developing countries were limited, discriminatingly applied, and of questionable value to eligible countries. Separate preference schemes have been implemented for ACP, Mediterranean and other developing countries, with preference margins declining in that order. In a nutshell, all preference agreements have provided low or even zero margins for developing countries' important export products, such as agricultural products, or have served to limit eligibility for narrow tariff quotas, as in the case of competitive suppliers such as the Asian newly industrialised countries and nearly industrialised countries. Preferences were plentiful for countries such as those from the ACP region which cannot supply manufactured exports in significant numbers because of domestic policy distortions. For these reasons, the trade effects of the GSP and other related agreements have remained negligible, as unused preferences and/or imports in excess of tariff quotas amply demonstrate.

In summary, the answer to the first question asked above is that EC member countries have digressed considerably from free trade principles to the detriment of developing countries. Despite some concessions in the GSP and vis-à-vis Mediterranean and ACP countries, there seems to have been an increase in the overall level of protectionism applied against developing countries. This new wave of protectionism did not however hurt all developing countries alike. Import barriers focused on newly industrialised countries in general and on Asian newly industrialised countries in particular, but also on some second-generation exporters when they emerged as competitive suppliers of certain products on EC markets.

Prospects for the future access of developing countries to the EC hinge on the outcome of the Uruguay round and on the shape of trade policies implemented after 1992. Concerning the Uruguay round, all available information seems to suggest that the EC will neither deviate much from its protectionist stance in agriculture nor give up the principle of special treatment and selectivity. The massive agricultural lobby within the EC determines the negotiating position of the EC. This lobby is supported by other countries with high rates of agricultural protectionism, such as Japan, and by quite a number of developing countries which are beneficiaries of special EC import regulations or are traditional net food importers. That potential winners of a liberalisation of agricultural trade could easily compensate potential losers does not seem to be a sufficient condition for achieving free trade in agriculture.

In conjunction with the former colonies of EC member countries, and under pressure from industrial lobbies, the EC will also not be prepared to abolish special treatment of developing countries under the GSP and the special Lomé and Mediterranean Preferences, special treatment of Eastern European countries, political preferences for sectoral arrangements and safeguard protection on a selective basis within the GATT framework. With respect to developing countries, the EC has shown an inclination to substitute some trade preferences by resource transfers, but a basic reform towards separating trade from aid policies and returning to MFN treatment is not in sight.

A glimmer of hope lies in the steps being taken towards a liberalisation of trade in services. A relaxation of trade barriers in this sector is one of the key ingredients of the 1992 operation and is likely to spill over to trade with non-member countries, since both suppliers and consumers within the EC have been pushing in this direction by exploiting loopholes to circumvent existing controls. Furthermore the EC will have to offer some concessions if it is to continue to resist a reduction in agricultural protectionism.

Concerning 1992, the bright prospect of a prosperous single EC market is dimmed by the fear that economic integration among the core members, together with the accession of Spain and Portugal, may only be accomplished at the expense of restricting the access of non-members, that is, by building a 'Fortress Europe'. The completion of the single market marks the third stage in the integration process of the EC. Having already established a free trade area and customs union, the liberalisation of services and of factor movement will make the EC into a truly common market. Monetary integration would then advance the process towards economic union. Looking at European integration from this 'stages approach', the opportunities and risks for third countries can be sketched in a relatively clear-cut way.

The completion of the third stage will stimulate structural change in the EC and accelerate economic growth. This holds true in particular for the tertiary sector, which lagged behind in its development because of massive barriers to market entry. On the supply side, competition for risk capital within the EC between the core regions and the periphery will be enhanced, and the initial inflow of capital into the periphery will lead to rising prices for non-tradables relative to tradables (real appreciation) in these countries. Labour costs would rise and the participation of the periphery countries in the European monetary system would remove the option of fighting rising labour costs by adjusting the exchange rate. This process could be enhanced by political pressure towards 'social harmonisation' within the EC so that differences in labour costs between the centre and the periphery would be leveled further. Under this scenario, relatively labour-intensive production in the periphery would lose competitiveness and would be shifted to countries outside the EC, that is, mainly to developing countries.

On the demand side, import absorption can be expected to increase because of higher growth. In cumulative terms, this effect weighs more than the 'once and for all' decline in extra-EC trade (trade diversion) as the result of changing relative prices.

Risks arise because customs union has not been accomplished in the new member states, Spain and Portugal, as well as in some so-called sensitive areas such as the textiles and clothing sector, some steel products, some agricultural products and in the entire service sector. Thus there is an adjustment jam as the liberalisation steps of the second and third stages of integration coincide. This jam provokes political resistance in new and old member states in which remaining protection in product as well as in factor markets is relatively high (for example in France and Italy). Attempts are being made to shift parts of the adjustment burden of internal liberalisation to third countries. Yet in a single market such shifts can only be implemented if the relatively open EC member countries such as Germany agree, and this will bring the EC into conflict with the targets of the Uruguay round which runs parallel to the single market process.

To summarise, from the macroeconomic viewpoint the single market can and no doubt will stimulate structural change and economic growth in the world economy, while concerns about continued protectionism are justified from the microeconomic point of view. The answer to the second question is therefore that it remains to be seen whether compromises on a common policy for the EC after 1992 will offer developing countries what is now being proposed: true access to a single market as opposed to a segmented market distorted by differing national policies.

Bibliography

Part I: Japan's Trade Policies towards Developing Countries

Australian Bureau of Agricultural and Resource Economics (1988) *Agricultural Policies in Japan* (Canberra).

Chenery, H. B. and M. Syrquin (1980) 'A Comparative Analysis of Industrial Growth', *American Economic Review*, May.

Cline, W. R. (1990) *Japan's Trade Policies*, paper presented at the Symposium on 'Toward New Rules for World Trade', 31 May and 1 June, organised by the Research Institute of International Trade and Industry, Ministry of International Trade and Industry, Tokyo.

Corker, R. (1989) 'External Adjustment and the Strong Yen: Recent Japanese Experience', *International Monetary Fund Staff Papers*, vol. 36, no. 2, pp. 464–93.

Economic Planning Agency, Research Department (1989) *Nihon Keizai no Genkyo* (The Current Situation of the Japanese Economy), (Tokyo).

Economic Planning Agency (1989) *Bukka Report* (Report on Prices), (Tokyo: Keizai Kikaku Kyokai).

Economic Planning Board of Korea (1989) *Major Statistics of the Korean Economy*.

Export-Import Bank of Japan (1989) *Kaigai Toshi Kenkyusho Ho*, vol. 15, no. 5, May.

Fair Trade Commission of Japan (1987) *Yunyu So-dairiten Seido oyobi Heiko Yunyu to Kyoso Seisaku* (Sole Agent Import System, Parallel Imports and Competition Policy) (Tokyo).

Fitchett, D. A. (1988) 'Agricultural Trade Protectionism in Japan: A Survey', *World Bank Discussion Papers*, no. 28 (Washington, DC).

Ito, Mitsuharu (1989) 'Nichi-bei Kozo Kyogi ni Igi ari' (Comments on Structural Impediments Initiative Talks between Japan and the US), *Sekai*, November.

Ito, Motoshige (1989) Comments to R. Harris, 'Market Access in International Trade', in R. M. Stern (1989).

Ito, Motoshige and A. Matsui (1989) 'Kigyo: Nihon-teki Torihiki Keitai' (Enterprises: the Japanese Way of Transactions), in Motoshige Ito and K. Nishimura (eds), *Oyo Mikuro Keizai-gaku* (Applied Micro-economics) (Tokyo: University of Tokyo Press).

Japan Department Stores Association (1989) *Showa 63-nendo ni okeru Hyakkaten no Seihin Yunyu, Kaihatsu Yunyu Jittai Chosa Kekka* (The Results of a Survey on Manufactured Imports and Development Imports by Department Stores in Fiscal Year 1988)(Tokyo).

Japan External Trade Organization (1989) *Nihon no Seihin Yunyu Doko* (Current Situation of Japan's Manufactured Imports) (Tokyo).

Japan Tariff Association, *Customs Tariff Schedules of Japan*, various issues.

Japan Tariff Association, *All about Revised Tariffs*, various issues.

Japan Tariff Association (ed.) (1985) *Ippan Tokkei Kanzei Seido no Keizai*

Koka (Economic Effects of the General System of Preferences) (Tokyo).

Japan Tariff Association (1989) *Summary Report of Japan's External Trade*, December.

Kohama, H. (1989) 'Nihon Keizai no Kozo Henka to Higashi-Tonan-Ajia' (Structural Change in the Japanese Economy and East and South-east Asia), in K. Watanabe and H. Kohama (eds), *Kokusai Kankei no Shiza Tenkan* (1989) (Tokyo: Hakuju Shuppan).

Manufactured Imports Promotion Organization (1988) *Shohisha no Yunyuhin ni taisuru Ishiki Chosa* (A Survey on Consumers' Attitude toward Imported Products) (Tokyo).

Maruyama, M. (1989) 'Ryutsu=Hikanzei-shoheki Ron wa Ayamari da' (Arguing Japan's Distribution Systems, a Non-tariff Barrier is Wrong), *Shukan Toyo Keizai*.

Maruyama, M. (1990) 'Nichi-bei Kouzou Kyogi to Ryutsu Mondai' (Structural Impediments Talks and Japan's Distribution System), *Keizai Seminar*, February.

Ministry of International Trade and Industry, *White Paper on International Trade*, various issues.

Ministry of International Trade and Industry (1989) *Kyujunen-dai no Ryutsu Bijon* (Visions for Distribution Industries in the 1990s) (Tokyo: Tsusho Sangyo Chosa-kai).

Miyazawa, K. (ed.) (1989) *Ryutsu Shisutemu no Sai-kochiku* (Reconstruction of the Japanese Distribution System) (Tokyo: Commercial Law Centre).

Nihon Keizai Shimbun (1989) *Nichi-bei Masatsu* (Japan–US Frictions) (Tokyo).

Organization for Economic Cooperation and Development (1987), *National Policies and Agricultural Trade: Japan* (Paris).

Ryutsu Keizai Kenkyusho (1989) *Ryutsu Tokei Shiryo-shu* (Statistical Handbook of Retail and Wholesale Trade) (Tokyo).

Sakaiya, T. (1990) 'Revision/Abolition of the Large-Scale Retail Store Law Will Reduce Land Prices' (in Japanese), *Voice*, July 1990, pp. 124–40.

Saxonhouse, G. and R. M. Stern (1989), 'An Analytical Survey of Formal and Informal Barriers to International Trade and Investment in the US, Canada, and Japan', in R. M. Stern (1989).

Sazanami, Y. (1989) 'Trade and Investment Patterns and Trade Barriers in the US, Canada, and Japan', in R. M. Stern (1989).

Stern, R. M. (ed.) (1989) *Trade and Investment Relations among the US, Canada, and Japan* (University of Chicago Press).

Takeuchi, K. (1989) 'Problems in Expanding Japan's Imports of Manufactures from Developing Countries: A Survey', *The Asian Economic Journal*, September.

Takeuchi, K. (1990) 'Does Japan Import Less Than It Should?: A Review of the Econometric Literature', *The Asian Economic Journal*, January.

Tsuruta, T. (1989) 'Kokusai-ka Jidai no Daiten-ho wa dou aru bekika' (Large-scale Retail Store Law in the Globalisation Era), *Economist*, 12 December.

United States Trade Representatives Office, US Office (1989), *1989 National Trade Estimate Report on Foreign Trade Barriers* (Washington, DC: Government Printing Office).

Urata, S. (1987) 'Sources of Economic Growth and Structural Change in China: 1956–81', *Journal of Comparative Economics*, vol. 11, no. 1, March, pp. 96–115.

Urata, S. (1989) 'The Rapid Increase of Direct Investment Abroad and Structural Change in Japan', East–West Center, mimeo.

Working Group on Market Liberalization (ed.) (1985) *Action Program* (Tokyo).

Yamazawa, I. (1986) *Kokusai Keizai-gaku* (International Economics), (Tokyo: Toyo Keizai Shimpo-sha).

Yamazawa, I. (1988) 'The Generalized System of Preferences and Japan's Imports from Developing Countries', *Hitotsubashi Journal of Economics*, vol. 29, no. 2, December.

Yamazawa I. and H. Kohama (1985) 'Trading Companies and the Expansion of Foreign Trade: Japan, Korea, and Thailand', in K. Ohkawa and G. Ranis (eds), *Japan and the Developing Countries* (Oxford: Basil Blackwell).

Part II: US Trade Policy towards Developing Countries

Akiyama, T. and P. Varagis (1989) *Impact of the International Coffee Agreement's Export Quota System on the World's Coffee Market* (Washington, DC: World Bank) February.

Alexander, Mudge Rose Guthrie et al. (1989) 'Statement of United States Association of Importers of Textiles and Apparel on Reduction of Duties and Elimination of Non-Tariff Measures in the Uruguay Round', Trade Policy Staff Committees, 16 October, mimeo.

American Textile Manufacturers Institute (1989) *Textile and Apparel Imports: A National Concern* (Washington, DC) October.

The Atlantic Council of the US (1987) *The Uruguay Round of Multilateral Trade Negotiations Under GATT* (Washington, DC).

Avery, Graham J. L. (1985) 'Enhancing Competitiveness: International Economic Policies', *Competing in the World Marketplace: The Challenge for American Agriculture*, mimeo.

Bailey, Kenneth W. (1989) *An Analysis of the Export Enhancement Program for Wheat*, mimeo.

Baldwin, Robert E. and J. David Richardson (eds) (1988) *Issues in the Uruguay Round*, NBER Conference Report.

Bryant, Ralph C., Gerald Holtham and Peter Hooper (eds) (1988) *External Deficits and the Dollar* (Washington, DC: Brookings Institution).

Bryant, Ralph C. and Gerald Holtham (1988) 'The US External Deficit: Diagnosis, Prognosis, and Cure', in Ralph C. Bryant, Gerald Holtham and Peter Hooper (eds), *External Deficits and the Dollar* (Washington, DC: Brookings Institution).

Bureau of National Affairs (1989) *International Trade Reporter* (Washington, DC) 27 September.

Castells, Manuel and Laura D'Andrea Tyson (1988) 'High Technology Choices Ahead: Restructuring Interdependence', in John W. Sewell and Stuart K. Tucker (eds), *Growth, Exports, and Jobs in a Changing World*

Economy: Agenda 1988 (Washington, DC: Overseas Development Council).

Cline, William (1987) *The Future of World Trade in Textiles and Apparel* (Washington, DC: Institute of International Economics).

Cloud, David S. (1989) 'Export Subsidies Attacked for Failing to Meet Goal', *Congressional Quarterly* (Washington, DC) 24 June.

Destler, I. M. and John S. Odell (1987) *Anti-Protection: Changing Forces in United States Trade Politics* (Washington, DC: Institute for International Economics).

Destler, I. M. and John S. Odell (1987) *Anti-Protection: Changing Forces in United States Trade Politics* (Washington: Institute for International Economics).

Erzan, Refik and Guy Karsenty (1989) 'Products Facing High Tariffs in Major Developed Market-Economy Countries: An Area of Priority for Developing Countries in the Uruguay Round', *UNCTAD Review*, vol. 1, no. 1.

'False Security', *The Economist* (London) 17 December 1988.

Feinberg, Richard E. and Richard Newfarmer (1980) 'Caribbean Basin Initiative: Bold Plan or Empty Promise?', in Richard Newfarmer (ed.), *From Gunboats to Diplomacy: New US Policies for Latin America* (Baltimore: Johns Hopkins University Press).

Feinberg, Richard E. (1982) *Subsidizing Success: The Export-Import Bank in the US Economy* (Cambridge MA: Cambridge University Press).

Finlayson, Jock A. and Mark W. Zacher (1988) *Managing International Markets* (New York: Columbia University Press).

Gadbaw, Michael R. and Timothy J. Richards (1988) *Intellectual Property Rights: Global Consensus, Global Conflict?* (Boulder: Westview Press).

Gardner, Bruce (1985) 'Economic Consequences of US Agricultural Policies', a background paper prepared for *World Development Report 1986*.

Ghadar, Fariborz, William H. Davidson and Charles S. Feigenoff (1987) *US International Competitiveness: The Case of the Textile and Apparel Industries* (Lexington: Lexington Books).

Giesse, Craig R. and Martin J. Lewin (1987) 'The Multifiber Arrangement: 'Temporary' Protection Run Amuck', in *Law and Policy in International Business*, vol. 19, no. 1.

Godshaw, Gerald Corri Pinon-Farah, Marco Pinon-Farah, George Schink and Virendra Singh (1988) *The Implication for the US Economy of Tariff Schedule Item 807 and Mexico's Maquila Program* (Washington, DC: WEFA Group) May.

Goto Junichi (1988) 'Effects of the Multifiber Arrangement on Developing Countries', *Working Papers* (World Bank).

Green, Paula L. and Janet Plume (1989) 'Coffee Market Hopes Prices Stabilize', *Journal of Commerce* (New York) 6 July.

Haq, Khadija (ed.) (1988) *Linking the World*, North-South Roundtable, Islamabad.

Hufbauer, Gary Clyde, Diane T. Berliner and Kimberly Ann Elliott (1985) *Trade Protection in the US: 31 Case Studies* (Washington, DC: Institute of International Economics).

International Monetary Fund (1987) *Government Finance Statistics Yearbook* (Washington, DC).

International Monetary Fund (1989) *Developments in International Exchange and Trade Systems* (Washington, DC) September.

International Monetary Fund (1989) *World Economic Outlook* (Washington, DC).

James, Canute (1986) 'Trade Preferences Scheme Under Fire', *Journal of Commerce* (New York) 1 October.

Kennedy, Paul (1987) *The Rise and Fall of the Great Powers: Economic Change and Military Conflicts from 1500 to 2000* (New York: Random House).

Krugman, Paul R. (1989) 'The J-Curve Illusion', *International Economy*, September/October.

Laird, Sam and Alexander Yeats (1988) *Trends in Nontariff Barriers of Developed Countries*, World Bank PPR working paper series no. 137 (Washington, DC) December.

Laird, Sam and Alexander Yeats (1989) *Quantitative Methods for Trade Barrier Analysis* (Washington, DC: World Bank).

Lewis, John P. and Valeriana Kallab (eds) (1983) *US Foreign Policy and the Third World: Agenda 1983* (New York: Praeger Publishers for the Overseas Development Council).

Malmgren, Harold B. (1986) 'Negotiating International Rules for Trade in Services', *Economic Impact*, no. 5.

Mellor, John W. (1983) 'Agriculture on the Road to Industrialization', in John P. Lewis and Valeriana Kallab (eds), *Development Strategies Reconsidered* (Washington, DC: Overseas Development Council).

Mudge, Rose, Guthrie Alexander and Ferdon (1989) 'Statement of US Association of Importers of Textiles and Apparel on Reduction of Duties and Elimination of Non-Tariff Measures in the Uruguay Round', before the Trade Policy Staff Committee, 16 October.

Nogues, Julio J., Andrzej Olechowski and L. Alan Winters (1989) *The Extent of Nontariff Barriers to Imports of Industrial Countries*, World Bank staff working paper no. 789 (Washington, DC).

North-South Institute (1988) 'Commodity Trade: The Harsh Realities', *Briefing*, May.

Organization for Economic Cooperation and Development, *Development Cooperation Report* (Paris) various issues.

Paarlberg, Robert L. (1987) 'US Agriculture and the Developing World: Partners or Competitors?', in Randall B. Purcell and Elizabeth Morrison (eds), *US Agriculture and Third World Development: The Critical Linkage* (Washington and Boulder: Lynne Reinner Publishers for the Curry Foundation).

Paarlberg, Robert L. (1989) 'A Closer Look at EEP', mimeo, November.

Pearson, Charles (1989) *Free Trade, Fair Trade?* (Washington, DC: Johns Hopkins Foreign Policy Institute).

Pelzman, Joseph (1983) *The US Generalized System of Preferences: An Evaluation and an Examination of Alternative Graduation Programs*, Report prepared for the US Department of Labor, October.

Retail Industry Trade Action Coalition (1986) *The Politics of US Textile*

Trade Policy: Two Centuries of Temporary Protection (Washington, DC).

Rodrigues, Rita M. (ed.) (1986) *The Export-Import Bank at Fifty* (Lexington: Lexington Books).

Rudolph, Barbara (1988) 'Bitter Standoff in Montreal', *Time*, 19 December.

Sampson, Gary P. (1987) 'Pseudo-economics of the MFA – A Proposal for Reform', *World Economy*, vol. 10, December.

Sapir, Andre (1985) 'North–South Issues in Trade in Services', *World Economy*, vol. 8, March.

Schoepfle, Gregory K. and Jorge F. Perez-Lopez (1988) *Offshore Assembly in Mexico and the Caribbean and its Implications for the US and Host Countries*, paper presented at the North American Economics and Finance Association meetings, New York, December.

Schott, Jeffrey J. (1989) *More Free Trade Areas?* (Institute of International Economics) May.

Sewell, John W. (1988) 'The Dual Challenge: Managing the Economic Crisis and Technological Change', in John W. Sewell and Stuart K. Tucker (eds), *Growth, Exports, and Jobs in a Changing World Economy: Agenda 1988*, (Brunswick, New Jersey: Transaction Books in Cooperation with the Overseas Development Council).

Shapiro, Robert J. (1988), 'A Battle Royal Over Food', *US News & World Report*, 23 May.

The Stern Group (1989) *Rebuilding American Manufacturing in the 1990s: The Case Against Steel VRAs* (Washington, DC) February.

Stokes, Bruce (1989) 'Pressures Bank Home', *The National Journal*, 4 February.

Strange, Marty (1989) *The Great Trade Debate* (Center for Rural Affairs).

Trela, Irene and John Whalley (1988) *Do Developing Countries Lose from the MFA?*, NBER working paper no. 2618, June.

Tucker, Stuart K. (1984) 'The US GSP Program: Trade Preferences and Development, *ODC Policy Focus*, no. 6 (Washington, DC: Overseas Development Council) September.

Tucker, Stuart K. (1986) *Update: Costs to the US of the Recession in developing Countries*, ODC Working Paper, no. 10 (Washington, DC: Overseas Development Council) January.

Tucker, Stuart K. (1986) 'Non-Tariff Barriers: Growing Obstacles to US–Third World Trade', *ODC Policy Focus*, no. 4 (Washington, DC: Overseas Development Council) July.

Tucker, Stuart K. (1988) *The Costs of Third World Debt: The Loss of US Jobs*, mimeo.

Tucker, Stuart K. (1989) *The Caribbean Basin Initiative and Job Creation in the Basin*, paper presented at the meeting of the Latin American Studies Association, Miami, December.

Tucker, Stuart K. (1989) 'Rapporteur's Report', in Stuart K. Tucker (ed.), *Beyond Subsistence: Labor Standards and Third World Development* (Washington, DC: US Department of Labor and the Overseas Development Council).

Tucker, Stuart K. (1989) 'Trade Unshackled: Assessing the Value of the Caribbean Basin Initiative', in William Ascher and Ann Hubbard (eds), *Central American Recovery and Development: Task Force Report to the*

International Commission for Central American Recovery and Development (Durham, NC: Duke University Press).

Tucker, Stuart K. and Maiko Chambers (1989) 'US Sugar Quotas and the Caribbean Basin', ODC *Policy Focus*, no. 6 (Washington, DC: Overseas Development Council) December.

UNCTAD (1986) *Protectionism and Structural Adjustment*.

UNICEF (1988) *State of the World's Children 1988*.

UNICEF (1989) *State of the World's Children 1989*.

US Department of Agriculture (1987) 'Current Issues in the World Sugar Economy', *Food Policy*, May.

US Department of Agriculture (1987) *Government Intervention in Agriculture: Measurement, Evaluation, and Implications for Trade Negotiations*, Economic Research Service, staff report no. AGES 861216 (Washington, DC).

US Department of Agriculture (1988) *Estimates of Producer and Consumer Subsidy Equivalents: Government Intervention in Agriculture, 1982–86*, Economic Research Service, staff report no. AGES 880127 (Washington, DC).

US Department of Agriculture (1989) *Agricultural Outlook* October.

US Department of Commerce (1988) *Caribbean Basin Investment Survey* (Washington, DC) November.

US General Accounting Office (1985) *Agriculture Overview: US Food/Agriculture in a Volatile World Economy*, GAO/RCED-86-3BR (Washington, DC) November.

US General Accounting Office (1989) *The Health of the US Steel Industry*, GAO-NSIAD-89-193, July.

US International Trade Commission (1987) *Annual Report on the Impact of the Caribbean Basin Economic Recovery Act on US Industries and Consumers: Second Report 1986*, September.

US International Trade Commission (1989) *The Pros and Cons of Entering into Negotiations of Free Trade Area Agreements with Taiwan, The Republic of Korea, and ASEAN, or the Pacific Rim Region in General*, USITC Publication No. 2166, March.

US International Trade Commission (1989) *US Imports of Textiles and Apparel Under the Multifiber Arrangement: Statistical Report Through 1988* (Washington, DC) June.

US International Trade Commission (1989) *Annual Report on the Impact of the Caribbean Basin Economic Recovery Act on US Industries and Consumers: Fourth Report 1988*, September.

US International Trade Commission (1989) *The Economic Effects of Significant US Import Restraints, Phase I: Manufacturing*, USITC Publication No. 2222, October.

van Leeuwen, Pieter and Andrew R. Wechsler (1988) 'US Trade Reform and the Third World, *ODC Policy Focus*, no. 5 (Washington, DC: Overseas Development Council) October.

Wells, Louis T. Jr. (1989) 'Intellectual Property and Developing Countries: Options for US Policy', *ODC Policy Focus*, no. 5 (Washington, DC: Overseas Development Council) October.

Whalley, John (ed.) (1988) *The Small Among the Big* (London, Ontario:

Center for the Study of International Economic Relations).
Whalley, John (ed.) (1988) *Rules, Power and Credibility* (London, Ontario: Center for the Study of International Economic Relations).
Womach, Jasper (1989) 'Sugar Policy Issues', *CRS Issue Brief* (Washington, DC: Congressional Research Service) 20 March.
World Bank (1986) *World Development Report 1986* (Washington, DC).
World Bank (1988) *Social Indicators of Development* (Washington, DC).
Zeitz, Joachim and Alberto Valdés (1986) *The Costs of Protectionism to Developing Countries*, World Bank Staff Working Paper no. 769 (World Bank).

Part III: European Trade Policies towards Developing Countries

Agarwal, Jamuna P., Martin Dippl and Rolf J. Langhammer (1985) 'EC Trade Polices Towards Associated Developing Countries, Barriers to Success', *Kieler Studien*, no. 193 (Tübingen).
Agra-Europe, *Unabhängiger Europäischer Presse- und Informationsdienst für Agrarpolitik und Agrarwirtschaft* (Bonn) various issues.
Amelung, Torsten and Rolf J. Langhammer (1989) *ACP Exports and EC Trade Preferences Revisited*, Kiel working paper no. 373 (Kiel) May.
Amtsblatt der Europäischen Gemeinschaften (Abl) (Brussels) various issues.
Bachmann, Ernst-Udo (1981) 'Die Präferenzregelungen der Europäischen Gemeinschaft (Teil II)', *Zeitschrift für Zölle und Verbrauchssteuern*, vol. 65, pp. 34–44.
Bakhoven, Anton F. (1989) *An Alternative Assessment of Macroeconomic Effects of 'Europe 1992'*, paper presented at the Kiel Week Conference on 'The Completion of the Internal Market', 21–3 June.
Baldwin, Robert E. and Tracy Murray (1977) 'MFN Tariff Reductions and Developing Country Trade Benefits Under the GSP', *Economic Journal*, vol. 87, March, pp. 30–46.
Borrmann, Axel et al. (1979) *Das Allgemeine Zollpräferenzsystem der EG* (Hamburg).
Borrmann, Axel, Christine Borrmann, Christian Langer and Karl-Wolfgang Menck (1985) *The Significance of the EEC's Generalised System of Preferences* (Hamburg).
Buigues, Pierre and Philippe Goybet (1985) 'Competitiveness of European Industry: Situation to Date', *European Economy*, no. 25, September, pp. 9–33
Bundesverband des Deutschen Exporthandels e.V., Verband der Fertigwaren e.V. (1988) *Auswirkungen des EG-Binnenmarktes auf die Drittländerbeziehungen*, mimeo, September.
Bureau of Agricultural Economics (BAE) (1985) *Agricultural Policies in the European Community (their origins, nature and effects in production and trade)* (Canberra).
Burniaux, Jean-Marc and Jean Waelbroeck (1988) 'Agricultural Protection in Europe: Its Impact on Developing Countries', in: Rolf J. Langhammer and Hans Christoph Rieger (eds), *ASEAN and EC Trade in Tropical Agricultural Products* (Singapore: Institute of Southeast Asian Studies) pp. 129–54.

Cable, Vincent (1989) *1992 and Its Implications for Developing Countries*, paper presented at the Kiel Week Conference on 'The Completion of the Internal Market' (Kiel) 21–3 June.

Cecchini, Paolo (1988) *The European Challenge, 1992 – The Benefits of a Single Market* (Aldershot).

Commission of the European Communities (CEC), (1988a), 'The Economics of 1992. An Assessment of the Potential Economic Effects of Completing the Internal Market of the European Community', *European Economy*, no. 35, March.

Commission of the European Communities (1988b) 'The Lomé trade arrangements: What do they do for the ACP's?; *The Courier*, no. 109, May–June, pp. 5–10.

Cooper, Richard N. (1972) 'The European Community's System of Generalized Tariff Preferences', *The Journal of Development Studies*, vol. 9, pp. 380–94.

Davenport, Michael and Sheila Page (1989) *Regional Trading Agreements: The Impact of the Implementations of the Single European Market on Developing Countries*, report prepared for UNCTAD (London: Overseas Development Institute).

Deardorff, Alan V. and Robert M. Stern (1985) *Methods of Measurement of Non-Tariff Barriers*, United Nations Conference on Trade and Development (UNCTAD), St./MD/28 (Geneva).

Demekas, Dimitrios G. et al (1988) 'The Effects of the Common Agricultural Policy of the European Community: A Survey of the Literature', *Journal of Common Market Studies*, vol. 27, pp. 113–45.

Deutsche Bundesbank (1988) Fachserie 17, Reihe 8, Preise und Preisindizes für die Ein- und Ausfuhr (Frankfurt) October.

Dicke, Hugo et al. (1987) 'EG-Politik auf dem Prüfstand', *Kieler Studien*, no. 209 (Tübingen).

Dihm, Martin (1989) *Zolleskalation und die Agrarexporte der Entwicklungsländer. Eine Analyse der Wirkungen von Verarbeitungsprotektion unter besonderer Berücksichtigung des Handels mit Kakao, Soja- und Palmöl* (Kiel).

Donges, Juergen B., Klaus-Dieter Schmidt et al. (1988) 'Mehr Strukturwandel für Wachstum und Beschäftigung – die deutsche Wirtschaft im Anpassungsstau', *Kieler Studien*, no. 216 (Tübingen).

Donges, Juergen B., and Hans Hinrich Glismann (1987) *Industrial Adjustment in Western Europe*, Kiel working paper, no. 280, March.

EG-Kommission (1989) *Die Lage der Landwirtschaft in der Gemeinschaft*, Bericht 1988 (Brussels).

Finger, J. Michael and Andrzej Olechowski (eds) (1987) *The Uruguay Round. A Handbook on the Multilateral Trade Negotiations* (Washington, DC: The World Bank).

GATT (The General Agreement on Tariffs and Trade), *International Trade* (Geneva) various issues.

GATT (1986) Press Communiqué. GATT/1390 (Geneva) 4 August.

Göbel, Heike Rolf J. Langhammer and Frank Weiß (1988) 'Wachstum im asiatisch-pazifischen Raum. Implikationen für die internationale Arbeitsteilung', *Kieler Studien*, no. 222 (Tübingen).

Gruber, Ludwig (1987a) 'Landwirtschaftliche Kooperation zwischen Europäischer Gemeinschaft und Afrika im Rahmen der Lomé-Abkommen. Fallstudien zum Zucker- und Rindfleischhandel', *Hamburger Beiträge zur Afrika-Kunde*, no. 30 (Institut für Afrika-Kunde, Hamburg).

Gruber, Ludwig (1987b) *Landwirtschaftliche Kooperation der Europäischen Gemeinschaft mit Entwicklungsländern am Beispiel der Lomé-Verträge.* (Ebenhausen: Stiftung Wissenschaft und Politik).

Hamilton, Carl (1988) 'An Assessment of Voluntary Restraints on Hong Kong Exports to Europe and the USA', *Economica*, vol. 53, pp. 339–50.

Hartmann, Monika and Peter-Michael Schmitz (1987) 'Effects of the Common Agricultural Price Policy on the Third World', *Quarterly Journal of International Agriculture*, vol. 26, no. 4, pp. 341–54.

Hartwig, Bettina and Stefan Tangermann (1987) *Legal Aspects of Restricting Manioc Trade Between Thailand and the EC* (Kiel).

Hein, Catherine (1988) *Multinational Enterprises and Employment in the Mauritian Export Processing Zone*, ILO Multinational Enterprises Programme, working paper, no. 52 (Geneva).

Hewitt, Adrian and Christopher Stevens (1981) 'The Second Lomë Convention', in: Christopher Stevens (ed.), *EEC and the Third World: A Survey*, vol. 1 (London) pp. 30–59.

Hiemenz, Ulrich and Rolf J. Langhammer (1988) *ASEAN and the EC. Institutions and Structural Change in the European Community* (Singapore: Institute of Southeast Asian Studies [ISEAS]).

IMF (International Monetary Fund) (1988) *International Financial Statistics 1988 Yearbook* (Washington).

Jungnickel, Rolf (1989) *Neue Technologien und Produktionsverlagerungen.* (Hamburg: Forschungsauftrag des Bundeswirtschaftsministeriums) forthcoming.

Koester, Ulrich and Roland Herrmann (1987) *The EC-ACP Convention of Lomé* (Kiel).

Koester, Ulrich et al. (1988) *Disharmonies in EC and US Agricultural Policy Measures*, report prepared for the Commission of the European Community (Brussels: EC Commission).

Krenzler, Horst G. (1988) 'Zwischen Protektionismus und Liberalismus. Europäischer Binnenmarkt und Drittlandsbeziehungen', *EuropaArchiv*, no. 9, pp. 241–48.

Krueger, Anne O., Maurice W. Schiff and Alberto Valdez (1988) 'Agricultural Incentives in Developing Countries: Measuring the Effect of Sectoral and Economy-wide Policies', *The World Bank Economic Review*, vol. 2, no. 3, pp. 255–71.

Laird, Samuel and Alexander Yeats (1987) 'Tariff Cutting Formulas and Complications', in: J. Michael Finger and Andrzej Olechowski (eds) *The Uruguay Round. A Handbook on the Multilateral Trade Negotiations* (Washington, DC: The World Bank) pp. 89–100.

Lamusse, Roland (1989) *Adjustment to Structural Change in Manufacturing in a North–South Perspective: The Case of the Clothing Export Sector in Mauritius*, ILO World Employment Programme Research, working paper, no. 27 (Geneva).

Langhammer, Rolf J. (1981) 'Nationaler Protektionismus im Rahmen der EG-Handelspolitik, dargestellt am Beispiel der Industriegüterimporte aus ASEAN-Ländern', *Die Weltwirtschaft*, no. 1, pp. 74–93.

Langhammer, Rolf J. (1983) *Years of the EEC's Generalised System of Preferences for Developing Countries: Success or Failure?*, Kiel working Paper, no. 183 (Kiel) September.

Langhammer, Rolf J. (1988) 'The EEC Trade Policies in Manufactures, the Mediterranean Market', in, Ilam Greilsammer and Joseph H. H. Weiler (eds), *Europe and Israel: Troubled Neighbours* (Berlin) pp. 195–211.

Langhammer, Rolf J. (1989a) 'North-South Trade in Services. Some Empirical Evidence', in: Herbert Giersch (ed.), *Services in World Economic Growth. Symposium 1988* (Tübingen) pp. 248–71.

Langhammer, Rolf J. (1989b) *Patterns of Trade in Services Between ASEAN Countries and EC Member States. Case Studies for West Germany, France and Netherlands* (Singapore: Institute of Southeast Asian Studies) forthcoming.

Langhammer, Rolf J. (1990) 'Europe 1992 and the Developing Countries. Fuelling a New Engine of Growth or Separating Europe from Non-Europe', *Journal of Common Market Studies*, vol. 29, December.

Langhammer, Rolf J. and André Sapir (1987) 'Economic Impact of Generalised Tariff Preferences, *Thames Essays*, no. 49 (London).

Massow, Valentin V. (1984) 'Einfuhrbegünstigungen und Ausfuhrpolitik der EG bei Rindfleisch', *Agrarökonomische Studien*, vol. 6 (Kiel).

Mathew, Samuel (1989) *Air Transport in Europe After 1992: Implications and Responses*, paper presented at the Colloquium on 'ASEAN and Europe 1992. Implications and Response', convened by the Institute of Strategic and International Studies, Kuala Lumpur, 10–11 July.

Matthews, Alan (1985) *The Common Agricultural Policy and the Less Developed Countries* (Dublin).

Menzler-Hokkanen, Ingeborg (1988) 'EC Trade Policies in Tropical Agricultural Products', in: Rolf J. Langhammer and Hans Christoph Rieger (eds), *ASEAN and the EC Trade in Tropical Agricultural Products* (Singapore: Institute of Southeast Asian Studies), pp. 60–115.

Messerlin, Patrick A. (1989) 'The EC Antidumping Regulations: A First Economic Appraisal, 1980–85', *Weltwirtschaftliches Archiv*, vol. 125, 1989, pp. 563–87.

Mishalani, Philip et al. (1981) 'The Pyramid of Privilege', in: Christopher Stevens (ed.), *EEC and the Third World: A Survey*, vol. 1 (London) pp. 60–82.

Mody, Ashoka and David Wheeler (1987) 'Towards a Vanishing Middle: Competition in the World Garment Industry', *World Development*, vol. 15, pp. 1269–84.

Musto, Stefan A. (1988) 'The Common Agricultural Policy and the Mediterranean', *The Jerusalem Journal of International Relaticns*, vol. 10, no. 3, pp. 55–84.

Nelson, Gerald C. (1989) 'Rentseeking in North–South agricultural trade', *European Review of Agricultural Economics*, vol. 16, pp. 53–64.

Neundörfer, Konrad (1987) 'Das vierte Welttextilabkommen', *Schriften zur Textilpolitik*, no. 4 (Frankfurt).

Nogués, Julio J., Andrzej Olechowski and L. Alan Winters (1985) *The Extent of Non-Tariff Barriers to Industrial Countries' Imports*, World Bank report no. DRDJ115, discussion paper (Washington, DC) January.

Noichl, Agnes (1985) 'European Trade Regulations for Bananas and Imports from Developing Countries', *Quarterly Journal of International Agriculture*, vol. 24, no. 1, pp. 63–77.

OECD (1979) *The Impact of the Newly Industrialising Countries on Production and Trade in Manufactures* (Paris).

OECD (1986) *The OECD Compatible Trade and Production Data Base 1970–1983*, working paper, no. 31 (Paris) March.

OECD (1987) *National Policies and Agricultural Trade. Study on the European Community* (Paris).

OECD (1988) *The Newly Industrialising Countries: Challenge and Opportunity for OECD Industries* (Paris).

OECD (1989) *Agricultural Policies, Markets and Trade. Monitoring and Outlook* (Paris).

OECD *National Accounts, Main Aggregates* (Paris) various issues.

Parikh, Kirit S., Günther Fischer, Klaus Frohberg and Odd Gulbrandsen (1988) *Towards Free Trade in Agriculture* (Dordrecht, Boston, Lancaster).

Patterson, Gardner (1983) 'The European Community as a Threat to the System', in: William L. Cline (ed.), *Trade Policy in the 1980s* (Washington, DC) pp. 233–42.

Pelkmans, Jacques (1986) *Completing the Internal Market for Industrial Products* (Luxembourg).

Pelkmans, Jacques (1987) 'The European Community's Trade Policy Towards Developing Countries', in: Christopher Stevens and Joan Verhoven van Themaat (eds), *Europe and the International Division of Labour. EEC and the Third World: A Survey*, vol. 6 (London) pp. 15–43.

Pomfret, Richard (1986) *Mediterranean Policy of the European Community. A Study of Discrimination in Trade* (London: Trade Policy Research Centre).

Sapir, André (1981) 'Trade Benefits Under the EEC Generalized System of Preferences', *European Economic Review*, vol. 15, no. 3, pp. 339–55.

Sathirathai, Surakiart and Ammar Siamwalla (1987) 'GATT Law, Agricultural Trade, and Developing Countries: Lessons from Two Case Studies', *The World Bank Economic Review*, vol. 1, no. 4, September, pp. 595–618.

Schnoor, Anke (1989) *Die Lomé Politik der Europäischen Gemeinschaft gegenüber afrikanischen Rindfleisch-Exportstaaten*, diplomarbeit (Universität Göttingen).

Schrader, Jörg-Volker (1982) 'Interdependenzen zwischen EG-Zuckerpolitik und Preis- oder Mengenschwankungen auf dem Weltmarkt', *Agrarwirtschaft*, vol. 31, no. 1, pp. 6–15.

Schumacher, Dieter (1981) 'Handel mit Entwicklungsländern und Beschäftigung in der Europäischen Gemeinschaft. Eine vergleichende Analyse für sechs EC-Länder anhand aktueller Import-/Exportströme im Handel mit Industrieprodukten', *DIW-Beiträge zur Strukturwirtschaft*, no. 66 (Berlin).

Siebert, Horst (1989) *The Harmonisation Issue in Europe: Prior Agreement or a Competitive Process?*, paper presented at the Kiel Week Conference on 'The Completion of the Internal Market' (Kiel) 21–3 June.

Spinanger, Dean (1989) 'Is the EC Foreshadowing a Fortress Europe in 1992? Examining Implications of 1992 and Current EC Trade Restrictions in PACRIM Countries', *PRICES*, paper no. 1 (Kiel).

Spinanger, Dean and Joachim Zietz (1986) 'Managing Trade but Mangling the Consumer: Reflections of the EEC's and West Germany's Experience with the MFA', *Außenwirtschaft*, vol. 41, no. 4, pp. 511–31.

Tangermann, Stefan (1988) 'International coordination of agricultural policy adjustments', *European Review of Agricultural Economics*, vol. 15, no.4, pp. 309–26.

Tangermann, Stefan, Timothy E. Josling and Scott R. Pearson (1987) 'Multilateral Negotiations on Farm-support Levels', *The World Economy*, vol. 10, no. 3, pp. 265–81.

Tyers, Rodney and Kim Anderson (1986) *Distortions in world food markets: a quantitative assessment*, World Development background paper (Washington, DC: The World Bank).

Tyers, Rodney and Kim Anderson (1988) 'Liberalizing OECD Agricultural Policies in the Uruguay Round: Effects on Trade and Welfare', *Journal of Agricultural Economics*, vol. 39, no. 2, pp. 197–216.

UN, *Monthly Bulletin of Statistics* (New York) various issues.

UNCTAD, *Handbook of International Trade and Development Statistics* (New York) various issues.

UNIDO (1989) data base: information supplied by the Statistical Office of the United Nations with estimates by the UNIDO secretariat (Vienna).

US Department of Agriculture (USDA) *Foreign Agricultural Services, Series: Grains and Oilseeds*, various issues.

US Department of Commerce (1986) *International Trade Administration 1984*, major shippers report – category and country (Washington, DC).

US Department of Commerce, *Survey of Current Business*, various issues.

Valdés, Alberto (1987) 'Agriculture in the Uruguay Round: Interests of Developing Countries', *The World Bank Economic Review*, vol. 1, no. 4, pp. 571–94.

Weinmüller, Egon (1984) *Außenwirtschaftliche Aspekte der EG-Agrarpolitik* (Kiel).

Weston, Ann, Vincent Cable and Adrian Hewitt (1980) *The EEC's Generalized System of Preferences. Evaluation and Recommendations for Change* (London: Overseas Development Institute).

Wilson, Dick (1988) 'Asian textiles and 1992', *Textile Asia* (Hongkong) November, pp. 22–4.

Winters, L. Alan (1987) 'The Economic Consequences of Agricultural Support: A Survey', *OECD Economic Studies*, vol. 9, pp. 7–54.

Wissenschaftlicher Beirat beim Bundesminister für Ernährung, Landwirtschaft und Forsten, Aktuelle Fragen der Ordnung des internationalen Agrarhandels (1988) Reihe A. Angewandte Wissenschaft, H. 362, (Münster-Hiltrup).

Wolf, Martin (1987) 'An Unholy Alliance: The European Community and Developing Countries in the International Trading System', *Außenwirtschaft*, vol. 42, pp. 41–64.

World Bank, *World Development Report* (Washington, DC) various issues.

World Bank (1988) *World Tables 1987*, 4th edition (Washington, DC).

Yeats, Alexander (1987) 'The Escalation of Trade Barriers', in J. Michael Finger and Andrzej Olechowski (eds), *The Uruguay Round. A Handbook on the Multilateral Trade Negotiations* (Washington, DC: The World Bank) pp. 110–20.

Index